Theories of
the State

B

To my parents

ANDREW VINCENT

Theories of the State

BLACKWELL
Oxford UK & Cambridge USA

First published 1987
Reprinted 1990, 1993, 1994

Blackwell Publishers
108 Cowley Road, Oxford, OX4 1JF, UK

238 Main Street
Cambridge, Massachusetts 02142, USA

British Library Cataloguing in Publication Data

Vincent, Andrew
Theories of the state.
1. State, The
I. Title.
   320.1′01   JC11
   ISBN 0–631–14729–2 Pbk

Library of Congress Cataloging in Publication Data

Vincent, Andrew,
   Theories of the state.
   Bibliography: p.
   Includes index.
   1. State, The.   I. Title.
JC325.V55   1987   320.1   87–5149
ISBN 0–631–14729–2 (pbk.)

Typeset in 10½ on 12pt Baskerville
by Columns of Reading
Printed and bound in Great Britain by
Hartnolls Ltd, Bodmin, Cornwall

This book is printed on acid-free paper

Contents

Preface   vii

1 The Nature of the State   1

   Introduction   1
   Formal Features of the Modern European State   19
   The State and Other Collectivities   22
   Cognate Concepts of the State   32
   Theory and the State   40
   Conclusion   44

2 The Absolutist Theory of the State   45

   Introduction   45
   Absolute Sovereignty   51
   Property Theory and Absolutism   61
   Divine Right and Absolutism   65
   Raison d'état and Absolutism   69
   Personality Theory and Absolutism   73
   Conclusion   75

3 The Constitutional Theory of the State   77

   Introduction   77
   Origins of the Constitutional Theory of the State   82
   Theories of Limitation and Diversification of Authority   91
   Orderly Change and the Maintenance of Values   114
   Conclusion   116

4 The Ethical Theory of the State   119

   Introduction   119
   Metaphysics and the System of Philosophy   123
   The Individual and the Social World   128

Forms of State   131
The External State   134
The Political State   136
The Ethical State   139
Conclusion   143

5 The Class Theory of the State   147

Introduction   147
The Traditional Class Theory of the State   152
Gramsci and the State: Theoretician of the Superstructure   164
Structuralism and the State   171
Conclusion   175

6 The Pluralist Theory of the State   181

Introduction   181
Variations on a Pluralistic Theme   189
Liberty and Groups   193
The Problem of Sovereignty   198
Real Personality and Groups   203
The Pluralist State   210
Conclusion   215

7 Do We Need a Theory of the State?   218

Notes   226

Bibliography   230

Index   241

Preface

I owe a considerable debt to a large number of people in writing this book. First of all I would like to thank the Nuffield Foundation for providing financial assistance in the initial research stages of the book. Within my own department at Cardiff Roy Jones has patiently put up with my regular interjections into his busy timetable with my tortuous thoughts on the State. I am certain that he will not agree with me, except perhaps on the importance of the State. John Cross and Barry Jones have also made helpful comments on earlier drafts of chapters as well as providing intellectual support and encouragement. Finally, I would particularly like to express my sincere thanks to Maurice Goldsmith, Jeremy Jennings, Peter Nicholson, Neil Harding, Terrell Carver, David Nicholls and Thomas Watkins, for their helpful comments and advice on sections of the manuscript.

The final responsibility, of course, is my own and on so broad a topic as the State I have found this, at times, a rather heavy one. Some of my judgements may appear to compress a lot of material. I confess that I have tried to impose some order and sense onto a very complex field. The literature on the State can have a rather daunting effect on the interested student. There are not many books that I have encountered on normative theories of the State which make concessions to the non-specialist reader. I have tried to overcome, as far as possible, this initial problem by presenting the arguments and problems in a very much more structured form. My purpose has been throughout to provide an introduction to normative theories of the State for the student of politics. If some interest, however critical, is generated on the issue of the State, then my purpose will have been accomplished.

Andrew Vincent
Cardiff

1

The Nature of the State

The history of how the modern state emerged is of course itself a
moral history.

MacIntyre, *After Virtue: A Study in Moral Theory*

INTRODUCTION

What is the State? This is one of the most simple yet elusive
questions that can be asked in politics. It is tempting to give an
equally elusive or alternatively simplistic answer. The central thesis
of this book is that an understanding of the State is crucial to the
grasp of nineteenth- and twentieth-century political thought and
practice. Even in those traditions which have reacted most critically
against the State, such as Marxism or anarchism, there is still
reflection on its profound significance. Despite this it can be said
that the State is now being slowly rediscovered by political theorists,
often by those working from a Marxist perspective. This is not
to say that we ever lost the concept, but rather, for a variety of
reasons, in the English speaking world it fell into disuse in academic
circles in the twentieth century. Oddly this has coincided with a
remarkable increase in the practical role and function of the State.
This lack of discussion, I would stress, has not been the case in
France, Germany and Italy. It is in Britain and America this century
that the academic climate has been generally unreceptive to any
general discussion on the nature of the State. The reasons for this are
again complex, many of them historical. For example some of the
most profound theorizing arose in Germany in the nineteenth
century. Even one of the most severe critics of the State, Karl Marx,
still worked within the parameters of Germanic preoccupations.
There has been a vague association between Germanic and European

interests in the State and the rise of nationalism and international aggression this century. G. W. F. Hegel (1770–1831) is often taken as one of the key offenders in this area. He is sometimes portrayed as the arrogant megalomaniac who offers the world the culminating philosophy, towards which all previous thought had been aiming. All contradictions are resolved in the Prussian State. Thus in the inter-war years the American philosopher John Dewey articulated the sentiments of many of his contemporaries when he wrote that 'The moment we utter the words "the state" a score of intellectual ghosts rise to obscure our vision' (1927, pp. 8–9). In fact the fate of the idea of the State this century has been to be either overinflated and sanctified or totally misunderstood. It is difficult to find a balanced assessment.

In Britain and America the reasons for this suspicion of the State run very deep. On one count neither society has a strong State tradition. There is very little self-consciousness of being in a State tradition. This is reflected at all levels of society, from government ministers, civil servants and lawyers to ordinary citizens. Further, the academic preoccupation of philosophers, historians and social scientists has usually been with the empirical appraisal of the State, as, for example, a stage in the broader development of societies. The predominance of linguistic and analytic philosophy has also led to a mistrust of broad-ranging metaphysical or juristic theories. Political philosophers since the 1940s have given their attention, by and large, to more precise, smaller-scale issues, such as the analysis of rights or obligations. Normative political theory has been generally avoided. The task of political philosophy was not limited to analysis in the more classical writers – Hobbes, Locke, Rousseau and Hegel. Classical political philosophy had an avowed normative task. It was concerned to reflect on practices such as citizenship, the family and forms of constitution, usually within a broad over-arching account of the State, its nature and purpose. Most theories of the State are to be found in the classical tradition of political philosophy.

There are a number of reasons why it is important to think carefully about the State. On a very practical level, it is now difficult to conceive of life without it. Statehood not only represents a set of institutions but also a body of attitudes, practices and codes of behaviour, in short civility, which we associate correctly with civilization. Certainly there are some 'State sceptics', from various ideological positions, who have tried to formulate ideas on Stateless societies, but on a more immediate level the State subtly penetrates much of our lives. We begin and end our lives within its confines. Thus, as well as being a complex concept, it is also an everyday reality that we cannot ignore. Before we can speculate about our relation to the State we need to know something of the theory of States.

Secondly, the State is neither a neutral institution which we can afford to ignore nor has it arisen out of pure chance or accident. There are customary features which have come about slowly by accretion. However, much of its form and structure can only be understood completely by grasping the legal and political theories embodied within them. Sometimes this is *ex post facto* theorizing trying to comprehend the actual structures that have arisen; however, at other points it is the theory itself which has given rise to the development of specific institutions. Since it is ideas of the State which often determine both the form of the State and our attitude to it, it is crucial that some grasp of the basic theories of the State be part of any political education.

Thirdly, there is often considerable conceptual puzzlement surrounding the idea of the State, specifically in relation to other concepts such as society, community, nation, government, crown, sovereignty and so on. Often these concepts are muddled together with the notion of the State. This muddle is often the result of inattention to the diverse uses of these concepts within differing theoretical contexts. An acquaintance with some of the strands of argumentation in various theories will throw considerable light on these issues and hopefully elucidate some of the problems.

Finally, one of the paradoxical aspects of much recent political theorizing is that it is premised on the State. Reflection on concepts such as law, rights and obligations implies the existence of some form of State; these concepts are meshed into the State. Thus it would seem to be an essential preliminary to any study of such concepts to gain some familiarity with theories of the State. However, apart from the critical studies of some political sociologists and Marxists, there is very little work on the State.

When dealing with the State we must be aware that it is the most problematic concept in politics. Anyone who has studied it in any depth will have become aware of this fact. This is not only because of its rather tortured history or its central importance to our present political circumstances. It is rather the problem of its ambivalence – its certainty and yet its elusiveness. It has a tendency to slip in and out of many practices and concepts with alarming ease. The State is not something which reveals itself at the first look. Despite its apparent solidity (try not paying taxes or leaving the country without a passport) it is none the less difficult to identify – an idea or cluster of concepts, values and ideas about social existence.

This point connects up with one of the deterrents to dealing with the State, namely the complex character of much of the theorizing. This problem can be met in two ways. First, by delimiting the field of study and focusing on some of the most well-known accounts. Admittedly this misses much of the richness of reflection on the State as detailed, for example, in Kenneth Dyson's recent book (Dyson, 1980), but at least it provides readers with a chance to develop interests in the subject to follow up if they wish. This book thus adopts the following pattern. The bulk of the introduction will be taken up with clarifying the origin of the word and history of the idea of the State, discussing its relation to cognate concepts, looking at alternative approaches to the State and finally examining the problems of theory in relation to the State. The subsequent chapters will consider a number of major theories of the State. The final chapter will consider the question: do we need a theory of the State?

The problem of the complexity of the State can be met, secondly, by showing a developmental interrelation and pattern between some of these theories. The constitutional theory of the State, for example, developed against the background of absolutism. The class theory developed in the nineteenth century against the backcloth of the constitutional and ethical theories and so forth. The interrelation and critical contrasts will facilitate the understanding of the uninitiated reader.

It is important, however, to stress the limitations of this book. It has no pretensions except to an overview of some key theories of the State. It isolates landmarks in theory. At most points in the study this involves compression, simplification and a broad brush stroke. It attempts to give the student of politics an introduction to State theory – nothing more.

Is politics about the State?

Political Science in the proper sense is the science which is concerned with the State.

Bluntschli, *The Theory of the State*

These opening lines to Bluntschli's large tome on the State echo a concern which goes back to Aristotle's *Politics*. The word politics derives from the Greek word *polis*, basically standing for 'city'; and to Aristotle the task of political science was to examine the *polis*. It was virtually impossible to conceive of civilized and free life outside the *polis*, therefore it was perfectly reasonable to conceive of politics as being about existence in a city. If it is the case that politics is about the State, and one further admits that the Greek *polis* is – in the modern sense – a State, then the great difficulty in writing about the State is to try to avoid writing a history of political thought from the Greeks to the present. This is something to be avoided in the present study.

Bluntschli's view of politics is echoed in some comparatively recent texts in political theory, for example, D. D. Raphael comments that the 'political is whatever concerns the state' (1970, p. 27), or N. P. Barry that 'the history of political theory has been mainly concerned with the state' (1981, p. 46). Many might now add the term nation to State, thus we might conclude that politics *only* exists in nation States. International politics exists between nation States. All the problems of politics including justice, freedom and rights are in the end State-related.

Some critics would not be so happy with this view. There are a number of reasons why one might object to the conflation of politics with the State. If one defined politics, as for example in Michael Oakeshott's famous definition, as 'the activity of attending to the general arrangements of a set of people whom chance or choice has brought together' (1956, p. 2), then this includes everything from the activities of families, tribes, clans, clubs and trade unions to every large-scale democracy or autocracy. It is difficult to say, without some further explanation, how this is all bound up with the State. In short, politics can be considered as broader than just the State. In fact the concept of politics may be, and has been, defined in a variety of ways which do not coincide with the State. To take this point one step further, many anthropologists and sociologists would argue that there is a rich array of pre-State or Stateless societies. Most scholars now agree that the State is a comparatively recent phenomenon in terms of the long history of social existence. If these societies were subject to some authority and rules, it is feasible to speak of politics existing but not the State.

A further reason for denying the conflation of politics and the State is that groups, associations and communities can have a complex life within themselves which may have nothing whatsoever to do with the State. Surely it is possible to say that politics exists within and between groups? Critics might argue at this point that the State has been given too central a role. Not all problems of group life or even individual life, liberty or justice can simply be rolled into the State. Such a philosophical benediction on the State makes the contingent appear necessary. To delimit politics to the State is to constrict the reality of politics. Many, at this point, might call for a liberation of politics from the State. This view is partially formulated in the classical liberal distinction between the political and social spheres or the public and private. In this argument what takes place in the family or the economy should be classed as private and therefore beyond the reach of the State.

Some of the above points have undoubted cogency. Historically politics does have a wider scope than the State. Yet in a contemporary sense it is difficult to see politics existing apart from the State or the aspiration to Statehood. Politics now is intrinsic to the State. However this does not limit politics to one particular entity. The State is not clearly one thing. This book investigates theories of the State not the theory. The diversity of State theory is a major factor of the philosophical appraisal of the State and the diverse values attached to it. The State is a complex of ideas and values, some of which have an institutional reality. These ideas are dense in texture and diverse in interpretation. To try to grasp them is to understand much of the European political experience in the last four centuries. Politics therefore encapsulates the richness and variety of State theory. There is no sense in which politics is delimited if conflated with the State. Philosophical Statism is bound up with reflection on the nature and ends of social existence.

States, the State and the idea of the State

> The first thing to be said about *the* modern State is that it does not exist and never has existed. What has existed historically is a great number of modern states, with very varied constitutions.
>
> Lubasz, *The Development of the Modern State*

It is often rather misleading to speak of theories of the State. The singular nature of the noun State implies something which is consistent, the same, identifiable throughout all the various theories. There is some truth in this consistency, but it has to be treated very carefully. There are three objections to the singular use of the 'the State' which are empirical, historical and conceptual.

The first relies on common sense and observation. If we look around us we see States with different structures, political institutions, cultures and values. We do not see 'the State'. The empirical observation of actual States must lead to the conclusion that no one specific model is characteristic of all States. At most it could be said that there are some resemblances. The differing historical experiences have led to differing perceptions and practices. One important counter-claim is that some of these resemblances are remarkably strong, for example, every State in fact has a territory, legal system, judiciary and monopoly of force and so on. However, there is one further objection which needs to be considered here. Often critics of the singular use of 'the State' have been objecting to something slightly different – what I would call 'the idea of the State'. It is not so much the formal features of resemblance which are targets for criticism, but rather the idea that there is a normative theory of the State embodying values, ideas and a conception of the common good (see Dyson, 1980, pp. 2–3). This is the State of the political philosopher. The 'idea of the State' is given too singular and sacred a status, as though it were a role model to imitate. Thus, as one critic put it, 'The isolation of the State imagined by the philosophers has made the description of *the* state more and more inapplicable to any single actual specimen' (Delisle-Burns, 1915–16, p. 294). This particular criticism, written in 1915 in the heyday of the Hegelian theory of the State, with Bernard Bosanquet looming large in the foreground, is probably not so appropriate today. There is no one dominant philosophical theory now.

The second objection focuses on the issue of the continuity of the State in history. It is very tempting to slip into a developmental or evolutionary terminology when speaking of the State. It is, however, an unwarranted assumption to suppose automatically a development of the modern State either from the Greek *polis* or the absolutist State of the sixteenth century. It is also wrong to assume that the European State should act as a model for developing countries, although such an assumption has had a considerable impact on both the domestic and foreign policies of developing nations.

One of the major problem in dealing with, for example, thinkers like Hobbes or Bodin, is to know whether one is being unhistorical in speaking of *their* theories of the State. This is so because: (1) the actual concept of the State did not really exist as a commonplace concept in the political vocabulary of the time; (2) their theories and authorial intentions have strong connections to the historical context in which they arose. These kinds of points arise in debates on historical purism or impurism, textualism and contextualism,

specifically in the wake of the methodological work of writers such as
Q. Skinner (see David Boucher, 1985). Surprisingly Skinner himself
in his substantive historical work *does* offer a developmental
perspective on the State, which is not what one is led to expect from
his methodological writings.[1]

When offering an account of the State one is inevitably faced with
such questions as: are Bodin and Hegel addressing the same entity
when they discuss the State? Is a critical enquiry into the theory of
the State advancing an argument at the cost of historical purity or
accuracy? However, it does appear foolish to deny a State tradition
going back to the sixteenth century. The character of the State – an
entity which has developed apace over the last four centuries in
Europe – has been under permanent scrutiny and debate. Its essence
and nature has been continually disputed, partly because it reflects
such fundamental values. Although Bodin's and Hegel's arguments
must be viewed ultimately against the background of their time,
none the less they were putting forward arguments which were and
are part of a tradition of discourse, which we are still part of. There
are certain discernible patterns of thought and language which
reoccur around the idea of the State. This is partly because theorists
tend to refer back to previous accounts. For example, where
sixteenth-century theorists referred back to Aristotle, the old and new
Testament and civil and canon law, nineteenth- and twentieth-
century theorists refer back to Hobbes, Locke and Rousseau, as well
as to Aristotle. There is no ineluctable sense of progress here, as in
the Whig theory of history (see Butterfield, 1950), rather a common
range of problems and patterns of reference (see Tierney, 1982, pp.
viii, 104–5).

The third objection relates to the use of the concept of the State.
When we speak of the State performing actions we personify it. We
attribute to it a status equivalent to a unique personality – an agent
or subject which acts. Acts in law specifically are attributed to the
State as though it were a distinct entity. When we say 'the State
killed x' or 'one State negotiates with another', we might be tempted
to say that these are, in Gilbert Ryle's phrase, 'systematically
misleading expressions'. The explanation of the personification of the
State lies in the fact that the individuals holding state offices do not
(or should not) act in a private capacity and do not personally own
their offices or the power, yet they still act *for* the State. Thus we
have the phrase 'servant of the State', or more conventionally, civil
servant. The State, through its offices, is seen to have a superpersonal
quality. The reality behind this is the legal character of public

authority. The person acts on behalf of the State. The mistake is to see the State as a person subsisting in its own right. This is legal mysticism. The State has no innate essence, it is a tool which can be used in appropriate contexts. It is thus no use searching for the meaning of the word in isolation from these contexts. The word is used in many different contexts. The legal philosopher Alf Ross developed this line of argument in the 1960s, arguing that 'The question what "the State" stands for as an acting subject is without meaning. This term cannot be defined by substitution, but only by naming the conditions under which statements regarding "the State" as an acting subject are held to be true' (1961, p. 123) The meaning of the word State 'is precisely the conditions that must be fulfilled . . . in order to make it possible to hold the statement to be true' (p. 124). The shade of Frege looms over Ross's analysis, specifically Frege's famous principle – 'never ask for the meaning of a word in isolation, but only in the context of a proposition' (1950). The sentences in which the concept State occurs are the units of meaning *not* the word itself. In fact Ross goes on to echo Frege precisely, arguing that the grammatical form of sentences in which the word State occurs are different from the logical form. Grammatically a sentence such as 'the State killed Mrs. Murrell' is the same as 'John built the house', both sentences have a definite subject. Logically, however, the State is a very different type of subject.

Ross's analysis might be perfectly acceptable to many British and American lawyers, but it is trying to examine the issue of State personality which was developed in a different philosophical tradition. We will return to personality theory in subsequent chapters. Yet it is far from clear that Ross really answers the problems which the personality theory attempts to solve. Legally, how can the State act or be liable for anything unless it has some kind of personal or subject status? It is no use speaking of differing types of statement – there must be some continuity and consistency between all the acts of the State, otherwise it would not be recognized as the State.

It can be seen, from these empirical, historical and conceptual objections, why many might be wary of using the singular noun 'State'. To avoid terminological problems in the book it will be assumed that there is some common entity which theorists are addressing, however their accounts of it often differ. Thus there are 'theories of the State'.

Stateless societies and the State tradition

The primary concern of this study is the State. However, for the sake
of clarity the category of Stateless societies will be examined. This is
not the place to engage in a full—scale anthropological discussion of
such societies, yet it is worth stating the central thesis of this book,
namely that the State is a comparatively recent phenomenon dating
from the sixteenth century. There is no Greek or medieval State, at
least not as we understand it: these are misnomers. The State is not,
apart from unavoidable conventional usage, the same as the ruling
council of a tribe or an empire. Thus there is a great deal to be
included under the rubric of a 'Stateless society'.

There are four very basic categories of Stateless society. The first of
these incorporates the vast range of anthropological literature on
'primitive' communities. Anthropologists and sociologists often tend
to view the State as one way of organizing society, which is found in
certain societies (see Krader 1968, pp. vii–viii). Stateless societies are
seen as organized by such categories as clan, blood ties or lineage,
the extended family or simply mutual help. Evans-Pritchard's
ground-breaking studies of the Nuer (1940) are typical of the analysis
of such acephalous societies (societies without an identifiable head or
ruler). These groups sometimes will have forms of government and
established rules, but nothing that is recognizably State-like.

The second category incorporates developed political organizations
which pre-date the State. The Greek *polis*, empires and medieval
political organizations are included here. Some of the characteristics
of these forms approximate to the State but most commentators have
been justifiably hesitant about calling them States. This category will
be discussed in more detail later in this chapter.

The next category is more speculative and Utopian. It includes the
Stateless visions of certain nineteenth- and twentieth-century ideologies, specifically anarchism, libertarianism and communism. The
idealization of the life of the freely subsisting commune, often
involving the praise of 'primitive' forms of community, is seen as
essentially Stateless. The State is seen as the primary cause of human
misery (see Kropotkin, 1903).

The final category covers those modern societies which do not have
a tradition of Statehood. These societies 'lack a historical and legal
tradition of the State as an institution that "acts" in the name of the
public authority . . . as well as a tradition of continuous intellectual
preoccupation with the idea of the state' (Dyson, 1980, p. viii). There
are two primary determinants of this lack of a State tradition; firstly,

institutional structures and secondly, juristic and ideological traditions. On the first point, the United States of America, with its federal structure, does not foster a 'sense' of the central State. Federalism encourages centrifugal forces, distinct legal structures and a general mistrust of centralism. The State, in its historical development, has been a centripetal force; the balance of forces rest at the centre, even though a State may *tolerate* or even encourage some local autonomy. There is a growing ambiguity in the case of the European community. It will be fascinating to see how the strong State tradition in Europe reacts in the next few decades to the idea of federalism. We are already witnessing some of the implicit tensions. The second major determinant is the juristic and ideological tradition. In the United Kingdom we can see the specific case of the juristic tradition. The common-law perspective from the middle ages and the general lack of separation between public and private law has tended historically (contrary to the Roman law tradition of Europe) to diminish the significance and function of the State. Law was seen not so much to emanate from the State as to grow out of the habits and customs of the people over generations. Custom formed the basis of equity and fairness. Judges such as Bracton and Coke articulated these views. Law was independent, Parliament was there in a declaratory not a creative role. This point can, however, be overemphasized. Britain and the USA do have some sense of the State. There is a firm grasp of territorial integrity, sovereignty, citizenship and the rule of law and the like. The actual powers of the State in practice remain untouched. However such powers are not reflected on. The State is not seen as a public power which acts (see Dyson, 1980, p. 20 note 2). Such an idea is usually treated with some embarrassment.

Antecedents to the State

There has been a strong tendency to identify the Greek *polis* as the earliest form of State in Europe. Certainly it was a unique form of political organization which shares some characteristics with the modern State. Yet many of these characteristics are partially an imposition of the present onto the past.

The origin and development of the city-state dates from approximately 800 BC to 500 BC. It developed from family and tribal units which united together in fortified settlements. The form and size of the *polis* was usually determined by geographical conditions. Most were very small comparative to modern States. The city incorporated families and clans into its structure. The clan, usually under the leadership of a family with a religious cult, was the result of more settled conditions. Close in structure to the clan was the *phratry*, which went beyond simple blood connections to bonds of fellowship. This bond of fellowship was influenced by another earlier form of grouping, the *heteiria*, literally associations of soldiers sharing the same tent. The *phratry* and *heteiria* were often integrated into the tribe (*phyle*) and eventually into clans. It is this complex network of kinship, military and fellowship groups which formed the network of relations within the city-state. The early city-states had their own religious cults. This common centre of belief, coupled with mutual military service in the *phalanx*, tended to cement social relations. The nature of Greek warfare was such that each hoplite soldier relied on the shield of his fellow to protect his life. Most commentators see a gradual movement from a more primitive migratory tribal unit, *ethnos*, in Western Greece toward the permanently settled community, based on a specific territory and almost always grouped around a city with a citadel. This was the *polis* (Ehrenburg, 1960).

It is very tempting to use contemporary terminology in discussing the Greek city-state, for example the Greek word for city and state is the same – namely *polis*. The Greek term *politeia* could refer to the idea of citizenship, the constitution of a city or the whole structure of the community. Similar problems occur with other Greek terms like *koinonia* which is often translated as community. Finley remarks that *koinonia* 'has a cluster of meanings, including, for example, business partnership, but here we must think of community with a strong inflection, as in the early Christian community, in which the bonds were not merely propinquity and a common way of life but also consciousness of common destiny, common faith' (1973, p. 29). Thus some care must be exercised with regard to terminology.

There are some formal similarities between the Greek *polis* and the modern State; for example, both have a definite territory, a specific population, the idea of citizenship and a conception of the rule of law. Nevertheless, it is still a mistake to see the Greek city as a simple analogue for the modern State. Both Plato and Aristotle argued for limitations on size in any city-state. Plato, in the *Laws*, mentions the figure 5040 citizens (see Plato, 1970, p. 249). The Greek cities were heavily reliant on slavery, specifically for agriculture. Up to half the population were slaves and therefore not citizens. For Aristotle and Plato, the aim of the *polis* was to develop the 'good life' for citizens. Political science, the science of the *polis*, was aiming at the development of virtue and happiness. The *polis* was seen to embrace the entire life of the citizen – religion, culture, politics and personal activity interpenetrated each other. Priesthood could virtually be described as a political office (Bultmann, 1956, p. 129). This was a totally integrated life, much admired by later generations of scholars and thinkers. The good of the individual was inseparable from the good of the society. Ethics was integral to politics. This led to another important dimension of the *polis* which is hard to compare with the modern State. There was no recognition whatsoever of either 'society' or individualism. Nothing existed apart from the *polis*. There was no realm of privacy, personal rights or freedoms. Individuals only had claims as full citizens and there could be no conception of any distinction between public or private law. Law (*nomos*) was integral to religion, morality and the constitution. The city was prior to any individual. Man had a natural need for the *polis*. He existed within it as a cell or organ within a body. As R. G. Mulgan has argued Aristotle 'considers the *polis* as if it were a biological organism and tries to discover its nature by examining the pattern of its growth and development' (1977, p. 20).

Public authority, specifically in Athens, was exercised by great popular assemblies. There was no separation of functions of government – for example, legislative and executive. All were exercised by a common authority. The constitution was not a legalistic entity but rather the way the city lived, a manner of life characterized by a moral and legal order (see Barker, 1979, pp. 6–7). This is not the more modern understanding of constitutional theory, which tends to divorce legal from ethical concerns. Aristotle explicitly links up constitutions with social values. There are institutional aspects to Aristotle's account; he does discuss various functions of government, however he had no conception of separate legislative or executive spheres. In Mulgan's words, he would not see legislation 'as an especially significant part of the day-to-day workings of government and would not agree with the constitutional theory that considers legislation to be the main method of declaring public policy' (1977, p. 58). Thus, overall, it is justifiable to be suspicious of any attempt to equate the Greek *polis* with the modern State.

Whereas many commentators would agree that it is stretching the imagination to characterize the *polis* as a State proper, there is some division of opinion on medieval political organization. One virtually uncontested point is that some form of recognizable State existed in the late medieval period, namely the 1500s. However, the real debate is about when we date its inception. Scholars have varied from the 900s up to the 1600s.[2] It is also difficult to ascertain as to whether the word 'State' existed prior to or simultaneously with some institutional manifestation. Without going into the minutiae of the enormous erudition on this topic, the debate can broadly be subdivided into two categories, firstly those who deny that the State existed through the bulk of the middle ages and secondly those who see some form of State present during that period.

Many notable scholars have denied that the omnicompetent State existed in the middle ages. Ullman, for example, argued that the concept with which the medieval period before the thirteenth century was not familar was that of the State. It was remote from the medieval mind (1975, p. 137). In one sense this position is strengthened by the fact that the word State did not exist in political parlance till the 1500s, and it seems inappropriate to use a concept to talk about a world in which it *did* not exist (see Cheyette, 1978, p. 1). The etymology of the word will be looked at in the next section, however it is clear that such non-existence has not deterred some proponents of the medieval State, for example the German historian H. Mitteis, from arguing that the State pre-existed the consciously formulated idea by several centuries (Mitteis, 1975).

There are a number of factors which tend to undermine the credibility of the idea of a medieval State. Primarily the feudal system itself tended to have a fragmenting effect on political organization. It was essentially a complex and rather loose structure of contractual or mutual obligations existing throughout a complex social hierarchy. These contracts were symbiotic – including the monarch. The monarch was in no special sovereign position; he was part of and reliant upon the community of the realm and was consequently under the law, not the source of it. No unitary sovereign was possible under such a system, which fostered what Ullman called the massive sublife of 'numberless associations' (Ullman, 1975). Many of the more significant groups – the large estates, the clergy, guilds and nobility – generated their own systems of rules and courts – Church Canon law is the best-known example. Such law was seen as customary and prior to the existence of a monarch. The monarch in the early middle ages was also generally regarded as an 'elected' officer and not necessarily hereditary. The larger bodies, like the nobility and the Church, also convened their own representative bodies to advise the monarch. Before the State developed 'power-wielding deliberative assemblies were acting at all levels of political life from the village council to the Electors of the Empire' (Tilley, 1975, p. 22). These feudal assemblies 'melted' into Parliaments and Estates Assemblies, carrying on the task of defending and maintaining certain privileges and immunities for sections of the population. Medieval society was criss-crossed with overlapping groups and conflicting loyalties and bodies of rules. This makes it impossible, in a different sense to the Greeks, to speak of a separation between State and society. The categories simply did not exist in theory or practice.

Coupled with the above point, it is also difficult to identify any clearly defined territorial units with a consistent loyal population. The only loyalty which transcended local group attachments was to the Church. All citizens lived in the *Respublica Christiana*; all authority was from God. Ultimately the Church and clergy, as the spiritual body, were higher than the civil authorities – an idea which was no doubt fostered by their dominance of education and learning. Society was lowered in significance. The most important fact was personal salvation. The Church was not only higher and more important than civil authority, but also to an extent incorporated it. The Church and Christianity were co-extensive with citizenship. Politics was a branch of theology and consequently the clergy enjoyed privileges. The Pope was envisaged as the ruler of the spiritual and temporal realm, a universal society. The Holy Roman Empire was the universal society ruled by one emperor and transcending all smaller political units, although its effect on the smaller units was negligible. Theoretically, if the Emperor and Pope or two rulers quarrelled, it was within the same unit. It was crucial for this vision to break down before independent political units could develop. Also, with a vast, complex, hierarchical structure of interlocking groups, no clear sovereign, the predominance of customary law, no clearly defined population and the over-arching legal, religious and moral conceptions of the Church and empire, it is difficult to envisage the existence of the State.

Apart from these points, certain historians have been impressed by the claim that some form of State existed in the early medieval period. The historian Gaines Post, for example, thinks that historians of political thought have been too obsessed with the plural, cellular structure of medieval society. Roman and Canon law had established ideas of some kind of transcendant public welfare. In a sense the acceptance of monarchy as a mode of rule was indicative of the search for some form of central authority. For Gaines Post the *raison d'être* of kings was the maintance and preservation of public welfare. The medieval State may not have been as centralized as the modern State but jurists 'were approaching the identification of the State (Republic or Realm) with the supreme authority vested in the government of the prince' (1964, p. 365). Public law and conceptions of public welfare were transformed from the papacy and empire to feudal monarchies. Thus, for Post, 'independent sovereign states were coming into being in the twelfth and thirteenth centuries' (1964, p. 496). By 1300 the State had been created in the image of the empire, via theories of Roman law and corporation theory. Oddly Post also thinks that nationalism was present in medieval States in the thirteenth century, which does seem to be pushing his argument too far.

Yet, even if we disregard the previous arguments, the medieval use of the word State (*status*), was very different to the modern sense (see Skinner, 1978, Vol 2, p. 352). The understanding of 'public welfare' is also not necessarily anything more than a partial aspect of the sixteenth-century State. We neglect at our cost the actual history of the word State.

Etymology of the word State

The word State derives from the Latin *stare* (to stand), and more specifically from *status* (a standing or condition). We still use the word status in approximately the same sense as the Latin. Usually status applies to something that is established, recognized as fixed or permanent in a particular position, as in the derivative English words static or stable. There is subtle and fascinating movement of this concept from a purely personal level of reference to one of institutions and political rule.

It was a perfectly legitimate use of the term status to speak of the standing or condition of a kingdom or ruler, whether Pope or emperor, in the same way as one might refer to the status or state of any person or an object in the world. We speak, for example, of an object being in a 'state of inertia'. With reference to rulers one not only refers to their situation or condition, in a more adjectival sense, but also in a noun sense. They were established, fixed and stable. It is in these senses that Roman writers, like Cicero and Ulpian, as well as early medieval lawyers, used the term in phrases such as *status civitatis* or *status regni*. The complex of ideas implied here, in status, is that one might be referring to the condition or situation, the fact of possessing stability or the things necessary for standing or stability. One important and subtle implication of the latter point is that if order is necessary for, and part of, stability and standing, and they are necessary for the welfare of the whole, then a connection is forged between *status* and the public welfare. This had momentous significance in the sixteenth century and after.

Another broad strand within the meaning of *status* is that 'standing' is always in relation *to* something. In other words, one must ask what are the criteria which establish the condition or standing of something. Some rough criteria of such standing, specifically in the medieval period, are property, family and sex, class or position and one's occupation or profession. Property, especially land, was the most fundamental determinant of status and one's 'estate'. The possession of property in the feudal era also carried unavoidable obligations and duties as well as rights. Hereditary and kinship factors were also closely tied to property. One's family background could be the key factor to one's status in society. Finally, occupation and profession could be a clear determinant of status. In fact, in old French, the word *estat* and the modern French *état* (as opposed to Louis XIV's capitalized *Etat*) imply a profession, calling or station in life. There is in fact no clear distinction in French between estate and state, as is also the case in the Spanish *estado*. This was the case in England. Dyson comments that 'in English state was a contraction from the word estate' (1980, chap. 1), and Ernest Barker that 'The words "State" and "estate", which are etymologically the same word, flow easily into one another' (1967, p. 91). Initially, therefore, different groups had status or estate. Thus we have the idea of the 'estates of the realm'. This point is behind Figgis's comment that 'there is an *état* which belongs to the king; but there is also an *Etat de la Republique*, while even a lawyer in the Paris Parlement has his *état*' (1956, p. 10). Status or standing was in relation to specific qualities. One's status was one's estate. This notion of 'standing' comes out well in the German word for estate – *Stand*, or *Stände* in the plural, which is distinct from *Staat* (State).

One important implication of these points is the link between land ownership, property, birth, rank and so on, and authority and ruling. Generally the highest estate was the ruling group, family or monarch. The highest status (state or estate) had potentially greatest authority and power and often perpetuated itself. It could afford to impress and be *stately*. It was thus feasible to call the monarch the highest estate. Also, referring back to the previous sense discussed, the monarch could be said to embody stability and order, therefore, implicitly the public welfare.

It was this complex of ideas which was established in the medieval period. Status meant one's position in society and the duties and privileges associated with it. It implied notions of rank, power and office. It was also connected to property, specifically in land, and would often be indicated by insignia, crests and so forth showing one's stateliness (see Dowdall, 1923; Dyson, 1980, pp. 25–8).

The question remains as to how much of the above had anything to do with modern idea of the State? On the one hand there are those like Gaines Post who argue that the independent nation State existed in the twelfth century. On the other hand there are those who argue that from Cicero to Grotius there is no single instance 'in which the word *status* standing alone is used for state' (Dowdall, 1923, p. 100). Dowdall's assessment in fact appears much safer than Post's. The medieval use of *status*, estate or state implied the condition or standing of a ruler, a realm or a principality. These uses were underpinned by the complex baggage of meanings discussed above. This line of argument squares with the now more common judgement that the first use of the word State is a much later product of the Renaissance. Although this argument does not deny the important fact that many of the traditional senses of *status* and estate were carried over into the theory and practice of the modern State.

The traditional view represented, for example, by Friedrich Meinecke and Ernst Cassirer, is that in Machiavelli we encounter the first modern use of the word State (*lo stato*), meaning a public power which acts separately from both ruler and ruled and constitutes the central locus of institutionalized power. Cassirer remarks, for example, that Machiavelli's fascination with Cesare Borgia 'is only understandable if we bear in mind that the real source of Machiavelli's admiration was not the man himself but *the structure of the new state* that had been created by him. Machiavelli was the first thinker who completely realised what this new structure meant. He anticipated in his thought the whole course of the future political life of Europe' (Cassirer, 1946, p. 134).

This view has been criticized in recent years. The first and most comprehensive challenge was by J. H. Hexter, who carefully identified and unpacked all the 115 uses of *lo stato* in the Italian text of *The Prince*. He maintains that if we look at these carefully, we must conclude that Machiavelli did not use the term State in a modern juridical sense. In fact Machiavelli's *lo stato* relates more precisely to the medieval idea of 'standing' or 'condition' as in the term *status regni*. In *The Prince* the word *lo stato* is hardly ever an active subject for verbs: 110 of the 115 uses are passive. Machiavelli seems much more concerned with the majesty or standing of the prince. We have tended to inject modern meanings into Machiavelli ignoring the way in which he uses the word (see Hexter, 1973; Dyson, 1980, p. 27) The modern idea of the State was hammered out after Machiavelli by the heirs of the late Italian humanists in France. Skinner follows this judgement by Hexter, pinpointing French sixteenth-century thinkers like Du Haillan, Budé and Bodin as the formulators of the modern idea (see Skinner, 1978, Vol. 2, pp. 354–5; Church, 1972; Dyson, 1980, p. 28). Machiavelli's impact, however, was to stimulate later thinkers and politicians, such as Richelieu, to consider the nature of the State. He may not have understood the nature of the modern State, but his imaginative and brilliant writings helped generate ideas in later thinkers. This present book follows the conclusions of Hexter, Skinner, Dyson and Church that the first uses (in the modern sense) of the word State are in the sixteenth century. It is from this point that one finds the word appearing more frequently in European languages, although in England there was still a preference for words such as commonwealth, kingdom or realm in mainstream political thought.

FORMAL FEATURES OF THE MODERN EUROPEAN STATE

This section will outline some formal, identifiable features of the State. Many of these formal abstract features can easily slip over into normative appraisals of a particular theory of the State. My argument is that these formal characteristics constitute a backcloth against which theorizing on the nature of the State takes place. In one sense, they are prerequisites for theorizing. They do not, however, constitute the essence of the State. The most crucial of these features is the idea of the State as a continuous public power above both ruler and ruled.

Primarily a State exists in a geographically identifiable territory over which it holds jurisdiction. Within this territory there exists a population, many of whom will be classed as citizens – namely they have specific rights and immunities within that territory. Territory is, of course, not an entirely safe or definite guide since States will often disagree on boundaries and claim quasi-jurisdictional interests beyond their boundaries.

A State will usually claim hegemony or predominance within a given territory over all other associations, organizations or groups within it. The motto 'thou shalt have no other association but me' is the conventional approach to group/State relations. However this supremacy is *legal* – it is based on rules which have some degree of universal recognition within the territory. In other words, the rules are not just the whims of the ruler. Thus exclusive power to determine rights and duties within a territorial limit is both *de facto* and *de jure*. Such an idea runs up against a multitude of problems. Since the advent of international legal, political, economic, military and cultural organization – for example, the existence of international law and courts, the United Nations, the EEC, GATT, NATO and the Warsaw Pact, as well as multinational companies and so on – it is less easy to speak of the dominance of a State even within its own territory. Despite this point there is still a formal acknowledgement that States have legal supremacy within their territory and that they are independent of external powers.

In comparison to groups within the State, it is generally true that the State has the maximal control over resources and force. At the same time it is not simply a power system. The forces of the State are regulated by rules, which of course can be distorted. However, the monopoly of force is tied to specific ends, namely the maintenance of internal order and external defence. The notion of internal order and defence are open to interpretation. The idea of legitimacy is important here since force exercised by the State is usually recognized by the population as distinct from other types of force. The State possesses authority to carry out actions. Its monopoly is recognized formally as necessary and *de jure*.

The State as supreme authority claims sole *imperium* within a territory. It is sovereign. This is an extremely problematic concept which will be touched upon throughout the book. On a very simplistic level what is meant here is two things: first, within a territory, the State has no rivals – it is predominant; second, externally, a State is sovereign if it is recognized by other States as a separate unit. This often boils down to the somewhat fuzzy notion of territorial integrity.

The State is the source of law or at least its very nature is tied up with the existence of law.[3] Law originates with the State. The most extreme version of this is the school of legal positivism. The State is recognized as the only source of compulsory rules. There are problems with this idea partly because it is now generally recognized that there are other traditions, such as natural law and customary law, which do not identify the State as the source of law. The whole point of the natural law approach is to argue that the State is subject *to* law or law pre-dates the State. However, even within legal positivism there is some recognition of different types of legal rule, some of which are not so susceptible to change by the State. H. L. A. Hart's ideas on secondary rules is a case in point (Hart, 1961).

The State tends to have wider or more comprehensive aims than most associations or groups. Its fundamental aim, in traditional terminology, is to promote the commonwealth or common good – although these terms are equally open to considerable interpretation. Furthermore, whereas most groups have a voluntary nature, the State in seeking it broad aims claims compulsion. No one can usually choose not to abide by traffic laws. Yet the voluntary and limited character of some groups is in doubt. No one can choose to be a member of a family. Many groups have complex rules which demand conformity and can, if disobeyed, result in punishment. If one were a member of the Catholic Church or the Mafia such punishments could have mortal significance. However, it is an approximate truth that States usually have broader and more comprehensive aims.

The really crucial formal feature of the State, which has most continuity and certainty in all States, is that it is a continuous public power. This public power is formally distinct from both ruler and ruled. Its acts have legal authority and are distinct from the intentions of individual agents or groups. Thus the State, as public power, embodies offices and roles which carry the authority of the State. Since this appears to give the State an autonomy apart from private individuals, many theorists have been led to accord the State a personality. It allows one to talk with ease of the State acting – an idea which will be discussed in later chapters where we shall see that a lot hangs on it. Many, however, find this idea abhorrent or simply incomprehensible. The main question which this book addresses is: what is this continuous public power? Formally, we can identify it as a crucial feature; however, the substantive answer to the question leads us directly into theories of the State. The main chapters of this book are answers to this central question. In other words, there are a number of different accounts of the nature of this public power which constitute theories of the State.

There are other apparently formal features which will not be discussed in this section since they are either highly contestable or deeply ambiguous – for example, the idea that all States are nations, centres of loyalty and patriotism, that States are organisms, or as the German theorist Bluntschli maintained, that the State is a masculine organism. If one delves into the diverse and often perverse literature on the State in the nineteenth and twentieth centuries there is no end to the oddities one can find on what is apparently essential to the State.

THE STATE AND OTHER COLLECTIVITIES

The concept of the State is often spoken of synonymously or in tandem with a number of concepts. This section will discuss the concepts of society, community, nation and government. It is hard in ordinary speech to avoid speaking of societies, nations or governments, when one means the State. There is nothing intrinsically wrong with this, but it is wise to be aware of the diverse uses of such concepts.

Society and the State

The manner in which we often speak of society and State as synonymous is confusing since the distinction between State and society has been of central importance to classical liberal thought. However it is explicable in another context. With the rise of sociology as a method of study – via such writers as Marx, Durkheim, Duguit and MacIver – the State was viewed increasingly as a subsystem of society. Studies centred on society as a self-sufficient entity, an encompassing network of relations with internal structures. The State was explained through society, it was not separate and distinct. Yet, if we look carefully at the concept of society we can identify a number of different senses in which it is used, some overlapping or coinciding, others distinct from the State.

There was no concept of society in Greek thought. Admittedly Aristotle had spoken of the *polis* as deriving out of the family (a characteristic 'society-orientated group'), yet he would not have acknowledged separate spheres of activity. The *polis* was a religious, ethical, communal, kin and military grouping rooted in human sociability. The first appearance of the word society is in Roman law, in the late Republic and early Empire, with the term *societas*.[4] A *societas* was a partnership, or more precisely a consensual contract, between freemen or citizens who were capable of sueing or being sued. It was a relation of free will based on a reciprocal agreement or contract for joint, mutually beneficial, action. The agreement entailed both parties becoming *socii* – partners. It was a relation dissolvable at will by the partners. It was contrasted to another type of grouping in law, the *universitas*. *Universitates* were groups whose unity and status was conferred on them by law from a higher authority. They could not be dissolved at will. Both *societas* and *universitas* were modes of association. Both were, more specifically, legal concepts.

Societas, however, was used during the middle ages to describe political organizations. It was convenient to describe the whole of a political grouping as a series of agreements or contracts. This was peculiarly appropriate to the feudal structure. On the other hand there were groups such as Guilds, cathedral chapters and universities which were described as *universitas*, although it is doubtful that they accepted the Roman law thesis that their unity was conferred on them and could simply be dissolved by a higher authority. *Societas* was also used by Stoic and Christian writers to describe relations going on beyond the *civitas*, in terms of a universal society. However, the application of *societas* to a whole political organization has been taken up again recently by the political philosopher Michael Oakeshott to describe a particular type of modern European State – a civil association manifesting civil privatism (Oakeshott, 1975).

In the eighteenth century a closely related but subtly different idea of society was used. Society was seen to be constituted by contracting individuals. No intermediate groups existed, rather society was seen as an aggregate of atomic individuals. This society is distinct from what might be called the State. It is an idea which has strong affinities with the classical liberal tradition of the nineteenth century. The most extreme version of this idea can be seen in the work of the modern American libertarian writer Murray Rothbard, who, from his extreme individualistic position, even chaffs at the very term 'society' as being too much of a collective fiction. For Rothbard only individuals exist and nothing else (Rothbard, 1978, p. 39). A subtle but important variant on this idea is that society is constituted *not* by individuals but by groups. Society is thus the collectivity of groups. This notion can found in the writings of Otto von Gierke, F. W. Maitland, J. N. Figgis and the young H. J. Laski. Variants of it can also be found in syndicalism and guild Socialism.

One final sense of society, which will be taken up in the next section, is as a synonym for the concept of community. The reason for this lies in group theory in the nineteenth century, as well as in the ambiguity of both concepts. Society was envisaged as a fellowship, a communal bond of shared values. This, of course, conflicts violently with the individualist notion of society which conceived of purely contractual relations between individuals.

In sum we have society understood as: (1) characterizing any social unit from the family to international society; (2) the Roman law sense, a legalistic way of characterizing certain groups; (3) society used to describe a particular type of civil State; (4) society as an aggregate of contracting individuals independent of the State; (5)

society seen as a collection of groups as in the pluralist tradition; (6) society taken as synonymous with community.[5]

From these various senses it can be seen that society can either overlap or be distinct from the State. In many ways State and society are intimately bound to each other. The definition of each and their relation changes within the general theory in which they are discussed. For example, if the State is regarded as a sovereign corporate entity then it could be said to create all subgroups or associations. In this sense, society, including the so-called natural groups like the family, are offspring from the State. They have no independent life. On the other hand, if sovereignty is said to reside in the collectivity of individuals or groups who create the State for certain limited ends, then the whole argument is reversed, society becomes an independent entity. In this sense it is difficult to separate the normative and descriptive uses of the concept. The significance which is attributed to State and society at various points in history may reflect an oscillating or shifting pattern of involvement between public and private goods or collective and individual goals, which has been suggested in recent years from an economic perspective by A. Hirschman (1982) and an ideological perspective by W. H. Greenleaf (1983, Vol. 2).

Community and the State

Community suffers from the ambiguity of society. This is specifically the case when community is used as a synonym for society. Society can be characterized by shared common ends or feelings. On the other hand community can take on more the contractual features of civil society in phrases such as the 'community of nations' or 'political community'.

Most commentators see the origins of the discussion of community at the close of the eighteenth century in Germany. Community was contrasted to the contractualism and individualism of the Enlightenment. It denoted a new type of legitimacy which was purportedly more natural to humans. It implied fellowship, personal intimacy and wholeness, moral commitment and social cohesiveness. In community, citizens found an identity and purpose. As Nisbet argued, community 'is a fusion of tradition and commitment, of membership and volition' (1970, p. 48). The distinction between a natural, harmonious community as against an imposed artificial and disruptive order haunts many thinkers from the eighteenth century to the present. Burke's vision of a traditionalist society based on a natural hierarchy is contrasted to a rootless, democratically levelled society upset by rampant individualism, as in revolutionary France. Hegel also had set an ethical community against the rootlessness of civil society. Gierke praised the communal fellowship of *Genossenschaft* as against the divisiveness of *Herrschaft*. In Britain, Coleridge's, Disraeli's and later T. S. Eliot's barely disguised contempt for commercial individualistic society is confronted by their traditional pastoral vision of one nation, a latter-day medieval nostalgia, reflected also in the work of William Morris, the Guild Socialists and even in Tawney's distinction between an 'acquisitive' as against a 'functional' society (see Tawney 1921).

The most famous rendering of this type of distinction is by the German sociologist F. Tönnies in his book *Community and Association* (1955). Although Tönnies, influenced by Gierke's idea of the *Genossenschaft*, had an undoubted nostalgia for community as a better way of life, it is important to note that he employed the terms 'community' and 'association' as social scientific categories. He was not writing an ethical treatise on community.

Simply put, *Gemeinschaft* (community) implied a face-to-face relationship based on family, kinship, neighbourhood and friendship. *Gesellschaft* can be translated as society, although association is more usual. It implies a more formal, legalistic, impersonal relation which is individualistic and contractual in character. This fits closely to the Roman view of *societas*. *Gesellschaft* is not morally undesirable for Tönnies. It is in fact the basis for the development of modern life and industry. Most of the arts and sciences develop in the the context of 'association'. *Gesellschaft* embodies the critical rational intelligence of which Tönnies's own book was a product. Yet the development of *Gesellschaft*, which means the advance of the State, bureaucratization and rational civilization – something that Max Weber was to expand – would also lead to the decline of community. There is thus a sense of gloom in Tönnies's study. States will artifically try to re-create communal sentiments via social security, welfare and insurance, but this is doomed to failure. Unlike Marx, Tönnies thought that capitalism and all the values it encouraged was caused *by* the loss of community and not vice versa. He also did not share Marx's or Gierke's optimism that community could be recovered in the future. Thus, for Tönnies, community was distinct from both the State and society relations.

European thought has been divided on the issue of community. Writers such as Durkheim read 'society' through communitarian ideas. Society was not a constellation of private contractual interests.

It was a corporate whole with a collective conscience. The human being was knowable only as a manifestation of the community. The function of the division of labour in modern society was social integration (see Durkheim, 1967). The heavy emphasis on the values of communal life has also been more recently investigated in the writings of theorists such as A. Maslow, H. Marcuse and E. Fromm. The liberal individualistic tradition from Locke and Bentham up to Hayek emphasizes the idea of society as an aggregative notion and is consequently deeply critical of communitarianism. This has been very much the case in the post-Nazi era. Thinkers such as R. Dahrendorf have seen communitarian ideas as potentially profoundly illiberal, reactionary and disturbing (see Plant, 1974, pp. 33–4).

Community, *prima facie*, implies some sense of belonging, locality, a shared set of values, beliefs or purposes. This may lead us to the conclusion that community is opposed to, or markedly distinct from, the State. This would however only be a half-truth. A lot again depends upon one's theory of the State. If the State is regarded as simply a bureaucratic and governmental order or body of institutions, then it could be said to be distinct from community. On the other hand, if we regard the State as a more total order embracing all social relationships and embodying common ethical ideals, then in an important sense it could be said to embrace community. Thus the meaning of community, like society, ties in closely with how one theorizes the State.

Nation and State

The term nation State has become a commonplace in political discussion in the twentieth century. There are approximately 150 entities calling themselves nation States; we also have a United Nations, transnational and multinational groups, nationality laws and so on. In fact the term nation has become a shorthand for State. But what is nationalism and where does it derive from?

Nationalism is a comparatively recent phenomenon dating from the late eighteenth and early nineteenth century. It derived from a number of sources. Popular sovereignty ideas, which identified the 'whole' people as sovereign, as in Rousseau's general will, formed a somewhat confused background to many eighteenth- and nineteenth-century democratic revolutions, beginning with the French revolution. The French revolutionaries were the the first to speak of a 'national assembly', an assembly which declared in 1789 that 'sovereignty . . . belongs to the entire nation'. Absolute monarchy had prepared the ground for this, since it established settled boundaries, centralized rule and bureaucracy, a uniform language and consequently reduced the heterogeneity and localism of feudalism. The breakdown of feudalism and localism was also necessary to incubate nationalistic ideas. Thus absolutism is sometimes seen as the cradle of nationalism. Irish nationalism dates from 1815, stimulated by French ideas. Most other European countries soon followed. In France Napoleon was to declare himself as different from all other dictators. He was the first 'popular' dictator, something that Benjamin Constant and other liberals were to criticize (see Dodge, 1980, pp. 24–5).

Another major source of nationalistic ideas was the reaction to the Enlightenment and cosmopolitanism that can be found in the German romantic and historicist traditions. Thinkers such as Herder, Fichte, and the young Hegel, spoke in organicist terms of 'people's spirits' (*Volkgeist*). Early theories of racial typology and linguistic and cultural identity were formulated which rejected universalism. As Herder stated 'The savage who loves himself, his wife and his child . . . and works for the good of his tribe as for his own . . . is in my view more genuine than that human ghost, the . . . citizen of the world, who, burning with love for all his fellow ghosts, loves a chimera. The savage in his hut has room for any stranger. . . . The saturated heart of the idle cosmopolitan is a home for no one' (quoted in Dunn, 1979, p. 77). These ideas were developed in the nineteenth century by racial theorists such as Gobineau. Undoubtedly there were many politicians who saw these ideas as useful tools to combine with juridical theories of the State. It gave their actions an added purpose and lustre. The development of the power and resources of States through industrialization in the nineteenth century only increased the use of nationalism as a unifying tool. Socialist movements and the working class fell in line with this pattern. Some political scientists have linked up nationalism with the thesis of modernization. It is viewed as one way of maintaining cohesiveness and identity during a period of modernization and structural upheaval.

Nationalism usually functions in three areas, with varying emphasis. It explains the common origin of a particular group, sometimes in relation to a particular place; it provides a sense of identity to a group and legitimates the ruling authorities; it also usually proposes certain ideals to aspire to. In working though these areas it manipulates myth, symbols, feelings, often utilizing religion, culture, tradition, history and language. In the late nineteenth and twentieth centuries spurious socio-biological theories were also brought into play. Thus nationalism is not simply affection for one's culture, language or neighbourhood. It is far stronger and less comprehensible than patriotism, loyalty or kinship affection. Therefore, for the proponent of nationalism it explains the natural basis of the State and its boundaries. It gives an account of beliefs and the destiny of a people. For social scientists and historians nationalism functions to unify a group internally by encouraging a sense of homogeneity. It may overcome class divisions and help to mobilize a population, especially in times of crisis. With the loss of more traditional beliefs through the advance of secularization and literacy it may also help to knit a society together (see Gellner, 1983).

One general point to note here is that nationalism can serve many different masters. Although initially in the 1830s being associated with more liberal and democratic movements it could also be reactionary, negative and regressive. As the former German Chancellor, Prince von Bülow, observed: 'It was the liberals who first expressed the idea of German unity and spread it through the people. . . . The goal could not be reached by the course which they followed. Then conservative policy had to step in, in order, as Bismarck expressed it, to realise the literal idea by means of conservative action' (quoted in Jay, 1984, p. 196). Nationalism has become the tool of all powerful States in the twentieth century, of whatever political complexion.

The classifications of nationalism are also many and various. The simplest distinction is between the ethnic and cultural nationalisms of the nineteenth century, which were liberal in demeanour, as against the post-war anti-colonial nationalisms, which were more limited in scope and less literate. Many might now add separatist or unificatory nationalisms within European societies. Much more sophisticated typologies have, however, been put forward in the last two decades (see Orridge, 1981).

What, however, is the relationship of nationalism to the State? Practically it would be hard for anyone to deny the impact of nationalism. In the gradual unification and development of States it was a vital tool for governments to exploit. It helped mobilize populations, providing an extremely effective rationale for geopolitical claims. It also provided reasons for overcoming internal divisions within the State, a process which had been going on from the sixteenth century. Nationalism met this general demand for uniformity in administration, taxation and political centralization. Theoretically it is a different case. Despite all the nationalistic myths, the State pre-dated the existence of nationalism. Nationalism would not really have made much sense to even late absolutist monarchs. Localism was still active and rife under one of the most absolutist of monarchs, Louis XIV. States quite clearly can exist without nationalism, although the converse is not true. Further, whereas States do exist and can be explained juridically, nations are emotive artifices. There are *no* adequate theories of nationalism, although there may be adequate theories *about* what nationalism does. Nationalism in itself is theoretically incoherent, if practically effective. States do not coincide with nations, in fact the majority of States embody multinational populations and whereas membership of a State is a matter of law, national membership is a crude amalgam of birth, bloodline, culture, tradition and so on.

Thus, despite the common usage of the term nation, specifically in the context 'nation State', and the fact that nationalism has been closely associated on a practical level with the State in the nineteenth and twentieth centuries, there is still no theoretical warrant for it. The State is a debatable concept, but it has an intellectual content. Nationalism, by comparison, is simplistic and inchoate. The coincidence between the two terms is thus a historical freak which it would be a relief to abandon.

Government, administration and the State

One of the most tempting synonyms for the State is the term government. In fact government is a far older term than State or administration. Government was usually employed in the middle ages for ruling, deriving from the Latin *gubernatio* or *gubernator*, to steer or a steersman. The term government seems to have come into English speech via the old French, *gouvernement*, in the 1500s.

Government can be understood in a number of senses. Firstly, it can refer to the person or persons who do the actual 'steering' at a particular point in time. It is thus simply equivalent to those who are ruling and declaring the law. In this sense, in England, it would have referred specifically to the monarch and also possibly Parliament. This is a very broad sense of the term. Secondly, with the comparatively late grasp of separate spheres of rule, it referred to the person or persons in the executive as distinct from the legislative. This sense of the term is still present today. A refinement of this second sense focuses on the 'offices' of the executive. The government is not so much the persons, but the offices responsible for ensuring that the declared laws are enforced. Another sense is that which views government as the policy-determining body which both declares and enforces the law. In Britain this tends to centre on Parliament, in J. S. Mill's terms a 'representative government'. This sense has increasingly centred on a small group within the representatives, the cabinet within the party, the inner cabinet or possibly just the Prime Minister. In this sense the cabinet or Prime Minister is the monarchy in commission, being advised by civil servants (see Dyson, 1980, p. 210). This can be refined again still further to say that government refers to the totality of continuing institutional machinery, incorporating all the varying offices and roles. One important point to note here is that none of these senses of government necessarily link up with the State.

In France and Germany the terms *gouvernement* and *Regierung* were and are very much narrower and more restricted in their usage than government in Britain. In France it has been by and large restricted to the executive, as in the Fifth Republic's *gouvernement présidentiel*, having powers distinct from the assembly. Government was thus restricted by the separation of powers. In Germany *Regierung*, apart from its older association with a ruler, came to be seen as an aspect of executive power not much different from administration (see Willoughby, 1896, chap. 2; Dyson, 1980, pp. 209–11). In France and Germany the notion of government was understood more narrowly in the context of an over-arching State. In Britain this is not the case, thus the term has tended to take on broader connotations. There is little sense in Britain of the State as a public power which acts and links government into a wider framework. The preference has been either to collapse the government into the State or to talk of fuzzy 'State substitutes' such as the Crown, which no one quite understands.

One further concept which should be kept distinct from both government and State is administration. Despite the use of the term 'new or old administration', referring to government, administration is distinct. It developed initially under the aegis of absolutist monarchy which broke down the feudal fealty relation and established officials, servants of the Crown, whose existence was dependent on service. The absolute monarchs required these officials to carry out the general services necessary for the maintenance of ordered rule on a day-by-day basis. This process was accelerated by the monarchy's demand for more centralized laws and taxes in order to carry out dynastic wars. Efficient collection of taxes needed administrators. Thus administration can be defined as the 'the sum of persons and bodies who are engaged, under the direction of government, in discharging the ordinary public services' (Barker,

1944, p. 3). Every right and duty has a corresponding service. In this manner administration is closer to a narrower sense of government in terms of a policy-enforcing executive. In practice, administration may play a more dynamic role in policy formulation, however this is not its *leitmotif*.

One final question remains here: why is it that many identify the State and government, in what a recent commentator has called such a 'slipshod' way (Siedentrop, 1983, p. 54)? A number of writers have however adopted this slipshod path. G. D. H. Cole spoke of the State as 'the national governmental machine' (1920, p. 86); H. J. Laski commented that a realistic analysis of the State suggests that 'State action is, in actual fact, action by the government' (1919, p. 30); and recently J. C. Rees suggested that in ordinary speech and sometimes political theory 'the word "State" has meant *government as an institution*' (1969, p. 216). A similar form of argument can be found in many anarchist, libertarian and communist writers. Some of the reasons for the synonymity do seem justifiable. The distinction between the two terms, as Laski (1935, p. 25) comments, is largely theoretical rather than practical. Most citizens do not perceive the State acting but rather 'persons in government'. The State is an abstraction which many find difficult to grasp. Anarchists, amongst others, would argue that this mystique of the State simply shields the people behind it in government. Another important reason for the synonymity is that in early forms of State, for example in absolutist monarchies, the sovereigns, as the governing authorities, consciously identified themselves with the State. The only way out from this impasse was to distinguish the *office* from the *person* of the sovereign, or the natural from the artificial person. This was often spoken of in terms of the king's two bodies (see Kantorowicz, 1957). This point will be explored in the next chapter.

Despite these points there are good reasons for keeping the two concepts distinct. Historically and anthropologically it is clear that both the concept and practice of government existed before the State. Government can and does exist without the State. In one sense the State can be viewed as a species of the genus government. There are thus non-State forms of government. Juristically most State theorists have seen the State as an inclusive public power which dignifies government. Government carries the authority of the State, a continuous authority which is above both ruler and ruled, which provides continuity and coherence to the political organization. One important value in distinguishing the State from the government is that it allows the structured changes and removal of governments to proceed while still maintaining the continuity and legitimacy of the social order. If government were totally identified with the State, then each removal of government would entail a crisis in the State. This point should also make us very wary of linking up all the practices of government with the State.

COGNATE CONCEPTS OF THE STATE

There are a number of concepts which are closely linked to the idea of the State. The concept of sovereignty is the best known. The term 'sovereign State' is part of our day-to-day political vocabulary. Yet what is sovereignty? Does a State have to be sovereign to be a State? Does sovereignty mean anything significant?

It is doubtful whether the concept of sovereignty was known in all its fullness before the fifteenth and sixteenth centuries. It was not an idea familiar to Greek, Roman or medieval thought, although there were many attributes familiar to these periods, which were discussed, and have subsequently been integrated into the discussion of sovereignty. For example, Aristotle clearly realized, in his study of various constitutions, that something needs to be 'superior' in a political unit, whether it be one, few or the many. This 'position of superiority', as an essential ingredient of any constitution, was accorded a certain dignity and majesty.

Roman law contributed most to the theory of sovereignty, specifically after its revival in European thought in the twelfth and thirteenth centuries. It provided a vocabulary for speaking of authority and power. For example, *potestas* denoted official legal power, which all magistrates possessed. *Potestas* was distinct from *auctoritas*, which meant influence or prestige, and ensured that one's view would be accepted. *Imperium* was a discretionary power to perform acts in the interest of the whole political organization. It was a right to command inherent in certain offices. Under the Roman Republic it was limited in scope. *Imperium* was usually obtained by a consul, and later by the emperor, from the senate, army or people via the famous doctrine of *lex regia*. This doctrine maintained that all powers were derived and conferred by the people. This was later systematized in the emperor Justinian's law codes. In the evolution of the Roman Empire the emperors increasingly took over the qualities which were supposedly confined to the people. In the Roman Republic leading statesmen had been called *principes*. The title was usually in recognition of their authority. The first emperors, like Augustus, called themselves *princeps* in consequence. It was often recognized, even in the Republic, that such men were potential dynasts, exercising illicit powers. Martial success was often supplemented with legal recognition. The *princeps* utilized his authority and *Imperium* and was consequently often referred to as *Imperator*. Despite the recognition by practitioners of Roman law up to the sixth century that the ultimate source of political power was the people, another important line of argument had gained credence, namely that political power was related in some way to the *Imperium*. It was recognized that political organization required a supreme will and that this will was the source of law. This was the doctrine of *legibus solutus* (what pleases the prince has the force of law). Emperors were sometimes referred to as 'living law'. Inherent in the office of the emperor was the right to command. Thus the emperor was legislator (literally *legis lator* – the proposer of the law). In the early period of the Empire there was not really a firm distinction between the doctrines of *lex regia* and *legibus solutus*. The emperor's power to enact law was seen to express and articulate the will of the people. Under the later Roman emperors, such as Constantine and Diocletian, as under the later absolute monarchs, the doctrine of *legibus solutus* was emphasized and *lex regia* diminished in significance. The former doctrine entailed, logically, that the emperor possessed *plenitudo potestatis*, or the fullness of legal power. He also possessed influence and the prestige to carry through measures, therefore he had authority (*auctoritas*). Thus during the late Roman Empire, legal and political superiority increasingly centred on the emperor as the linchpin of the whole organization, the centre of dignity and majesty, an office that was the source of law and not subject to it. This was effectively the first formulation of the theory of public power, later to be linked to sovereignty.

Despite the fact that papal rule tried to emulate many of the Roman law attributes of the emperor, something that secular rulers learned from the papacy, the middle ages was not a period of spectacular development in sovereignty theory. The feudal ruler did not really possess any *Imperium* and was not viewed as *legibus solutus*. Rulers were seen far more in contractual terms. This idea was also fostered in the Church by the conciliarist movement which envisaged authority to lie in the whole Church, not the Pope. Many monarchs were also regarded not as hereditary rulers, but rather as elective officers tied by coronation oaths. They were not the source of law but were rather constrained by customary law. The debate as to whether, for example, the English Parliament *made* law or *declared* existing law was active up to the eighteenth century. The existence of strong codes of customary law, the contractual character of feudalism, the resilience of the many and various estates' assemblies, guilds and towns did not foster the centralization of authority and power. If anything sovereignty was more diffuse, cellular and devolved to groups – an observation which was taken up by sixteenth-century critics of absolute monarchy and nineteenth century exponents of group theory such as Otto von Gierke. Forms of popular and group sovereignty were nourished by the communal life of towns and guilds from the thirteenth century, although the proponents would not have used the appellation 'sovereignty'.

The first real conscious and systematic use of the word sovereignty was by the French thinker Jean Bodin. He also seems to have associated it closely to the State, although there is some debate on this point. France was passing rapidly out of feudalism in the French Wars of Religion. The problem of order was paramount for many theorists. Bodin was a member of the *politiques*, a Catholic royalist group who advocated some toleration. Bodin's theory of sovereignty was fully formulated in his work *The Six Bookes of a Commonweale* (1576). It was designed to meet the problems of order, as well as to systematically explore the domain of politics. Sovereignty was described by Bodin as a 'supreme power over citizens and subjects unrestrained by law'. It was seen as essential to any commonwealth and by nature absolute, perpetual, indivisable, imprescriptible and inalienable. Sovereignty was the source of law and could not be restrained by law. Consequently, for Bodin the sovereign could not be resisted lawfully. The foundations were laid in this account for the absolutist theorists (see Skinner, 1978, Vol. 2, p. 287).[6] Bodin's and Thomas Hobbes' theories furnished the basis for later seventeenth- and eighteenth-century absolutism and also for modern discussions of sovereignty.

The opposition to this line of thought on sovereignty largely concentrated on forms of limited sovereignty, associated with the more constitutional tradition. Initially this was represented in a group called the Monarchomachs, whose most famous theorist was François Hotman. However, limited sovereignty theories also became absorbed into the mainstream of the natural right and contract theories and subsequently into classical liberal thought. Some of the key senses of sovereignty in contemporary usage will now be reviewed in relation to the idea of the State.

Sovereignty implies supremancy or superiority. The paradox of sovereignty is based on the fact that it is difficult to conceive of 'limited' supremacy. The logic of sovereignty is that something is

supreme or unlimited in every State. This is essentially the logic of
Bodin on sovereignty. In spite of this, Bodin and many others have
proposed diverse forms of limitation intrinsic to sovereignty. It is
important to point out that no sovereignty theorists, even absolutists,
were arguing that sovereignty is simply the *de facto* ability to coerce
persons or groups. Sovereignty was always understood as *de jure*.
Even if the sovereign was the source of law, which might lead to the
conclusion that sovereignty was not legal and therefore simply *de facto*
power, sovereignty was legalistic. As 'living law' the prince's
supremacy was seen as just. However, this does not overcome the
logical paradox that if the king is not subject to the law, how can
sovereignty be legal? Yet no sixteenth-century proponents of
sovereignty viewed it as anything other than *de jure*, and no monarchs
wanted to be seen as simply autocrats with an ability to coerce.

In the sixteenth century, sovereignty was initially thought of as the
supreme authority of a person, monarch or emperor. This followed
directly upon the later Roman law descriptions of the emperor. The
sovereign person might be viewed as a real person who possessed
sovereign power in land or property. On the other hand it could be
viewed as an artificial person – *persona ficta* – a creation of law. In this
latter sense the person is embodied in an office representing the
whole realm. In both senses, supremacy is embodied in the person.
The person is the living law. Sovereignty in this context also implied
the majesty, dignity and independence of the person, as well as the
special prerogatives and privileges accorded to the royal personage.

A second usage of sovereignty, which derives out of the attribution
of sovereignty to a person and ties closely to the State, is sovereignty
expressing the 'personality of the State'. In this idea the attributes of
the person, the capacity to perform duties and possess rights, the
ability to act and so forth, are attributed to the State. Sovereignty
indicates, in this usage, the completely independent personality of the
State. The personality is legal, not physical or psychological. It is, in
other words, an abstract person, not connected in any way with
individuals.

With the increasingly abstract quality to the State, sovereignty was
used to express more collective notions. The critics of absolute
sovereignty relied on the idea of the supremacy of the people and
their ultimate power and authority. This idea can be found in
embryo in the Roman law doctrine of *lex regia*, which argued that
power was conferred by the people or *populus*. Some absolutists who
acknowledged this point got round it by arguing that the people had
once and for all alienated their power and authority to the monarch.

Thus it could not be retrieved. This initiated a long-running debate as to whether power was really alienated or simply delegated for a period. The supremacy of the people, however, can be understood in a number of ways. It could mean that the 'whole' people, within a territory, possess sovereignty. Before the practice of democracy this might not mean very much. Secondly, the supremacy might lie with an electorate, which could of course vary in size considerably depending on how you define a voter. Thirdly, the people's authority could be represented in some form of assembley who speak as the sovereign. Fourthly, the people or *populus* could be said to include the king and his government, thus 'any corporatist definition of *populus* must include the king himself' (Wootton, 1986, p. 48). This idea entailed that the king could not be resisted in the name of the *populus*, which was the subtle idea explored by some writers in the English civil war. Finally, the people could be interpreted as a nation. Nation, if examined in racial terms, could presumably rule out sections of a people as aliens.

Another important use of sovereignty is in relation to the law. Sovereignty, in this sense, is supreme legal authority. Again this is rather ambivalent. Legal sovereignty could simply be an expression of the self-sufficiency of a legal order, possibly set against other legal units. This refers to the capacity of the order to create its own rules, rights and duties. A second sense of legal sovereignty is the legal omnicompetence of a legislative organ such as Parliament; thirdly, the existing body of laws and a linking norm in a legal hierarchy, as in Hans Kelsen's *Grundnorm* (1945). The fundamental norm in a legal hierarchy (*Grundnorm*) holds together the whole structure of rules and thus functions as a sovereign. This has close parallels with the oldest use of legal authority – namely the development out of the natural and customary law traditions – and also the idea of constitutional law. A constitution in this context would be a body of rules which is different in character to all other rules. These constitutional rules determine the way in which all other rules are identified, adjudicated and changed. They determine the structure of institutions, offices and roles and cannot be changed without fundamental and profound discussion. In this situation legal sovereignty refers specifically to the sovereignty of constitutional rules. The strongly moralistic character of much early consitutional thought also raises another slight variant, namely that constitutional laws are sovereign in so far as they are moral. Unlike the trend within legal positivism, early constitutional theorists would not have seen a separation between law and morality. Constitutional laws would be compatible with moral rules.

The most popular use of sovereignty since the seventeenth century, and theoretically one of the most odd, is that which argues that supremacy is shared amongst a number of elements. Its proponents tried to combine, in various ways, elements from ruler, popular and legal sovereignty. The British doctrine of the Crown in Parliament or the American separation of powers are typical examples. Dicey's discussion of the *legal* sovereignty of Parliament and the *political* sovereignty of the electorate, is another attempt to combine divers elements (Dicey, 1902). Sometimes sovereignty was seen in the mixture of elements – giving rise to the idea of the mixed constitution. Others tried to diversify and separate the legislative, executive and judicial elements. The oddity of these interpretations is to know where sovereignty lies or even whether it is worth discussing. They seem to defy the logic of sovereignty.

One final sense, which touches on the same problems as above, is the notion of the sovereignty of groups, in other words pluralized sovereignty. Sovereignty is here envisaged as being widely dispersed amongst groups; it is neither in institutions nor spheres of government. English pluralists and guild socialists were exponents of this idea.

The question remains: is sovereignty necessary to the State? Is State sovereignty a pleonasm? Again everything depends on one's view of 'sovereignty' and 'State'. If sovereignty implies a person with supreme authority or conversely the predominance of a series of constitutional rules, then clearly there are non-sovereign States. It is also questionable as to whether federal States can be classed as internally sovereign. On the other hand, certain absolutist theorists grasped the idea of the State solely in terms of the idea of sovereignty.

Authority, obligation and legitimacy

In contemporary discussion it is difficult to separate any of the above concepts from the the idea of the State. Admittedly all of them exist in non-State contexts. Questions of authority, obligation and legitimacy are always found where people gather together for some activity which depends on their several roles. However, we refer to them in their political setting. Authority originates in the Roman term *auctoritas* which meant the capacity to influence people. This was initially separate from the ideas of *Imperium* and *potestas*, and was gradually tied into the office of the emperor or ruler. Authority now usually implies some degree of official power, the obedience of others and specific functions, within the confines of certain rules. Someone in authority has a right of command. This is distinct from the simple exercise of power or force. Authority is, in a sense, the legitimate use of force.

Legitimacy derives from the Latin for law and is of the same root as the words legislator and legislation. A legitimate authority is one which is recognized as valid or justified by those to whom it applies. It is recognized as lawful, just or rightful. In this context coercion or force by a State authority is seen to be justified. The legitimacy of a political order is its worthiness, the sense in which it is a locus of the public will. The political order has a right to command and make rules which it expects will be complied with. It involves 'the capacity of the system to engender and maintain the belief that the existing political institutions are the most appropriate to one's society' (S. M. Lipset quoted in Connolly, 1984, p. 10). Admittedly there are different types of legitimacy, as in Weber's famous classification of charismatic, traditional and rational–legal. Also, many individuals obey simply out of apathy or unthinking acquiescence; however, all States – whatever their ideological complexion – will seek legitimacy from sections, if not the whole, of their populations. The quest for legitimacy is the provenance not only of liberal democratic States.

Some recent theorists, for example Jürgen Habermas and Klaus Offe, have given particular attention to the concept of legitimacy. In Habermas's terms the modern capitalist State is caught in a legitimation crisis. It is subject to contradictory imperatives. The State must on the one hand maintain the condition of capital accumulation and free enterprise. It must appease the interests of business and capital in order to retain its legitimacy. On the other hand, to avoid social crises and some of the dysfunctional effects of capitalism on other sectors of the poulation, the State must try to manage, steer and intervene in the economy. Capitalism, in generating expectations of increasing consumption, has increased pressure on governments to intervene in industry and maximize production. State involvement often generates a demand for more State involvement. If the State responds to one set of imperatives it undermines and produces a deficit on its legitimacy with other sectors of the society. This leads ultimately to crises of inflation, public finances and rational administration. Habermas also sees a motivational crisis in the population. Capitalism requires a basic moral and cultural consensus resting paradoxically on pre-capitalistic values of trust, honesty, fair-dealing, promise-keeping, and so on. Yet the values of capitalistic individualism, namely self-interest and instrumental rationality, undermine that cultural consensus necessary for the functioning of a capitalist order. This leads again to an increasing legitimation deficit (see Habermas, 1976; Plant, 1982; Connolly, 1984).

Both authority and legitimacy are closely tied to the concept of obligation. Authority embodies the presumption of legitimacy. In turn, legitimate authority presumes a right to act which correlates with the duty of obedience. As Hannah Pitkin argues 'To call something a legitimate authority is normally to imply that it ought to be obeyed. . . . Part of what "authority" means is that those subject to it are obligated' (1972, p. 77). This argument can be and has been taken to unwarranted lengths, where it is claimed that part of the meaning of the word State and authority (presumably semantically and practically) *is* that citizens are obligated. Thus there is no need to raise any further questions about why one obeys. There is no need to look any further than the semantic rules governing the meaning of the words involved. Theorists, for example Carole Pateman and Richard Flathman, have criticized this conclusion, arguing that it involves an uncritical acceptance of semantic rules and stretches conceptual analysis too far. Also, the concept obligation contains preceptive elements bound up with how 'good' or 'desirable' it is. These elements need to be evaluated. As Flathman argues: 'The fact that words have a certain established use is in itself hardly a reason for acting in a manner that affects other people. If instead of saying "That was what I was ordered to do" Eichman had said "That is what the words 'authoritative command' mean", he would hardly have added to the strength of his case' (1972, p. 105). For Flathman, Pitkin's position can lead to abject conformism to established usage. We need to reason critically about alternatives and to raise general questions about obligation. None the less obligation is still, for Flathman, a rule-governed practice which really only makes sense in the context of the State.

Without repeating this argument *ad infinitum*, a similar point holds for the concepts of law and rights. Apart from the natural law tradition, arguments on law and rights presume the existence of some notion of the State. This is specifically the case with the mainstream legal positivist tradition. Thus it is clear that the most important political concepts presume and subsist within the parameters of the State and will often change in character according to the State theory concerned.

THEORY AND THE STATE

> There never has been an age so theory-drenched as ours.
>
> Taylor, *Ideology, Philosophy and Politics*

A theory is essentially a systematic mesh of interconnected concepts which purports to characterize, describe and explain reality. It is a mental schema which makes sense of the world and may often prescribe courses of action. All theories are open to criticism, although some more than others. Social and political theories tend to differ from scientific theories. It is much harder to say that social and political theories are true or false, partly because the falsity of one theory will be premised on the assumption of another theory, assumptions which again may be judged as false by others. Social and political theories tend actually to constitute the reality of politics; there is no independent reality to which they apply or which will adjudicate between the competing claims to truth. We explain and understand ourselves in politics in theoretical terms. Theory thus has a constitutive role. Scientific theories, on the contrary, aim to establish the truth or falsity of their claims and are wary of saying that theory constitutes reality – although there seems to be some movement of science in this very direction, specifically at the sharp end of research into the physical structure of matter. Social and political theories, unlike those in science, are not really empirically testable. The test of social and political theory is rather its fruitfulness in explaining the social world, not its empirical adequacy. Further, unlike scientific theory, social and political theory will often prescribe conduct and change the social reality. This is because such theories are part of our self-understanding.

All theories involve certain elements. There are certain basic principles, axioms or assumptions involving definitions. These immediately delimit an area and impose an order on a multiplicity of details. Definition tells us how an author is using key terms and this involves considerable selection and abstraction. It is not the case that particular definitions and premises in discussion on the State will lead to similar conclusions. There is no necessary process of inference from premises to formal structures. Both Hobbes and Locke shared many individualistic assumptions, as also do John Rawls and Robert Nozick. However, in the case of Hobbes the contractual process leads to an absolute monarchy and in Locke to a rudimentary constitutional theory. In Rawls, the conclusion is a social democratic welfare State;

in Nozick, a minimalist State and a free market economy.

The initial assumptions and definitions will allow the theorist firstly to describe the world, although implicit within the description are certain parameters. The description will be closely tied to an explanation of what is going on. The theorist will not be satisfied with an endless narration of facts. All description is rooted in certain assumptions and it culminates in an attempt to make sense of the world by explanation. Social and political explanations tend to be very diverse. Unlike scientific theories the explanations of political reality are usually extremely varied and often conflicting.

Finally, theory in the social and political context, involves recommendations, normative assessments and prescriptions. The theorist will set standards and lay down forms of conduct which are desirable. This will often result in schematizing ideals to pursue forms of perfectibility which 'ought' to be sought. All social and political theory contains this normative component.

However, what of the claim that the factual elements should be kept clearly distinct from the more evaluative elements in a theory? A theory which becomes so absorbed in the normative component may not allow the evidence of facts to count against it. It will become a 'closed' theory. It might be argued that there are certain facts to be described in the State. The State, for example, involves the facts of government, a monopoly of force and a legal system. After the facts are established normative assessment arises. Yet can the judgement of what is factually the case be dissociated from the normative assessment? An anarchist may accept the description of the State as a monopoly of force. The description by the anarchist is typical of the nature of theory itself, which is a valued framework which secretes notions of 'good' and 'value' into the actual descriptive process. The anarchist's conclusions on the State are embodied in his theoretical premises. The description of the State, as a monopoly of force, lays the foundation for saying that if you value liberty or autonomy, and liberty is construed as contrary to 'being forced or coerced', then the less State the more liberty, which is precisely what the anarchist would prescribe to us. It might be argued at this point that there must be something, some facts, to which we attach the concept of the State. Yet the point is that *all* the concepts used to give factual sense to the State are themselves philosophically challengeable and normatively based. This point raises a question mark over factual description. Heuristically it is valuable to maintain the notion of description when breaking down the concept of theory, but it doubtful whether it can be separated from the normative component.

Thus it is virtually impossible to gain an empirical 'knock-out' of a theory. There are no independent facts to which it must correspond. The political world is already saturated with ideas and values. We must seek a certain coherence and consistency within a theoretical construct, as well as clarity of exposition, but even here it is difficult to gain any finally agreed conventions of explanatory adequacy, clarity or rationality since they will vary with the theory concerned. What is clarity to Karl Marx would be obfuscation to Hayek, what was lucidity itself to Heidegger would have been gibberish to J. L. Austin and vice versa.

Essential contestability and the State

State is a contested concept and, therefore, involves problems of meaning and application.

> Dyson, *The State Tradition in Western Europe*

There are a number of functions that the political theorist has always performed. One of these, which has been given a great deal of emphasis in the post-war period, is that of the analysis of concepts. There is considerable heuristic value to any student of politics in analysing and unpacking arguments and concepts to illustrate their various uses. It is now argued by some political theorists that many concepts in social and political life are subject to *continual* dispute and contestation. This is not simply a claim that the concept is contested or argued about and that a resolution may at some point be found; it is rather the case that the concepts are *essentially* contested. The proper use of these concepts inevitably involves endless disputation about their proper use. Even the criteria of their application are contested. For the proponents of this position essential contestability establishes the propriety and necessity of continual argument and disagreement about fundamentals (see Gallie, 1955–6; Connolly, 1983). One recognizes the permanent value of alternatives. Some theorists, for example W. B. Gallie, argue that such a recognition raises the quality of argument. There are obviously certain elements in common between positions, common resources of reason and evidence, which allow mutual recognition of a topic. In terms of the State these might be the 'formal features' outlined in an earlier section. However these are insufficient to reduce the variety of interpretations which are rationally defensible.

The State is a good example of such essential contestability. Yet one should be wary of holding to essential contestability as a dogmatic assumption. It is useful in educational terms to acknowledge that there are diverse views of the State which should be explicated. The State is certainly not one thing. It needs to be unpacked. But we do not need to go on from this to the conclusion that there are either in principle no grounds for finally adopting a particular view of the State or that the State *must* always, in all situations in the future, be subject to dispute. There are certain logical oddities in such a view which link up with a dogmatic adoption of essential contestability. There seems to be an implicit claim that all concepts now and in the future must in principle be subject to such dispute. This is an inverted form of 'essentialism' which makes the thesis of essential contestability self-refuting. A more balanced thesis is that at the present moment there are neither completely satisfactory explications of the State nor ultimate empirical grounds which can be agreed to test theories. We need to pay attention to the way in which the concept has been used. It reflects values and views of human nature and constitutes political reality. Since theories of the State reflect such fundamental values and self-images, it is important that they should be open to discussion, criticism and disagreement. To dispute about the nature of the State is to dispute about the character of social existence. It is doubtful whether endless dispute is either possible or fruitful.

Theories of human nature and the State

At the centre of political theory lies the effort to establish a relationship between human nature, however that is conceived, and the State.

Duncan, *Politics and Human Nature*

All classical political theorists make assumptions about human nature. Some are more explicit than others. The conception that we have of humanity will affect how we view the interrelation of individuals in social life as well as which institutions would be desirable or effective. There are no automatic inferences from certain premises about human nature to a theory of the State, but usually the theorist will want to tie in the account of human beings with the structure of political arrangements.

Human nature can be viewed as static or developmental, self-interested or altruistic, rational or irrational, perfectible or imperfectible. However, there is no guarantee what structure will arise from any of these assumptions. Hobbes, Bentham and Max Stirner may have viewed humans as largely self-interested, but whereas one saw absolute sovereignty as a governmental solution, another took the path of representative democracy and the other, anarchy. Even within one particular theory of the State, there are no grounds for trying to identify a consistent view of human nature. Human nature has no necesary connection with *a* theory of the State, thus it is an uncertain guide. For example, Bodin and Hobbes had very similar views on sovereignty, but Bodin would have been truly shocked and outraged with Hobbes's assumptions about human beings.

A rough and ready guide to human nature and State is that those who place a heavy emphasis on an ideology of order and a strong view of sovereignty and the State, tend to have some mistrust of the potentialities of human nature. A centralizing tendency usually, though not always, reflects some mistrust of human nature. On the other hand, those who have emphasized popular sovereignty and so forth, specifically in the context of a decentralized framework, usually seem to have a more optimistic view. Humans can, it is believed, act autonomously, responsibly, and virtuously without any over-arching structure of coercion. Most of us hover between this antinomy.

CONCLUSION

The first chapter has been trying to clear the ground on the nature of the State and to draw it distinct it from a large number of cognate concepts. The overall aim of the book is to review some of the main theoretical landmarks in State theory, not to provide a systematic survey of the whole of the literature on the State. In the following chapters absolutist, constitutional, ethical, class and pluralist theories will be discussed. These form substantive interpretations of the State understood formally as a public power. The final chapter will examine the question: do we need a theory of the State?

2

The Absolutist Theory
of the State

INTRODUCTION

Absolutism was a relatively late addition to the European political vocabulary. In one sense it was a retrospective judgement from the early eighteenth century, although the theories and practices of absolutism were well developed by the last quarter of the sixteenth century, primarily in France. Absolutism derived its terminology from sovereignty theory, specifically Jean Bodin's discussion of the *puissance absolue*. It is the central contention of this chapter that in absolutism we see the first theoretical and self-conscious formulation of the idea of the State. However, it is not a theory of the State which we would be wholly familiar with, in fact much of it is somewhat alien. Yet there are also elements of absolutism which have been retained and absorbed within later theories of the State. As a recent scholar has noted, to understand absolutism 'it is important to set aside the notion of the state as one organisation among others, one part of a complex social and economic structure' (Keohane, 1980, p. 18). It is not wise to bring in immediately the terminology of Marxism, liberalism or contemporary political science when discussing the nature of absolutism.

There are some common assumptions on the nature of absolutism which should be initially dispelled. First, it is not an antiquated doctrine which links up with the middle ages, whereas constitutionalism looks forward to some 'modern age'. In fact, *prima facie*, the reverse is the case. Constitutionalism has far more affinities with the middle ages, and absolutism is a far more decisive break with feudalism. In fact neither position is really satisfactory. Both ideas were rooted in the middle ages. The elements of both can be found in Roman law and some traditions of the middle ages. Also it is a mistake to see them as mutually exclusive doctrines.[1] In practice they subsist together even in the reign of one of the most absolute of all the monarchs, Louis XIV.

Although sovereignty theory is probably the most important element of absolutism it is not the only element. Absolutism is a far more complex theory than is often realized. Further, it is not intrinsically a religious doctrine, although there are powerful religious themes within it, as there are also in aspects of constitutionalism. Absolutism is very different from theocracy. Finally, it is important to dissociate it from a number of other ideas: despotism, enlightened despotism, dictatorship, simple personal rule, arbitrary tyranny or totalitarianism. Some historians see absolutism as being despotic in the sense of having unlimited rights over persons and property (see Mousnier, 1979). Others argue that enlightened despotism is the stage between the arbitrary tyranny of absolutism and the bourgeois monarchies of the eighteenth century (see Lousse, 1964, p. 58). The idea of enlightened despotism was developed by philosophes and physiocrats in the eighteenth century, identifying the monarch as the first servant of the realm, listening to reason and aided by a rational enlightened bureaucracy. The *Oxford English Dictionary* definition of a despot is an 'absolute ruler . . . hence, any ruler who governs tyrannically'. In this sense despotism, tyranny and absolutism are used synonymously with arbitrary rule. In fact absolutist monarchs did not usually accept the nomenclature 'first servant'. Furthermore, they were not generally regarded by their contemporaries as tyrannical, except of course by some of their constitutional critics.

The dictionary definitions seem unduly affected by a specific line of argument in political theory. Absolute monarchs regarded themselves and were regarded by most of their subjects as exponents of order, legality and justice. In comparison with the disorder of civil war in France in the sixteenth century, they certainly had a point (see Keohane, 1980, p. 1). Absolutism, in sum, was therefore not arbitrary rule or tyranny. It was also not necessarily oppressive or in violation of constitutional principle in its title to authority. Thus in terms of much of the theory and practice of absolutism, despotism and tyranny are peculiarly inappropriate synonyms. The same point holds for totalitarianism. Absolutists promoted centralized power, but the theoretical manner in which they did this is alien to the proponents of total rule in the twentieth century. Absolutism neither had the means nor the intention to mobilize a mass society or to establish a regime of complete terror. Absolute monarchs could not have penetrated all aspects of life, even if they had wanted to (see King, 1974, pp. 255–9).

Absolutism was formulated in an age which saw order and hierarchy in cosmic terms. Creation was envisaged as an ascending and descending scale. From inorganic matter up through all the varieties of organic life the work of an infinite designer could be discerned. Harmony and order could clearly be seen throughout the panoply. Jean Bodin had devoted a whole book (*Le Théâtre de la Nature Universelle*) to this point alone (see Greenleaf, 1973, pp. 23–5). Politics was seen in the context of this cosmic hierarchy. As the monistic God ruled the universe, so the earthly States were to be viewed as ruled by single fatherly rulers. The king was the head of the body and the shepherd of the flock (see Eccleshall, 1978). In the same manner as God does not ask the advice or seek the consent of 'lower' orders of creation, so genuine monarchs should not seek the consent of their subjects. Thus the definition we often find of absolutism is 'the idea that the ruler, however much he may be responsible to God . . . does not require the consent of any other human agent in making public policy' (Franklin, 1973a, p. 151) or that it is 'a form of monarchical government in which the prince's authority is in fact free (unbound, absolute) from check by any higher authority or organ of popular representation' (Lousse, 1964, p. 43). Most absolutists usually intermeshed these cosmic ideas with a juristic theory of sovereignty.

There is a sense in which absolutism remained in the realm of theory. Practically it is difficult to conclude that absolutism ever really existed. However, it is also true that all States exist in theory. Absolutism, however, as one recent scholar has argued, 'was always in the making but never made' (Parker, 1983, p. xvi). The theory was being constructed and built up well into the reign of Louis XIV. It did not achieve any finality in Bodin or Hobbes: they contributed fundamentally important elements to a larger theory.

The intellectual roots of absolutism are tangled and complex. Primarily the development of absolutism is integral to the critique of feudalism. Medieval theorists using Roman law systematically questioned the idea of feudal society and its understanding of leadership. Feudalism represented what Ullman called the 'ascending thesis' of government and society, namely that authority and power moved upward *to* the government. Absolutism was a classic case of the contrary 'descending thesis', where decisions were seen to move downwards from the centre. Although some commentators, for example M. P. Gilmore and Q. Skinner, have questioned the extent to which the renewed study of Roman law from the twelfth century onward furthered the development of absolutism, none the less certain Roman law ideas did play a key role. This is specifically the case with doctrines such as *plenitudo potestas* and *princeps legibus solutus est*. These doctrines tended to focus and concentrate power, authority and law into the ruler. These were attractive ideas to theorists looking for an alternative to the strife of civil war. Initially canon lawyers were fascinated by the use of such doctrines to describe papal rule. Papal monarchy was first formulated by Pope Leo I (440–6), although later, much more vigorous, formulations of it were offered by Popes Gregory VII and Innocent III.[2] The apostle Peter signified or embodied the church *in* his person. Popes saw themselves as the juristic successors to the powers and functions of St Peter. The debate was not a closed one since the very same lawyers who enthusiatically applied the doctrine of *plenitudo potestatis* to the papacy also discussed the question whether church authorities possessed power on *behalf* of the people. Such an idea placed limitation on papal rule. The continuing debate as to whether the Church's power was derived from the Pope or not, carried on into the debates on secular monarchy in the sixteenth and seventeenth centuries.

Religious discussions of papal sovereignty and the constitutional role of the Church were gradually laicized in the sixteenth century. The original role of the emperor facilitated this since he was generally regarded as a quasi-religious figure. This theocratic notion had considerable impact on the later idea of divine right. The transference of the attributes of the medieval Church and papacy to the more secular monarch was more completely, if unknowingly, accomplished during the Reformation by men such as Luther, Zwingli, and Calvin. As J. N. Figgis wrote 'Luther is . . . the spiritual ancestor of the high theory of the State' (1956, p. 59). Without Luther there would have been no Louis XIV. There are a number of reasons why the Reformation is significant in preparing the ground for secular absolutism. It undermined the independent role of the Church which was seen as a community of the faithful. Coercive authority was limited to the secular kings and magistrates. Luther also advocated passivity and non-resistance to secular rulers. The powers of the rulers were a gift of God and thus were not to be interfered with by any other authority. Monastic property was criticized, as well as feudal privileges. All should be subject to the authority of secular rulers who were accountable only to God. Like Machiavelli and later Renaissance writers, Luther was increasingly identifying the secular kingdom as the chief good for humanity.

There were a number of closely linked empirical factors which tended to hasten the concentration of power in the sixteenth century.[3]

The primary factor was war and disorder. Internally, civil war initiated a concern for strong central rule and diminishing the role for local powers. Externally, the authority and prestige of monarchs was dependent on their capacity to wage dynastic wars. The impact of war was, however, paradoxical. Authority was developed in conditions of war, yet war created the demand for finance. Finance required taxation and orderly collection of revenue. This process required, in turn, law and order, which was dependent on disciplined troops. But disciplined troops, which were also the prerequisite to war, also demanded adequate finance. But of course adequate finance was dependent on disciplined troops. Despite this paradox war did create standing armies (often mercenary), centred on the authority of the prince and not based on old feudal fealties. Standing armies required greater public expenditure from central government and thus more adequate collection of taxes. Such a process led to the development and evolution of a centralized corps of salaried officials, dependent and responsible to the prince and royal council. This centralized administration began to develop in France under Francis I (1515–47) and Henry II (1547–59). Many of the these officials were trained in Roman law at the University of Toulouse – a training which often provided the theoretical backing for absolutist rule.

With increased centralized power in raising taxation without consent, a bone of contention even in absolutist writers such as Bodin, the constitutional role of central and local assemblies diminished. Like the nobility in France they began to atrophy. From the reign of Francis I the French monarchy took an increasingly domineering attitude to both Parlements and assemblies. Absolutist apologists insisted that it was not the role of Parlements or any other body to ratify law or control monarchs (Skinner, 1978, Vol. 2, pp. 256–7). The absolutist monarchs, specifically under chancellors such as Mazarin, Colbert and Richelieu, also began to take an interest in the control of the economy. Mercantilism became the dominant economic practice.

These empirical factors only accelerated the ideological moves towards absolutism over the 1500s. Most historians, in discussing absolutism, have concentrated on the empirical factors. This present study will, however, focus on the major theoretical components of absolutism which have contributed towards its particular account of the State.

It is the contention of this chapter that there are five major elements to the full explication of the absolutist theory of the State; the theory of complete, absolute legislative sovereignty, property theory, divine right, reason of state, and personality theory. Each of these components will be discussed in the following sections.

Briefly though, sovereignty provided the linchpin of the absolutist theory of the State. The primary claim was that in order for there to be a State there must be a sovereign. Secondly, this sovereign was most adequately embodied in a monarchic person. Finally, it was the only theory to accept completely the logic of sovereignty itself – namely that sovereignty implies supremacy. The sovereign is the source of law and therefore above all law and responsible only to God. This consequently established the predominance of sovereignty both within the realm and in the actual definition of the State.

Property theory reinforced the identification of the sovereign with the State. The realm belonged to the monarch or sovereign, it was his property. This included goods and persons. Thus the monarch did not have to consult with anyone when taxing or using anything in the realm. The State was the property of the sovereign.

Divine right differs from the older theocratic ideas. It affirms that the sovereign rules by divine sanction. Laws promulgated by the monarch thus take on a strong religious significance. Non-resistance and passivity become religious duties. The sovereign virtually becomes, in Hobbes's phrase, a mortal god. When this theory was joined to the doctrines of reason of state a particularly powerful idea was formed. *Whatever* the sovereign decided, in the interests of State (which only he could ascertain), took on a religious significance. Since in theory the mortal god could not err, the sovereign's wish automatically became the State's interest.

Behind this movement of ideas we can find the personality theory of Roman law. How, it was asked, could the monarch be identified with the whole realm? This is in fact a central thesis of absolutism which is not often adequately grasped. The sovereign person *was* the State. The State *was* the person of the sovereign. Such an idea is not as bizarre as it sounds. Roman law theory had discussed the idea of legal personality. When we speak of a 'corporation' or 'corporate activity', the word derives from *corpus* (body). It implies a unity or identity which transcends, or is qualitatively different from, the members acting individually. Legal personality is a step beyond this, giving a legal identity to the body. As Hobbes argued, it is perfectly possible to see the sovereign as an artificial person, representing the totality of the realm. At this point the argument becomes complicated, since many later absolutists – specifically in the apogee of absolutism in France, for example Bossuet – move away from the fictional aspect of absolutism. At this stage many theorists, impressed by the logic of absolute sovereignty, property theory, divine right and reason of state arguments, identified the State with the real person of the sovereign. However, neither the fictional, artificial character of legal personality nor the 'office' theory of kingship were totally forgotten. One suspects that many of the arguments were never wholly clear in the protagonists minds.

It is important to realize that the impersonal State of the twentieth century originated in the personal State of the sixteenth century. It is also the case that the cohesive unity of the twentieth century State *is* the direct result of the personal theory. It is a short step from the actual person, to the fictional person and finally to the impersonal, especially when the initial monarchical person claims to be the essence and source of impartiality in law and justice. The use we make of the terms sovereign State and 'the sovereign' still reveals something of this particular ancestry. A heavy emphasis will be placed upon France in this chapter. The reason for this is that France first developed a theory of the State and also the first and most vigorous absolutist theory.

ABSOLUTE SOVEREIGNTY

The sovereign of Bodin embraces in his person all the functions of the State.

Franklin, 'Jean Bodin and the End of Medieval Constitutionalism'

The notion of absolute sovereignty is the key concept, the linchpin of the absolutist theory of the State. The major theorists who will be discussed are Jean Bodin and Thomas Hobbes. It is important to grasp that they are not exponents of the more complete account of absolutism. Also, although Bodin and Hobbes can be examined in terms of their contributions to sovereignty theory, it does not mean that their theories can be compared overall. Their respective conceptions of human nature are in fact markedly different. The intellectual context of their thought is also different. Bodin's ideas on politics were rooted in his interests in astrology, climatology, geography and cosmology. He thought, for example, that celestial factors, demons and the like, were relevant to the domain of politics. Hobbes's thought represents a much more rationalistic, utilitarian philosophy which was, minimally, sceptical about religion.

There is some debate on the situation in which absolute sovereignty arose. The debate centres on the fact that both Bodin's and Hobbes's accounts of sovereignty were formulated in the context of civil war: in Bodin's case the French Wars of Religion, and in Hobbes's, the English Civil War. Whereas some would argue that the concentration on absolute sovereignty was a response to the disorder, others would maintain that the basic arguments pre-dated the conflicts. There is more of a case to be made that Bodin's ideas are such a response. Hobbes is more problematic. For example, in the case of Bodin, some scholars have seen a definite shift from the more constitutionalist view of his earlier work the *Methodus* towards his later *The Six Bookes of a Commonweale*. However, this is a point of scholarly dispute. J. H. Franklin argues that the *Six Bookes* was 'a sudden and dramatic shift' from the earlier work (1973b, p. 41). Preston King also maintains that the *Six Bookes* simply 'argues more forcefully than the *Methodus* for unrestrained public power – not that it contains fewer arguments for greater restraint upon public power' (1974, p. 301). Scholars such as Franklin, Salmon and Skinner see the *Six Bookes* as a reaction to the views of Huguenot monarchomarch constitutionalism after 1572. In Hobbes's case it is difficult to ascertain who influenced his writings or why he developed ideas on absolute sovereignty, although undoubtedly in works like *Behemoth* he did examine the origin of the civil wars in the context of conflict over sovereignty.

The centrality of sovereignty

A. J. Carlyle and R. W. Carlyle remarked that the fundamental principle of Bodin's political theory was that 'there must be somewhere in the State a supreme and absolute authority. He is setting out what in later terms we should call the theory of sovereignty' (1936, Vol. 6, p. 419). In the 1606 Knolles translation and edition of the *Six Bookes*, the term sovereignty or *soveraingtie* is used fairly frequently. It is also used as an equivalent to 'majesty'. As Bodin put it, 'Maiestie or Soveraigntie is the most high, absolute, and perpetual power over the citizens and subjects in a commonweale' (1606, p. 84). Bodin also refers to sovereignty as the 'greatest power to command' and 'total power' (*toute puissance*). It is also implied that the sovereign is unlimited, his power is inalienable and indivisible. The core of these arguments can be found in Book 1, chapters 8 and 10 of *Six Bookes*.

What was new in this conception of sovereignty developed by Bodin? In his own terms, Bodin thought that he was discussing something hitherto uninvestigated. As he stated, 'it behoveth first to define what majestie or Soveraigntie is, which neither lawyer nor political philosopher hath yet defined: although it be the principall and most necessarie point for the understanding of the nature of a Commonweale' (1606, p. 84). The novelty of Bodin's, and to an extent Hobbes's, conception of sovereignty lay in five related points.[4]

Firstly, sovereignty was seen to be essentially legislative in character. The point of this is often missed or mixed up immediately with the 'command theory of law'. The middle ages usually discussed the power or majesty of a ruler in terms of the 'prerogatives' of the Crown, referring to a collection of rights and duties attached to monarchy or rulership. Some would argue that this set of prerogatives was still present in Bodin's earlier work the *Methodus*. Even in his later *Six Bookes*, Bodin still brings in the traditional scheme in terms of the 'marks of Sovereignty'. The monarch makes law, is a judicial authority, can confer power on judges and magistrates and has the power to make war and peace (see Skinner, 1978, Vol. 2, p. 289). This type of analysis of the marks of sovereignty was a traditional theme in the works of sixteenth century lawyers. Bodin stresses, however, that the most fundamental and crucial of these marks or rights is the power to make law. The other marks are relatively unimportant in comparison. Whereas in the late medieval conception, the sovereign could have been defined as the sum total of prerogatives and rights, Bodin sees the sovereign embodied in an absolute and perpetual legislative power. As Church has put it 'For him [Bodin] sovereignty and the power to make law were all but synonymous' (1941, p. 229). Supremacy was thus embodied in the right to make law.

This gave rise to a second novel feature in Bodin's view of sovereignty. The medieval period had seen rulers as basically judges and administrators. This was a pervasive theme well into the eighteenth century. English lawyers, for example Coke, saw the common law embodying fundamental rules which should be recognized by the court of Parliament. Bodin, although acknowledging the judicial and administrative role of the crown, none the less saw the legislative role as crucial. In fact the legislative role freed the monarch from the civil law and judicial limits, unless he voluntarily acquiesced to them. It is not certain that Bodin would have spoken of the sovereign in these terms. To concentrate on the legislative role assumes that there was a general consciousness of separate spheres such as administration, executive or judicial. This was not the case in the late middle ages. As Kenneth McRae has put it, theorists were 'still groping for a theoretical analysis which would fit the changed political structure. Bodin's work represents the culmination of a long development' (1962, p. 14). Bodin's concern, translated into legislative power, was that the sovereign should embody the ultimate and supreme right and authority to command over all groups, institutions or individuals within the realm. It was this idea which was eventually to translate into the theory that every legal system must analytically possess a supreme legal norm or procedure through which rules are identified, adjudicated, and co-ordinated. Another point to make on this is that the theory does ignore, to a degree, the role of customary, natural, fundamental and constitutional law. The sovereign in Bodin was not identified with these bodies of law, only civil law. This point will be returned to.

A third novel feature in Bodin's sovereign was his acceptance of the full logic of sovereignty, at least in a specific area. If something *was* supreme and the source of civil law, then law was the will of the sovereign who thus could not be subject to it. If the sovereign were subject to law he would no longer be the source of it and therefore not sovereign. Bodin's legal training had been in Roman law and he was familiar with the doctrines of the ruler's *imperium*, *suprema potestatis*, and *legibus solutus*. It is a matter of debate exactly how novel Bodin's doctrine was. As A. J. Carlyle and R. W. Carlyle remarked 'The theory of Bodin was . . . not, strictly speaking, new, but we think it may properly be said that it represents a much sharper and more dogmatic enunciation of the conception' (1936, Vol. 6, p. 420). Bodin does fit, although not without some qualification, into a tradition called legal positivism. To make civil law the will of the sovereign is to undermine some of the impact of customary and natural law. Effective law becomes the command of the sovereign. Customary or natural law becomes a rather weak side-constraint on the sovereign. Some have argued that Bodin should not be associated with this legal positivist and command theory tradition (see Lewis, 1968, p. 215). Bodin was not admittedly concerned to separate law and morality or to make *all* law the command of the sovereign. Yet he does insist the sovereign is the highest legal authority. This was the great novelty which he pointed out. That the sovereign could not be bound by law and non-resistance by all subjects in a realm was a logical implication for Bodin. Such ideas have led others to argue that Bodin had reached a 'distinctively modern legal-positivist conclusion' (Skinner, 1978, Vol. 2, p. 289). Thus although Bodin did not draw any distinction between law as it is and law as it ought to be, he did insist that effective civil law was the command of the sovereign. Hobbes on the other hand, provides a much clearer example of the legal positivist perspective. In fact he sometimes called the 'father of legal positivism' (Fuller, 1966, p. 19). Hobbes's theory of law was a direct refutation of common-law ideas. The function of magistrates for Hobbes would not be to continue working with precedent and case law but simply to act as ciphers for the king's statutes (see Peters, 1967, p. 212). If the sovereign delegated power it remained his possession. He did not alienate it to the magistrate. The relationship of Hobbes and Bodin on this and other points is problematic. It has been pointed out that it is a mistake to view Bodin as a stepping stone to Hobbes and Austin (Hinton 1973, p. 303). Bodin's views on human nature, family life, and groups are quite obviously different from those of Hobbes (Keohane, 1980, pp. 67–8; see also Salmon, 1959). Even in the area of sovereignty any limits which Bodin places around the sovereign are swept aside by Hobbes. Hobbes's logic of sovereignty is in fact 'cruelly complete', more thoroughgoing and absolutist (Merriam, 1900, p. 27).

Despite these qualifications, it theoretically remains the case that Bodin provided the first systematic exposition of the logic of sovereignty, a logic which Hobbes and later Austin took to its conclusion. In fact Hobbes, oddly, is not as explicit as Bodin on the features of sovereignty. Yet, as Preston King has pointed out, the adjectives that Bodin attaches to sovereignty are far from clear. Absolute power, for example, seems to be equated with the words highest, greatest, total and unlimited. Yet each of these terms have different, and at times overlapping, senses. Highest and greatest imply the apex of a hierarchy with other powers at different levels. Unlimited power is also distinct from total power, 'the latter implies that potential objects of control (like the possible openings in a game of chess) are finite, while the former implies that the potential objects of control are infinite' (King, 1974, p. 140). The concept of unlimited power seems distinctly unrealistic even in comparison to total power. No prince or ruler has in fact ever had unlimited power: it is an impossibility and illogical. The notion that it was perpetual power was really justifying the right of the monarch to rule in perpetuity. Such power was indivisible; thus Bodin set his face against any form of mixed or shared sovereignty. Mixed or shared sovereignty (shared or mixed between a monarch and assembly) was a contradiction in terms.[5]

Another feature of both Bodin's and Hobbes's view of sovereignty was that, by and large, a monarchy was preferable. Both, however, recognized some dangers implicit within it. The preference for monarchy was based on practical and normative grounds. Bodin is much clearer on this than Hobbes and favoured monarchy because one decision-maker was more in tune with the cosmic order. Harmony was seen in 'oneness' – one God and one king. Non-monarchical regimes were defective on this count. One unitary ruler meant greater moral and political stability. Bodin recognized other types of regime where, for example, aristocracy existed, but in his view they were less stable. Hobbes, on the other hand, had no real normative preference for monarchy. He did not believe in hereditary rule, divine right or patriarchalism. He also recognized, far more than Bodin, that a collective sovereign was feasible. It was difficult for one who lived under the English Parliament to say otherwise. Hobbes does imply that a monarchy is more convenient for peace and security (1968, chapter 19). However, he never questions the point that the artificial or natural representative person is crucial to the existence of the commonwealth.

The final and most distinctive element of Bodin's and Hobbes's theory is the identification of the sovereign with the State. This idea was carried to completion by later proponents of absolutism. It is not really developed by either theorist. There are places where the medieval traditions impinge strongly on Bodin's ideas. Bodin appears at times to be speaking of the sovereign as the supreme agent *within* the State. For example, when Bodin talks of the sovereign as the 'greatest power to commaund', it implies that he is the highest in a hierarchy (1606, p. 84). This fits in with the point that Bodin was tolerant of group life within the commonwealth. As he stated 'beside that soveraigntie of government thus by us set downe . . . many other things besides are of citizens to be had in common among themselves' (1606, p. 11). Bodin mentions markets, churches, walkways, customs, public building as well as colleges and corporations. Without these, he argues, 'a Commonweale cannot be so much as imagined' (1606, p. 11). The sovereign here seems to be envisaged as the formal seal put on the commonwealth, the highest in a hierarchy of groups and institutions. In other passages Bodin seems to use 'State' in the older Latinized sense of 'standing', for example when he says that the prince 'revengeth the publique injuries done against the state' (1606, p. 212), or that 'soveraigntie of government is the true foundation and hinge whereupon the State of a citie turneth' (1606, p. 10). In these senses the State is definitely not identified with or synonymous with the sovereign.

There are senses of the State in Bodin and Hobbes which do coincide with the idea of sovereignty. These are the more dominant ones. What one finds in Bodin specifically is the idea that absolute sovereignty is 'an analytical implication of the concept of the State'

(Skinner, 1978, Vol. 2, p. 287; see also Church, 1941, p. 226; Franklin, 1973b, pp. 23, 93). This notion is in the opening lines of Bodin's *Six Bookes* where he maintains that a commonwealth (or State) is 'a lawful government of many families . . . with a puissant soveraigntie' (1606, p. 1). A lawful government of many families implies an absolute sovereign and vice versa. In fact a sovereign encapsulates the entire body of authority necessary to bring a State into existence. The sovereign embodied the civil law as 'living law'; he is the linchpin which holds the whole together. As Bodin put it 'it is neither the wals, neither the persons, that make the citie, but the union of people under the same soveraigntie' (1606, p. 10). This doctrine derives from the Roman law ideas of *imperium* and *suprema potestatis*. A closely related idea to the above is that the sovereign embodies all the functions of the State, namely the maintenance of public rule as embodied in the role of the sovereign. Hobbes developed a slightly different idea of the sovereign/State identity in chapter XVI of *Leviathan*. For Hobbes, the sovereign is a legal person who represents the entire body of the realm, summing up the life of the body politic. A 'person [is one] whose words or actions are considered, either as his own, or as representing the words or actions of an other man' (1968, p. 217). When the words or actions are the person's, he is a natural person, when they are represented he is a '*Feigned* or *Artificial person*' (1968, p. 217). The person owning the the words or action is the author. If one covenants to such an artificial person, gives up one's natural rights to him, then that artifical person possesses those rights as an agent. This, crudely put, is the situation of the Hobbesian sovereign. The sovereign is authorized by a covenant with all individuals. Then, as Hobbes put it, 'A Multitude of men are made *One* Person, when they are by one man, or one Person, Represented . . . it is the *Unity* of the Representer not the *Unity* of the Represented, that maketh the Person *One*' (1968, p. 220). The people can become one, the State can only exist by virtue of one who represents them in the fictional person of the sovereign. A multitude can only become a corporate body via a sovereign. Thus in the representative sovereign the State exists. One corollary of this is all subgroups are seen as concessions from the sovereign. They cannot exist of their own right except through the sovereign. Hobbes took this representative doctrine directly, with his own modifications, from Roman law theory on the personality of associations. Austin, who is often linked with Hobbes, is slightly different again. In his *Lectures on Jurisprudence* Austin says that 'The State is usually synonymous with "*the* sovereign". This is the meaning which I annex to the term' (1880, Part 1, p. 95n.). Presumably he meant the king or ruling body, in Britain the king, Lords and Commons. Austin certainly conceived this sovereign to be absolute, but not in Hobbes's Roman law representative sense. Austin is in fact closer to Bodin's idea of the sovereign embodying the necessary logical prerequisite or precondition for there to be a State. Therefore, the State and sovereign are analytically tied. Austin, however, would not have accepted any of the moral or cosmic themes surrounding Bodin's ideas on sovereignty.

Austin's thesis on sovereignty also has close links with Bentham. Austin was seeking a tidy logical theory that would clarify the legal process and wipe out all its archaicism. Like Bentham's desire for codification of the law, Austin wanted to know precisely how and by whom positive law is promulgated and enforced. He wanted to cut through the baggage of natural, constitutional and customary law into the utilitarian essence of legal rules. In this sense Austin's theory is substantially different from that of both Bodin and Hobbes.

Some problematic limits on sovereignty

Before concluding this section attention will be drawn to some problems in Bodin's account of sovereignty. The remarks are addressed to two areas: the issue of limitations on the sovereign and secondly the tolerance of group life.

One difference between Bodin and Hobbes is that the former incorporates, quite unequivocally, limits to his absolute sovereign within his overall theory. Hobbes does not do this – apart from limits implicit in human nature and possibly prudence – and it appears deeply paradoxical to claim something as both absolute and limited. The limitations that Bodin envisages can be divided up into three broad categories: the constraints of natural and divine law, the basic historical limitations within French constitutional history, and finally the fundamental laws or *Leges Imperii* concerning the form and nature of government. Many of the natural law limitations can be traced back to Roman law, specifically the *Corpus Iuris* of Justinian (see Giesey, 1973). The constraints of natural and divine law bound the monarch to, for example, keep promises and fulfil covenants and to respect the institution of the family. In fact there was a whole complex of such laws which had been presented in Justinian's law codes. It is important to realize that these natural laws were not regarded lightly. In Bodin's time they formed a basic consensual morality. The second category is the complex array of constitutional constraints which had been built up over many decades in France, namely that private property was inviolable and taxation should not be considered without the consent specifically of the Estates. Bodin had been a vigorous defender of this right as embodied in the Estates-General. Finally the *Leges Imperii* contained the Salic law, which forbade female succession to the throne. The *Leges* also prohibited the monarch selling off his public domain or royal lands. The non-alienation of the public domain assured a smooth transmission of sovereignty and also guaranteed a continuing source of revenue for the crown (see McRae, 1962, pp. 16, 17).

Some of these limitations, particularly the *Leges Imperii*, were obscured by the development of popular sovereignty and the concentration on Hobbes's and Austin's speculations on power and sovereignty. There have been, however, three basic interpretions of the limitations on the Bodinian sovereign. The first is that Bodin was fundamentally confused, or at least that he did not adequately reconcile the limitations with his account of sovereignty. Either Bodin was 'verbally careless though fundamentally sound – or . . . he was verbally conclusive but doctrinally inconsistent' (Hinton, 1973, p. 303; see also Allen, 1957, p. 404). Hinton argues that the first interpretation is the result of trying to tie Bodin in too closely to Hobbes and Austin. The second interpretation swings to the opposite pole, playing down the idea of sovereignty and placing Bodin in a medieval constitutional context. The limitations are part of an embryonic medieval rule of law and custom controlling the burgeoning power of the sovereign. This view overemphasizes the limitations. It has led recent scholars to conclude tentatively that Bodin was 'working for limited and not absolute monarchy' (Giesey, 1973, p. 178). The dominant scholar in this area is Charles McIlwain in *Constitutionalism and the Changing World* (1939). The final interpretation, which now seems to be the more accepted line, is that the limitations are integral to the very idea of sovereignty. The sovereign was absolute, but within certain legal parameters. This is an implicit recognition that unlimited sovereignty is a logical and practical fiction. Bodin was not simply advocating that might is right. The *Leges Imperii* are seen as 'part of the sovereignty by which he [the sovereign] makes and breaks laws in other respects' (Burns, 1959, p. 176). In this sense he was probably more sophisticated than either Hobbes or Austin (see Lewis, 1968, pp. 213–5).

The second problem of limitation concerned the question of groups within the State. There is a marked difference between Hobbes and Bodin on this issue. Hobbes had contemptuously dismissed groups,

such as corporations, as 'worms in the entrails' of the body politic.
The reason for this is quite clear: Hobbes took seriously the logic of
sovereignty. Groups were artifical entities allowed or conceded by the
sovereign – they had no independent or autonomous life. If they were
allowed autonomy this would undermine the absoluteness of the
sovereign. For Hobbes, groups were simply aggregates of individuals.
In this sense there was no essential difference between a family, guild
or commonwealth. Hobbes, however, did admit that great monarchies
arose out of families. As he put it 'it is evident that dominion,
government, and laws, are far more ancient than history or any other
writing, and that the beginning of all dominion among men was in
families' (Hobbes, 1839, Vol. 6, p. 147). Yet in Hobbes's *De Cive*,
Leviathan, and *De Corpore Politico*, groups are seen as totally reliant on
the permission and concession of the sovereign. The latter position is
more consistent with absolute sovereignty. Hobbes's ambivalence on
the family does not appear in Bodin, or Sir Robert Filmer for that
matter. Bodin, like Aristotle, viewed society as built up and reliant
on a rich sublife of groups. Families, colleges, guilds, corporations –
whether social, religious or professional – were essential to the
commonwealth. Bodin's first definition of the State is that of a lawful
government of many families. The family is a natural society where
altruism and love exist. For Bodin and Filmer, the individual was
social by nature. Again this is alien to Hobbes (see Black, 1984, pp.
330–1). Bodin saw groups both as relatively independent but also
essential to the commonwealth (1606, p. 11). Admittedly the family
was more inviolable than the college or corporation – but as has been
recently argued – 'It is clear . . . that Bodin saw colleges as essential
partners to royal government in securing peace and social order . . .
he appears to have wanted to balance the concentration of legal
authority at the centre with a wide diffusion of associational life'
(Black, 1984, p. 131). Thus Bodin does not fall into the same view as
Hobbes on group life. Hobbes, however, does appear to be more
logically consistent in terms of sovereignty theory, whereas Bodin is
more sociologically astute. Theoretically, it is more difficult to
reconcile Bodin with absolutist theory. This is because he was more
aware than Hobbes that the State is a more complex phenomenon
than can be encompassed in a logically pure understanding of
sovereignty.

PROPERTY THEORY AND ABSOLUTISM

The second broad feature of the absolutist theory of the State is property theory.[6] The feudal understanding of property, very crudely, had been focused on land. Ownership of land, no matter how large or small, implied certain rights and duties. Property was thus a conditional right. *Status* or standing was closely linked to property. Property indicated one's estate. This linked up with one's position in society and the rights and duties associated with it. The highest estate in the realm was usually the ruling person, family or group. Yet even here property and power were conditional. Kingship was, in a sense, the highest tenure. One important implication of this line of thought was that the king or ruler tended to look at the realm through the eyes of a landed proprietor. He had both the privileges, but also the duties of such a proprietor. This idea is crucial when the concept of property and the nature of rule began to change. However, the important point is that the realm (or estate) was owned by the ruler within constituted conditional limits. Also the estate could be passed on in a hereditary sense.

Pre-existing these conditional feudal ideas were the conceptions of property embodied in Roman law. One of these was the patrimonial property which was possessed by the head of a family. This property was distinct from the public property (*res publica*) owned by the emperor. Patrimonial property could be used or abused by the father, whereas public property could not. There were, however, some limits to patrimonial property. If the father were to go insane or act in a prodigal manner, then a curator could be appointed to look after it for the family. Patrimonial property did have certain family expectations attached to it in law. The school of legists, in reviving Roman law study, attempted to apply the idea of patrimonial property, to which they gave the name *allodium*, to feudalism. Initially it did not fit. Freehold property was alien to the spirit of feudalism since it implied an unconditional right of ownership. Yet even within the feudal structure itself freehold allodial property began to be partially realized. In the late medieval and early modern period service in relation to land and fiefs became increasingly something in name only. Services were often commuted to money payments. In many cases, however, the land was seen as a permanent right and not linked to services (see Rowen, 1980, pp. 10–11). This fact, in itself, would have been less significant if the feudal mind had not already equated ruling with ownership in the realm as an estate. Where ownership implied detailed contractual obligations, as well as privileges, the idea was relatively innocuous. Yet when ownership was understood allodially, as a freehold right, with no implied duties and indivisible possession, then the effects were quite marked on kingship, specifically when it coincided with the changing concept of legislative sovereignty in the fifteenth and sixteenth centuries. The ideas of absolute sovereignty and indivisible ownership of the realm were, fortuitously, mutually reinforcing ideas. As Figgis argued 'When feudalism decayed and property became pure *dominium* under the influence of Roman law, the king's estate underwent the same change' (1956, p. 9).

One way of coping with the powerful implications of absolute sovereignty and freehold property in the realm had already been formulated by papal canon lawyers in the twelfth century (see Tierney, 1982, pp. 13–15). This was the office theory of rule. The idea was that an office could embody supreme authority and possibly even the realm or church; yet the authority was only present *in* the office. The office could not be owned or just used by an individual. As M. P. Gilmore succinctly put it 'The office cannot belong to the person but power can belong to the office' (1941, p. 108). The subtle point made here is that authority and sovereignty remain absolute, the realm as a whole is still equated with the monarch, but with the crucial proviso that the individual person in the office cannot use it for personal ends and cannot alienate or misuse the authority. Such constrictions can be found partially formulated in the *Leges Imperii* discussed earlier. Initially, therefore, the office theory did not overtly conflict with either the theory of absolute legislative sovereignty or the ownership of the realm. However, over the sixteenth and seventeenth centuries its use became equated more with constitutional writings, where the king in his office was seen as the first servant *of* the State, a kind of super-administrator, subject *to* the State. The reasons for this are that despite ownership of supreme public power, it is a power which is not personally owned and is constrained within limits. The power is not the person's, rather it exists to serve the whole realm. This is a subtle restatement of the older feudal notion of service and obligation implicit in ruling. It also implies a difference of public and private roles. The division between the public and private became a crucial plank in later constitutional and ultimately liberal thought. Thus, however indirectly, the office theory had an affinity with constitutional thought.

Yet the office theory was initially not strong enough to counteract the pressures of 'incipient allodialism'. As Herbert Rowen has argued 'royal absolutism was to become entangled in the question of the proprietory character of monarchy. Allodialism shaped the new absolutist theory of royalty by making sovereignty inherent in the king by right of birth, wholly personal' (1980, p. 30). The crucial question at the root of allodialism was: what was owned by the prince from birth? An office, by definition, could not be owned since it was distinct from personal property. The king, however, for many absolutists, was seen to own his domain. Domain could mean the sovereign public power and authority, the actual lives, possessions and territory, or a combination of both. Such an idea merged the public and personal capacities of the monarch. The sovereign authority, right to rule and territory were his property. Such an idea reinforced the latent identification of the State with the ruler. Absolute sovereignty was an 'analytical implication of the concept of the State' (Skinner, 1978, Vol. 2, p. 287), and sovereignty was co-extensive with monarchy. If the territory and authority of the monarch were his property then literally the State was identified totally with the sovereign: it was his property. There were no conditions or duties attached to this property. In this sense it was perfectly consistent with absolute legislative sovereignty. This did not mean that the medieval and office theories were abandoned, rather that they subsisted usually in a constitutional context in a tense relationship with allodialism and absolutism. The protagonists shifted in their vocabulary between executive and proprietorial ideas of sovereignty. However proprietorial ideas appeared in many countries during the sixteenth century, coinciding with the development of absolutism. James I, for example, in his *Trew Law of Free Monarchies* argued that monarchs were owners of their realms. Speaking to Parliament in 1609, he stated, 'Now a father may dispose of his Inheritance to his children, at his pleasure; yea, even disinherite the oldest upon just occasions, and prefer the youngest, according to his liking; make them beggars, or rich at his pleasure. . . . So may the king deale with his subjects' (James I, 1918, p. 308). However, he diplomatically coupled this proprietorial statement with the qualification that civil, natural and fundamental law would still be respected and this included respect for private property.

One of the key areas where the tension over proprietorial ownership of the kingdom came into sharp focus was over taxation. The key questions at issue were: was there a distinction between the king's private purse and the public purse? Could the monarch use all property in the realm as his own without seeking the consent of his subjects? The distinction between the private finance of the ruler and the public purse had existed in Roman law. The medieval legists took up the distinction, calling the public purse the *fisc*. In terms of the the office theory of kingship it was relatively easy to maintain the distinction. It was also possible to argue for consent to taxation, since private property was distinct from public property. However when absolute sovereignty was joined to the idea of allodial property and the realm, territory and possessions were seen as part and parcel of the king's domain, then, by definition, the king did not have to seek consent to use *his* own property. What was really at issue in this dispute was the nature and extent of political authority. The high point of such proprietorial claims to the wealth of the realm was in the reign of Louis XIV. Louis tended to regard the wealth of his subjects as his own. Taxation was simply transferring his property from one place to another. As Louis put it in his *Mémoires for the Dauphin* (1666): 'Kings are absolute Lords and by nature have complete and true disposition of all wealth owned either by churchmen or by layman . . . according to the general needs of their state' (quoted in Rowen, 1961, pp. 91–2). Subjects, therefore, must forego their property rights in the interests of State. As Louis continued, 'Everything within the boundaries of our states, no matter what its kind, belongs to us by the same title and should be equally dear to us' (quoted in Rowen, 1961, p. 92). In practice, however, Louis respected property rights far more than the theory would have us believe.

One important point is illustrated in this proprietorial theory. The apochryphal remark which is attributed, probably wrongly, to Louis XIV – '*L'Etat c'est moi*' – has often been a source of considerable puzzlement. How could the State *be* Louis? The answer to this puzzle lies in the theories of absolute sovereignty and property theory. Louis achieved a final confusion of public and private ownership. It was not a totally irretrievable confusion since he could still speak of interference in private property only in the 'interests of State', which is essentially the use of public power. Yet increasingly he associated the totality of the realm with his own person and will. Literally speaking, he *was* the State. As Louis put it in *Le Métier de Roi*: 'When we have the State in mind, we are working for ourselves. The welfare of the one creates the glory of the other. When the former is happy, lofty and powerful he who is the cause of it has glory' (quoted in Rowen, 1961, p. 79). In this passage Louis's 'I' and 'the State' are one. The idea seems to have been accepted by chancellors such as Mazarin and Richelieu, and theorists such as Loyseau and Bossuet, as well as in diplomatic circles (see Rowen, 1961, p. 95). We might find these remarks of Louis confusing or possibly abhorrent. The absolutist theory is, however, not so distant as we sometimes imagine. Louis began to rely on a growing administration and bureaucracy, which became part of his person and therefore the State. The State retained legislative sovereignty, centrality, and, to a large extent, its ownership of the kingdom; but with the increasing number of personnel in the administration, its nature became necessarily less personal and thus more abstract and impersonal. This process was accelerated by the 'office' theory which regarded the king as yet another servant of the State. There is thus a complex and subtle connection between the 'State as the monarch' and the 'State as standing over and above the monarch' and the 'impersonal abstract State'.

DIVINE RIGHT AND ABSOLUTISM

The identification of monarch and State was the ultimate in absolutism. When the identification was held to be sanctioned by God . . . the doctrine of absolutism and the divine right of kings was fused.

Fox, 'Louis XIV and the Theories of Absolutism and Divine Right'

Kingship and political rule have always had a close connection with religion. Kingship and priesthood were closely intertwined in early cultures and societies. In pre-Christian societies such an idea was relatively commonplace. Judaism and Christianity gave fresh impetus to this theme. The biblical ideas of divine Davidic kings, priest kings, and the stipulations of St Paul's Romans XIII and St Peter's Epistles, gave a strong impetus to the idea of God's sanction of the governing process (Figgis, 1922, pp. 17–19). In spite of the ancient origin of the idea it is important to remember that the divine right of kings was not the same as divine authorization or theocratic rule. To claim that a king was authorized to rule by the grace of God was different from arguing that a king, by hereditary succession, had a divine right to rule. Feudalism, for example, accepted the idea of God's grace on rulers and kings, but the rulers and kings were also hedged about by many obligations. As Ullman remarked 'The medieval corrective to royal theocracy was the king's function as a feudal overlord' (1975, p. 146). The mid-thirteenth-century lawyer, Henry Bracton, described the relation between lord and vassal as a legal bond which both sides must fulfil. Divine right aimed to make the monarch a virtual mortal god.

The preconditions necessary for divine right were the development of relatively independent territorial units, the breakdown of the power and influence of the Holy Roman Empire, and the declining influence of the papacy. The theocratic ideal of the Empire, the *Respublica Christiana* ruled over by Christ, through his vice-regents, the Pope and Emperor, implied two claimants to semi-divine status. Such an idea had to fragment before independent monarchs could claim divine right. On a theoretical level, Roman law – especially after its revival in the eleventh and twelfth centuries – gave rulers, initially Popes such as Innocent IV, a seemingly supreme unchallengeable status. This doctrine, as we have seen, was taken up enthusiastically by secular rulers. Also, the revival of interest, in the thirteenth century, in Aristotelianism initiated great interest in the idea of separate, autonomous political units, each with their own constitution. Politics was no longer just a staging post to heaven or hell, but rather an important area of human experience. Divine right undermined the role of the church and ecclesiatical supremacy by the gradual absorption of all public coercive power into a monarch chosen by God. This in turn undermined the older theocratic ideal of the 'two swords'. Finally, the position of divine right owed much to Renaissance thought which unified the imperial government of society with cosmological and religious themes. As Frances Yates has argued, 'the imperial idea in the Middle Ages and Renaissance . . . is a necessary preliminary to the study of the ethos and symbolism of the national monarchies of Europe' (1977, p. 28). Kingship provided a unity under a single head. It relied on arguments drawn from Roman law accounts of the imperial emperor. In Britain, for example, Tudor monarchs claimed imperial status. As Figgis remarked, 'there was a belief, that true sovereignty, i.e. independence and unquestioned authority, had been derived from an appropriation by each kingdom of rights originally confined to the Empire' (1922, p. 43 n. 3). Henry VIII and Elizabeth I both claimed Imperial status and 'it is as successors to the divine imperial power that kings claim the right to throw off papal suzerainty' (Yates, 1977, p. 39). Imperial symbolism was taken on board both by Tudor and Stuart monarchs. In terms of Elizabeth I it virtually became a religious cult (see Yates, 1977). Oddly Anglican royalists were in a far easier position than French or Gallican royalists such as the *Politiques*, since the latter, as Catholics, had in some way to accommodate papal authority with the absolute claims of their monarch. This was not the case in England.

Yet, paradoxically, despite that fact, absolutism made greater headway in France than England.

The impetus to the development of divine right was first, the advent of Lutheranism and the Reformation and secondly, in France, the catalyst of the French Wars of Religion (1585–93). Luther accelerated the fusion of religion and politics and the breakdown of the Empire and papal authority. Calvin and Zwingli after him reiterated the idea of the divine nature of civil authority. Rulers who had previously been in conflict with the Church now integrated it into civil authority and looked to it to condemn tyrannicide and disobedience. Thus the doctrines of the divine ordination of kings – that the ruler is accountable only to God and that subjects are enjoined to non-resistance and passive obedience – are attributed to Luther. All are central to the theory of the divine right of kings. This point lies behind Figgis's remark that 'Had there been no Luther there could never have been a Louis XIV' (1956, p. 62). The French Wars of Religion acted as a catalyst to a number of thinkers, most notably Jean Bodin. Reflecting on social and political disorder, the notion of legislative sovereignty made powerful headway. Although Bodin himself was not a proponent of divine right, his notion of sovereignty was quickly adorned with the robes of divinity by later thinkers. Theorists such as Adam Blackwood began to see the prince as a mortal god (see Church, 1941, p. 247). After Bodin, those who argued for legislative absolute sovereignty became divine rightists. As Church commented 'It would not be a great exaggeration to attribute the origins of seventeenth century absolutism to this union of concepts' (1941, p. 245). A similar fusion of legislative sovereignty and divine right can be found in the Royalist party in England – for example Dudley Digges's *The Unlawfulnes of Subjects taking up arms against the Sovereign*. Such ideas came to a head, as in France, during the civil war of the 1640s.

The basic arguments of divine right, which were taken in deadly earnest by its opponents (see Pocock, 1957, p. 189), were firstly that monarchy was ordained by God, and second that hereditary right was indefeasible. The king acquired his right by birth. Usurpation was not accepted. (This point alone put Hobbes outside the parameters of divine right theory since he acknowledged the possibility of sovereignty acquired by usurpation or conquest.) Thirdly, the king was accountable to God alone. He was beyond all legal limitation and could not alienate or limit his sovereignty. This point linked directly with absolute legislative sovereignty. Finally, the subjects were enjoined as a religious duty not to resist and to be passively obedient (see Figgis, 1922, pp. 5–6; Dickinson, 1977, pp. 15–16). The only redress against a wicked king was God and natural law. It is important to point out that this doctrine is not exactly the same as the theory of patriarchalism, as put forward by Sir Robert Filmer in *Patriarcha* in 1652. Patriarchalism was not divine right, although by the end of the 1600s in England it was its best theoretical support (see Figgis, 1922, p. 150). Filmer identified the kingdom as a family. Royal power was paternal, originating in Adam. Monarchy was the only proper form of government and as it was paternal and absolute it could never be tyrannical. The image of monarchical authority being paternal was an idea which pre-dated Filmer. Thomas Aquinas had referred to the father of a family as a 'petty monarch', and thinkers such as Marsilius of Padua, Suárez and even Bodin, had made use of the idea of kings as fathers. In patriarchalism, however, more naturalistic, almost anthropological, claims take precedence over the directly religious (see Schochet, 1975). Patriarchalism purported to give an account of how society and political rule came about via the development of the family. Oddly enough, this point makes it intrinsically more intelligible than contract theories which relied on the state of nature.

From Henry IV's reign (1589–1610) up to Louis XIV's (1643–1715), legislative absolute sovereignty gradually mutated into divine right. The king was regarded increasingly as a mortal god, anointed with holy oil from the sacred ampula at coronation time, and possessing the royal touch. French writers in the early 1600s such as Du Boys and Duchesne compared the king to a god on earth, a celestial soul or one made in the image of God (see Church, 1972, p. 30). The fusion of divinity with legislative sovereignty and property in the realm gave an added mystique to the State. The king, as a kind of superbeing, could literally embody the totality of the realm in his person. There was obviously no need for such an individual to consult his subjects, since he embodied public right and power and was guided by God. Adam Blackwood, for example, asserted that the king could take taxes on this basis (see Church, 1941, p. 259). The king was living law. Thus divine right theory reinforced the idea of property in the realm and legislative sovereignty and also gave an added credence and lustre to the idea that the monarch *was* the State. In this sense it is not often realized that divine right is a modern doctrine, a bridging point between the medieval and modern conceptions of politics. Right existed in the civil ruler. Papal and imperial authority had come to rest finally in the person of the king. In this context it was a highly successful idea. As Figgis has argued

'The theory of Divine right did not lose its popularity because it was absurd, but because its work was done' (1922, p. 263).

In England, divine right theory became part of the ideology of order of the Tory party. It had a sharp reverse in 1688 when the non-hereditary rulers William III and Mary assumed the throne. Yet it was not abandoned. Many Tories simply transferred the locus of sovereignty and religious sanctity. As H.T. Dickinson argued,

> By changing the location of sovereignty they found an absolute and irresistible power, the legislature, which was more able than an absolute monarch to protect the interests of propertied men. By abandoning indefeasible hereditary right and by accepting the Protestant succession they were in a better position to defend the privileged position of the Church of England than they had been under a Catholic ruler. (1977, p. 43)

The elements of divine right and absolute sovereignty became subtly integrated into the British political tradition, specifically in the Tory party.

RAISON D'ETAT AND ABSOLUTISM

The end-product of divine right sovereignty was reason of state.
McIlwain in Church, *Richelieu and Reason of State*

It was inevitable that reason of State would connect up with divine right. If the monarch as the living law was identified with the whole State and expressed the will of God, then whatever the king said was obviously in the interest of State. Reason of State was not always understandable by 'mere mortals', but in the high mystical realms of mortal gods, there was a divine sense to it.

The idea of reason of State (*ratio status, ragione di stato, raison d'état*) originated in sixteenth-century Italy, although subsequently it developed in France, specifically under the patronage of Cardinal Richelieu. Contrary to popular opinion, the first use of the term was not by Machiavelli. Guicciardini and Della Casa were the first to employ the term *ragione di stato*, indicating that good ends justify civil means.[7] The interest in the term accelerated after the publication of Machiavelli's *Prince* (1532) and the slightly later treatise by Botero in 1589 (see Skinner, 1978, Vol. 1, pp. 248–9; Church, 1972, p. 46). It is difficult to ascertain what sense of the word 'State' is being employed by Machiavelli and Guicciardini. Yet even if they used State in the older sense of 'standing in the realm', none the less the cause of a prince's 'standing' could still justify expedient measures. The notion, therefore, that the interests or ends of the State justify the means holds true, whether it is understood as standing, princely person or abstract authority.

Apart from the discussion of reason of State in Italy, Spain and the Low Countries, its firmest foothold was in France, after the Wars of Religion. This is the point at which we can see it linking up with divine right arguments. There were three different French translations of *The Prince* published in France before 1600, plus many pirated, popular abridgements and reprinted editions. Catherine of Medici and Richelieu were both reported to have been great admirers of the work, especially the latter. The Machiavelli that was known was not the historian but rather 'the projenitor of Machiavellianism. A scheme of politics that was totally secularised and sanctioned any methods that might contribute to the preservation of the state and its power' (Church, 1972, p. 47). The civil war experience, specifically in its religious context, led many to tie in justice and order with the mere survival and continuity of the State, and to reject claims that any Church, religious principle or natural law had precedence over the continuity of civil law and the sovereign prince. In this latter area Figgis (1956, p. 72) maintains that Luther and Machiavelli were oddly at one. Divine right overcame the problem of the religious critique of existing rulers by situating religious authority *in* the ruler. The survival of the ruler and consequently the State were superior reasons to all others and thus took priority. Even *Politique* writers such as Bodin, as well as Huguenot critics who were overtly critical of Machiavelli, reached the same conclusion, if by a different route. Divine right was thus an ideal legitimation for reason of State.

It is too easy to caricature and misunderstand the idea of reason of State. There are three ways in which it can be understood. The first and crudest notion is what Meinecke calls 'a materialistic ability for calculation' (1957, p. 194). This is the sense in which reason of State is regarded as pure expediency or manipulative means/end rationality. Political and personal survival, in the perception of the ruler, individual, or government, means that any type of action – no matter how immoral – can be performed. This is probably the crudest understanding of Machiavellianism, as virtually equivalent to political cynicism. With a deeply pessimistic view of human nature and State action, it presumes that there is no morality within or between States or individuals, only power, survival and the manipulation of one's own interest. Meinecke distances himself from this view. Reason of State is not necessarily naked cynicism. Yet Meinecke does argue that it is bound up with powerful 'instinctual' motives for self-preservation. The ultimate value for reason of State is the well-being and health of the whole State. This demands rationality and expediency in political conduct. It is not cynicism but realism. Exponents of reason of State, for example, Richelieu, were not to Meinecke just cynical diplomatists sold to the highest bidder, but rather devoted public servants who performed actions, in their perception, for the benefit of the whole State. Readers of Richelieu's *Testament Politique* will realize this to the full. Richelieu was zealous in public service. As H. B. Hall states 'the most enduring single impression to be gained from the *Testament* is the unintended self-portrait of its author – friendless, lonely, selfless, severe, distrustful, inflexible, indefatigable, devoted only to the welfare of the state as he saw it' (1961, p. x). Moderation or ruthlessness were equally possible and equally justifiable by reason of State.

The third sense of reason of State, which does not come out strongly enough in Meinecke's account, is that, for many, reason of State was divinely and morally legitimated. The monarch was the source of justice and law. He was a divinely appointed ruler cast in the image of God. The glory of God and the king were tied to the glory of the kingdom. Thus the ends of the State must be intrinsically religiously legitimate. The monarch, especially as the personification of the State, was the linchpin and full representative of political harmony and order. This was seen as practically and cosmically good. Whatever the monarch did in the interests of State must be in the interests of such order and therefore compatible with the central tenets of Christianity. Reason of the State in this context was not saying that the survival and health of the State is the primary concern, but that Christianity is fully compatible with reason of State. In this sense, there is no division between realism and morality in politics. The monarch as the embodiment of public authority and law represented the totality of the realm; being divinely chosen he could not err. In seeking the ends of the State, of which logically he is the best judge, and given the sinfulness and ignorance of the majority of his subjects, there could be no conflict between the monarch's personal interests and the interests of the whole polity. Such an idea is worlds apart from the means/end view of reason of State.

The development of reason of State is a later manifestation of absolutism. The more complete vision of the absolutist theory of the State is discernible in Richelieu and Bossuet, not Bodin. Richelieu and Bossuet explicitly identified the public State with the prince. In

Richelieu 'little attention was paid to the potential dissonance between the prince's personal desires and the good of the whole polity' (Keohane, 1980, p. 175). The monarch was the only true judge of the public interest. Although this was a bald statement of concentrated power, it was tied closely to religion. As Church remarked

> A majority of the writers who supported the Cardinal therefore sought to develop a concept of Reason of State that was grounded upon the religious nature and purposes of the French State and attempted to demonstrate that one of the objectives of royal policy was the benefit of universal Christendom. . . . Far from divorcing the interests of the state from organised religion, they defined the aims and ends of offical policy partially in religious terms. (1972, p. 44)

The good of the State was the good of religion. Richelieu wanted to build an effective State, to increase the power of administration and to ensure the continual obedience of the subjects. The higher morality and precept of the State might mean unusual courses of action against specifically treasonable action. In this case Richelieu suggested that normal legal processes should be bypassed. The concentration of power was continued up to the reign of Louis XIV and then reappeared in new forms after the Revolution of 1789. Louis could say with all honesty and no sense of unreality that when the State was his concern 'one works for oneself' (quoted in Church, 1969, p. 73).

Thus, as most recent scholars have noted, divine right – and behind this, legislative sovereignty and property theory – wedded itself to reason of State in the late 1600s (see Parker 1983, pp. 91–2; Keohane 1980, p. 241; Church 1972, p. 16; Fox 1960, p. 135). This formed a crucial addition to the absolutist theory of the State. Not only did the action of the prince, and thus the State, have a divine legitimacy, but theoretically whatever the State did was legitimated. The prince had the best of both worlds. His actions were not constrained by moral or religious principles, because they embodied religious and moral principles in their own right. This is the closest absolutism comes to despotism. This development of absolutism is important in the context of the subsequent theories of the State. Reason of the State in the context of absolutism gave the State a transcendental gloss, which although at times appearing patchy, has never quite worn off. The continuity and survival of the State is given a sacred mystique. Such an idea is not always as dangerous as it sounds except where it is linked with virulent jingoism, nationalism or territorial aggrandizement. It may also have dangerous implications if a ruler totally identifies his or her interest with the State's. Such dangers were identified in the sixteenth century by constitutionalist critics of absolutism. It is possible, however, to have constitutional reason of State, although it is not as easy. Reason of State, in order to function effectively, needs to minimize controls and constraints. Constitutional forms of rule exist in the context of such constraints – thus limiting the scope of reason of State. None the less, reason of State is still an active precept in world politics today and it shows very little sign of departing.

PERSONALITY THEORY AND ABSOLUTISM

One final element of the absolutist theory of the State, which can often be forgotten in the welter of arguments, is that the State was identified with the person of the ruler. The theory of the personification of the State is important since it provides the strong sense of identity and unity to something which otherwise might appear diffuse. The unity and concentrated power of the State is a direct legacy of this personification in the sovereign of absolutism.

The word person derives from the Latin *persona*, meaning a mask worn by actors. Actors were *personae*. There are direct parallels with the court-room, since legal roles were played on the juridical stage. Roman lawyers began to employ the term in this legal sense. One area in which it proved to be of particular use was in the characterization of groups. How does one deal with groups in law? One way is to see them as legal persons. This is origin of the term corporation, where a group is treated as a body with some kind of unity. The corporate entity was regarded as a *fictio juris* or *persona ficta* – fictional personality. The early use of legal personality goes back to the second and third centuries BC. It was later used in Justinian's *Institutes* and *Digest* and then the glossators and canon lawyers. By the eleventh and twelfth centuries, after the revival of interest in Roman law, it became part and parcel of legal discussion in Europe.

There are a number of senses in which we might understand the idea of person now. Pyschologically a person is usually identified by certain qualities, namely: the power and capacity of self-consciousness; the ability to form intentions; the ability to articulate these intentions, usually in language; the ability to determine their own behaviour according to their own interests; and the capacity of unified continuous reasoning and volition. The idea of a person can also be taken in a forensic ethical sense indicating a capacity for rationality and responsibilty or the ability to determine one's own action by moral categories or principles. The legal idea of personality is distinct again. It indicates a power or capacity for legal action and being a subject of rights and duties. The original Roman sense of this, as indicated, was a fictional personality conferred by a higher authority, so that the group could be legally identified. Such terminology was ideal for describing all forms of grouping or association from the State downwards. Hobbes, for example, brought the idea of State personality into sharp relief with his *persona civitatis*. Hobbes's sovereign was not necessarily an organic, pyschological or ethical entity. The artificial or natural person represents the whole realm; the multitude of separate individuals become as one in the sovereign. This is a distinctive account of legal personality and it is one in which absolutist theory personifies the State.

Absolutist theory at its apogee under Richelieu and later Louis XIV produced a different account of the personification of the State. Because of the identification of legislative sovereignty with the monarch, the melding of personal and public ownership and the lack of dissonance between the monarch's personal and public interests, the personal became less fictional and more focused on the actual person of the monarch. This was not a specifically psychological, ethical or fictional view. The monarch, partly because of his divine status, was viewed as a 'super-being'; Louis XIV seemed personally convinced of this. The State was thus encapsulated in the absolute sovereign. The realm was *his* property. The major problem with this was that it stretched credulity and theory too far. In fact it is questionable whether it can be grasped theoretically without moving either to the fictional theory of personality or the public office theory of rule. For example, if asked how the person could be the whole State, the apologist of Louis XIV could answer that: (1) it was a purely legal fiction; (2) Louis occupied a public office which was distinct from his private interests; and (3) Louis was the divine link which connected the whole together, he was omnipresent in the State. His person was uniquely chosen by God to be the mystical cohesive factor to the whole realm. The establishment of the United Provinces was a problematic example for apologists of Louis, since there did not seem to be a concrete person or sovereign to knit the whole together. The problem with (3) is that rather than making the State focus on the concrete person of the sovereign, it makes the sovereign person look more and more abstract and impersonal. No one could identify with such a super-person. This paved the way for later developments in the State. Although we have long since given up the vocabulary of absolutist theory, we can still in mundane political discussion speak of the State 'doing x', 'prosecuting y' or 'speaking to another State'. Such notions were facilitated by absolutist theory which provided a fictional and later 'real' person to be identified with the State. The personification makes sense of the above statements, although it might raise doubts in our minds about how we use such notions in contemporary discussion.

CONCLUSION

Absolutist theory developed slowly during the sixteenth century. It was gradually supplemented by property theory, divine right and the like. It is also paradoxical that at its apogee it was already theoretically and practically in difficulty. Theoretically, as argued in the previous section, the final result of such an intensive focus on the person of the monarch was to make him abstract, impersonal and somewhat improbable. The actual sense of the State in consequence began to change. With much of the official work being done largely by a corps of administrators the actual monarch became more and more a figurehead. The impersonality of the State was beginning to take over.

Logically sovereignty and divine right placed intolerable burdens on the monarch. No State or prince has ever been absolute. It was in practice an absurdity. The technique, capacities and energy for even an attempt at such control were lacking. Absolutist theorists based their theory on an impossibility. It is doubtful as to whether absolutism even existed at all. As David Parker has remarked, absolutism 'was always in the making, but never made' (1983, p. xvi). With the increasing financial burdens of warfare at the close of Louis XIV's reign falling on the shoulders of already impoverished subjects, many no longer identified the sovereign's will with their interest. For many there was a yawning gap which reason of State did not bridge. Also, with rival religious claims within the State, as well as from other dynastic monarchies, it was difficult to go on crediting one monarch with sole access to the creator. Often the extent of absolutist claims was dependent on the character of the sovereign, the economic circumstances of the realm, the international situation and the quality of support and advice from his ministers. Yet it is wrong to push these points too far. It is a mistake to believe that there was no really consistent theory of absolutism and that it was pragmatic and *ad hoc*. This is plainly false. The problem was that it was too consistent and logical to fit the messy realities of the the 1600s.

In practice it was also the case that limitations and constraints existed right through the absolutist era up to the reign of Louis XIV. Despite the attitude of absolute monarchs toward, for example, the various assemblies and the Parlements, they continued to exercise an important consultative role, if only via continual complaints and argument. Registration of the king's enactments by royal command as opposed to consultation was always regarded as contrary to good legal practice. Absolute monarchs never overcame this particular criticism. The nobility, Church and government officials retained and defended a considerable number of privileges which the monarch did not interfere with. At lower levels, local mutinies, attacks on soldiers, tax-collectors and government officials remained common practice in Louis XIV's reign. The *Fronde* revolts showed that active resistance was still a possibility despite the effort to control the population. Admittedly the cutting edge of consultative and consent-based traditions of feudal assemblies had been blunted under the absolutists, but by creating a large new group of officials and venal office-holders, the monarchs only created a new element of limitation on their powers. As Parker argues 'Royal policies reflected more than just the need to compromise. . . . They also show an underlying acceptance by the government of the corporate and hierachical organisation of French society' (1983, p. 139). Thus in France, the cockpit of the absolutist view of the State, the theory of absolutism was failing in its own terms. However it is clear that it did not simply disappear from European thought. Conversely many of its central precepts became deeply embedded in legal theory and practice and still underpin some of our vocabulary on the State.

3

The Constitutional Theory
of the State

INTRODUCTION

A philosophy of constitutionalism is not so much a mere
description of facts as it is a normative philosophy of the state.

Elliott, *The Pragmatic Revolt in Politics*

The idea of constitutionalism relates to the verb 'to constitute', from the
Latin *constituere* (to cause to stand, to found or to establish). That
which is set up is constituted, consequently the contents of that which is
established can be referred to as the constitution. To constitute is the
act of establishing – the constitution is the ordinance so established.

The constitutional theory of the State is a product of the eighteenth
century, although many of its elements and key arguments date back
to the middle ages. Some of the main themes of constitutional
thought pre-date the absolutist theory of the State by many centuries,
although unquestionably the absolutist theory provided the actual
foundation and groundwork for the development of constitutionalism.
Absolutism established the centralized and territorially unified
political order on which constitutional theories developed. With the
fading significance of kingship, the growth of an independent
administration serving the interests of the State and the development
of ideas of popular and later national sovereignty, a different account
of the State was needed. The first and most powerful view, in terms
of European thought, was the constitutional theory. It is a theory
which underpins much thinking about the State into the present
century.

Prima facie, the central feature of the constitutional theory, which
will be dealt with in some detail, is that it is a theory first and
foremost of limitation. Developing as it did in the context of
absolutism this became an overriding preoccupation. A central

ambiguity arises here which has to be dealt with. Conventionally the constitutional limits are sometimes seen to be limits *on* the State. The argument gives rise to the impression that constitutionalism is something 'attached' to a State, the State being an entity which by its nature desires more power and therefore needs controlling. Such an argument is given credence by the attempts in the sixteenth and seventeenth centuries to limit the scope of monarchical action. However this impression is false. A constitution is not an addendum *to* a State; it is part of a particular theory of the State. The limitations are intrinsically part of and identifying features of that theory – they are not independent of it. In this sense, limitation can be a misleading word.

What is sought for in the constitutional theory is some diversification and thus limitation of authority. This does, however, create another ambiguity. One of the most important claims which appears to be part of the constitutional theory is that a constitution is seen as in some way prior to the State. This is closely connected to the argument that limits are independent of the State. The priority may be temporal, legal or moral, but it is claimed that it is the fact of priority which marks out the constitutional theory. The constitution is prior to any particular government. It defines the authority, and gives to government the right to exercise its power. The validity of such constitutional rules is independent of the political system – their amendment or repeal is thus a matter of profound importance. The very essence of the constitutional rules is that they are above the whims of the actual law-makers. They are laws which govern the State, rather than law by which the State governs. Even if such an idea is largely fictional and dependent on the goodwill of the governors and the governed, it is, none the less, necessary to maintain the idea of such prior rules. It is this argument which makes constitutional theory distinct from all types of arbitrary government. It is also this analysis which contributed to the nineteenth century classical liberal judgement of the State as a threatening leviathan which should be minimalized and curtailed. Yet, as argued, this view is a fundamental misapprehension. The idea no doubt arose because absolutism associated the State so intensely with the person of the monarch that it was felt that 'the State' (i.e. the person of the monarch) had to be controlled. But institutional developments had moved well beyond this even before the decline of absolutism. The limitations were envisaged and constructed by those who were to be limited.

Apart from an ambiguity about what a constitution is and what are the limits implicit within constitutionalism, namely that a written constitution or body of rules is only *one* type of limitation within constitutionalism, there is still the point to be recognized that the constitution is part of the State. Even in conventional constitutional accounts, the State is constituted by the constitution. It is therefore created by a legal act of a specific character. As Ernest Barker argued, 'The State therefore exists to perform the legal or juridical purpose for which it was constituted. It declares and enforces, subject to the primary rule of the constitution, a body of secondary rules, or system of ordinary law, which regulates the relations of its members as "legal persons"' (1934, p. xxiii). Thus the key emphasis of constitutional theory is on the State as the guardian of the constitutional order. This is what marks out the constitutional theory. It embodies a complex hierachy of rules and norms which explain juridically and define the nature of the institutional structures. The priority is not on the State, but rather on the seriousness with which certain rules are taken in relation to the everyday legislative activity of the governers of a constitutional State.

It is important at this juncture to indicate the different senses of the concept of 'constitution'. Some of these will be explained in more detail in later sections. The oldest idea of a constitution, which is still embodied in current speech, implies the integuments or inner workings of an entity. It is thus referring to 'that which constitutes' the whole. This could be a motor car or a human body or analogically the body politic. Thus the constitution of a State would simply refer to that which constitutes it. A more limited sense of the term would indicate the type of government in a political structure. This is closest to the sense in which Aristotle employed the term. The study of constitutions can be summarized under such notions as democracy and aristocracy. Constitution is simply, in this sense, the type of government which characterizes or constitutes a particular city. These views of constitution are purely formal and descriptive.

A more normative and substantive usage refers to a body of basic, fundamental or customary laws. This idea, although not referred to as constitutional until fairly late in European thought, is the basis of the view of law in the middle ages and in fact up until the eighteenth century in some circles. It lies firmly within Bracton's and later Coke's defence of the common law in England. A variation on this theme, which is still praised as part of the British constitution, is the idea of a body of conventions. Conventions are seen as implicit, unwritten customs built into the behaviour and attitudes of political agents, which act to restrain their conduct. Another important variant of the doctrine of fundamental or customary law is the doctrine of the ancient constitution, which was the mainstay of many thinkers up until the eighteenth century. They maintained that there were certain substantive principles and rules to be deduced from the history of a people. As Lord Bolingbroke put it in 1733: 'By constitution we mean, whenever we speak with an exactness, that assemblage of laws, institutions and customs, derived from certain fixed principles of reason, directed to certain fixed objects of public good, that comprise the general system, according to which the community hath agreed to be governed' (quoted in McIlwain, 1940, p. 5). This is very close to Edmund Burke's notion of the constitution as the result of many ages of thought and practice, time out of mind, embodying deep-rooted conventions and customs. For Burke, the British constitution is viewed as virtually a divine creation – a partnership between the dead, living and future generations. Others argued that the constitution could be traced back with precision to the Anglo-Saxons or Franks. In France such arguments concentrated on the so-called Gothic constitution, specifically in Huguenot writers such as François Hotman. This idea of the ancient constitution was used by some of the radical groups, like the Levellers, during the English Civil War. John Locke is notable, however, for *not* using this sense of constitution.

During the eighteenth century the most well-known sense of constitution arose in America and France. This was the idea of a written document incorporating a Bill of Rights to which legislators and the judiciary deferred. This is a form of more rational constitutionalism which employs no mysticism about ancient rights. It rather offers a direct argument and defence of certain fundamental rights and freedoms in the present. This is the origin of the idea of the rights of man and also the current human rights conventions. When most laymen think today of a constitution, it is the American model which springs to mind most easily, although in terms of the history of constitutionalism it is a fairly late and specific use of the idea. In most eighteenth- and nineteenth-century constitutionalism such an idea was usually linked to another important sense of the term. Constitutionalism was most importantly an institutional arrangement to ensure the diversification of authority and the maintenance of orderly change in order to defend certain fundamental values such as liberty, equality and individual rights. The best known institutional arrangements include the doctrines of the separation of powers, checks and balances, the balanced constitution and federalism. It is this latter sense of constitutionalism which in fact incorporates many of the preceding ideas.

It is difficult to disentangle constitutionalism from many concepts and processes which are very familar to us in the twentieth century. From the seventeenth century it developed slowly with theories of popular sovereignty, individual rights, democratic enfranchisement and, most importantly, classical liberalism. By the mid-nineteenth century, to defend constitutionalism was to defend liberalism. The problem of this mixture of terms is that it inhibits our seeing these as separate entities. In the twentieth century we often end up with a pot-pourri. Constitutionalism has no intrinsic connection with liberalism or democracy. We often tend to run these various notions into each other with alarming ease. Arguments for obligation based on contract and consent have had a strong connection, from Locke, with constitutional thought, yet it must be recalled that absolutists also used contract and consent arguments. For example, absolutists sometimes claimed, via the Roman law doctrine of *lex regia*, that the people had once and for all consented to the absolute authority of the monarch. The argument with the constitutionalists was over whether it was a 'once and for all' delegation. Hobbes also uses many of the stock-in-trade contract arguments to give a very logical reading of absolute sovereignty. Similarly, popular sovereignty ideas have no necessary connection with constitutionalism or in fact democracy. The earliest exponents of popular sovereignty were neither democrats nor constitutionalists, as we might now understand the term. Constitutionalism was often, in its first uses, based on royalist premises, as in such thinkers as Bodin or Seyssel. It fits with many types of regime, monarchical and otherwise, although undoubtedly since the nineteenth century its strongest affinity has been with forms of liberalism.

Constitutionalism suffers many problems today. Despite the fact that the constitutional State is the most successful form of twentieth-century State and the model which many developing countries aspire to emulate, none the less it has fallen on hard times. There is a sense in which 'everyone is a constitutionalist now'. Whether one inhabits the USSR, China or South Africa, there are basic constitutions. Most commentators are now aware of the prevalence of façade constitutions. The popularization of constitutions has paradoxically led to their trivialization. This has created an indifference, apathy and cynicism about the whole constitutional idea. Many countries which have been devoted to constitutional practice, the notion of limited responsible government and the diversification of authority have not escaped this cynical malaise. Constitutionalism has in many cases been fixed into formal procedural devices. Institutional opposition, voting and the like have lost their significance and become empty procedures to be gone through. Those who might have defended it in the discipline of politics have often become engaged with supposedly non-normative amoral political science. The avowedly normative task of constitutionalism has fared ill under such an intellectual regime. Normative theorists have instead fixed it under a critical gaze as part of a general critique of liberalism. The notion of the limited responsible State has been seen historically to be a failure and inadequate to deal with the complexities of twentieth-century politics. Usually behind such criticism is a contrary normative theory of the State. On the other hand the defenders of liberalism have often in recent years displayed rather limited intellectual concerns and have shown little awareness of the broad historical sweep of liberal political thought.

This chapter will deal with constitutional theory primarily as a theory of limitation and diversification of authority and power. These limitations are historical/legal and moral/philosophical limitations. They are embodied within a theory of the State which is attempting to defend and maintain certain fundamental values. Before dealing with each of these, the origins of constitutional arguments will be examined.

ORIGINS OF THE CONSTITUTIONAL THEORY
OF THE STATE

When discussing the origins of constitutional theory it is important not to slip into what Herbert Butterfield called the 'Whig Theory of History'. There is really no inevitable progress of constitutional theory through history. Liberal democracy in the nineteenth and twentieth centuries is not sanctified by some kind of providential pattern. Yet it is also important not to underestimate the continuity of certain ideas. Conciliarists in the fifteenth century could not anticipate later developments, yet it is true that many ideas used by conciliarist writers had been discussed by twelfth-century canonists, and were later to be employed by sixteenth-century monarchomachs and other critics of extreme royalism. As Figgis remarked, 'It was the lament of an English royalist in the seventeenth century that the dangerous theories of rights of the people first became prevalent with the Conciliar movement' (1956, p. 36). Yet, in examining the continuity of some ideas, it should not be assumed, as pointed out in the previous section, that the use of constitutional themes necessarily implies a commitment to any overall position in politics. The fact that nineteenth-century constitutionalism became tied to democracy and individual rights, does not imply that previous constitutionalists were in any way committed to such ideas.

The origins of constitutional theory can be very roughly broken down into six broad categories: first, Graeco-Roman thought, specifically legal ideas from Rome; second, feudalism, as articulated by lawyers such as Bracton. This category is best seen as part of what Ullman called the 'ascending thesis' of government. Third, there is the fifteenth century Conciliarist movement in the Catholic Church; fourth, French constitutional theory in writers such as Seyssel; fifth, the religious and political controversies during the Reformation. Under this latter heading are included Lutheranism and Calvinistic theory, Huguenot and monarchomach ideas and counter-reformation scholasticism. Finally, there are the complex debates on mixed and limited monarchy during the English civil wars.

As argued in the previous section, the Greek sense of constitution, as we find it in Aristotle and Plato, is descriptive and usually refers to the whole structure of a city. Greek political life revolved around the the city in terms of religion, morality, politics and education. There was little or no conception of any distinction between the public and private realms; freedom was a social or communal phenomenon. Generally the Greeks thought of law in the context of the city, not vice versa. None the less in later Greek thought, specifically the Stoics, there were ideas of a fundamental law of nature transcending the city. This was not considered to be in any way constitutional. Greek thinkers such as Thales and Aristotle had seen certain regularities in nature; it was harmonious and purposive. Humans by nature were social creatures and the *polis* was designed to realize certain natural regularities in human nature. It was, however, Stoics such as Zeno and later Cicero, in Roman thought, who first developed the idea of a normative universal law of nature outside the city. Nature embodied reason and universal moral laws which could be perceived through the use of our rational faculties. Such ideas were transformed in Christian thought, although nature was not wholly trusted in the early Church, partly because of its theological linkage with the Fall and human sin. Yet it was still argued that underlying all legal arrangements were certain universal ethical and spiritual principles to be perceived by reason. What is significant in this early view of natural law is that within the reasonable framework of social life there were rules and principles which even rulers had to obey.

Initially, in Roman thought, the term constitutional had a technical sense referring to acts of legislation by an emperor, a sense which the Church later borrowed for ecclesiastical regulation. This use of constitution, an equivalent to the word 'edict' (*edictum*) in Imperial Rome, was still prevalent up to the thirteenth century, where constitutional administrative enactments were distinguished from customary law (McIlwain, 1940, p. 24). It is fairly common in historical scholarship to see Roman law, specifically in Justinian's law codes, as linked to later absolutism. Doctrines like *legibus solutus* are used to support this assertion. Such an argument neglects the doctrine of *lex regia*. However, it should also be noted that in traditional Roman law, rulers or emperors did articulate the will of the *populus*. Power (*potestas*) and *ius* were ultimately derived from the people. In fact many medieval and later absolutist writers often confused the subtle distinction between *lex* and *ius*, which we might translate as law and justice. Law (*lex*) became identified with *ius*. What was lawful was right and just. Further, Roman lawyers were the first to develop the distinction between public and private law, which was crucial to the later development of constitutional ideas, although at the time the appellation constitutional had a different meaning. The rights of individuals as private citizens had to be conceptualized before they could be discussed. Within this system of private law, specifically in Justinian's codes, were justifications for resistance to unjust magistrates, a point picked up by commentators in the eleventh and twelfth centuries. Also the famous doctrine of *Merum Imperium*, describing the nature of public power usually in terms of the emperor, was also intepreted by some later jurists to mean that even inferior magistrates could wield the sword of authority. Authority and legal capacity, in other words, were not just situated in the emperor (see Skinner, 1978, Vol. 2, pp. 124–7). Thus Roman law had distinct constitutional implications which were realized by lawyers from the eleventh and twelfth centuries onwards. Roman law was influential on both absolutist and constitutional theory (see Skinner, 1978, Vol. 2, p. 124; Tierney, 1982, pp. 31–2; McIlwain, 1940, p. 42).

The deep roots of constitutional theory lie in the middle ages, specifically in the feudal perspective. Feudalism, although difficult to define, broadly involved a complex web of duties and obligations. Power was neither absolute nor curtailed but diffused. Despite the absolutist and theocratic ambitions of some monarchs, the feudal period was characterized by limitations on authority: kings were not regarded as 'living law', standing above the realm. In feudal Europe, beside canon and Roman law stood customary law, in England the 'law of the land' (Ullman, 1975, pp. 150–1). Customary law was not created but declared by a king or Parliament.

The medieval jurist, Henry Bracton, utilized the constitutional implications of the Roman law doctrines such as *lex regia* to explain coronation oaths. The king receives authority from the people after making a series of promises. McIlwain argues that Bracton drew a distinction between *gubernatio* and *jurisdictio*. In jurisdiction, which embraces all the king's authority, 'the king was bound by his oath to proceed by law and not otherwise' (McIlwain, 1940, p. 86). In governing, however, the king's right was absolute, as long as it did not infringe his jurisdiction. The idea of jurisdiction thus set limitations or parameters within which the monarch acted. Essentially the king was under the law as well as being the promulgator of law. He was viewed as part of the 'community of the realm', not – as later absolutists were to claim – standing above the law and the realm. The king's authority was thus conditional upon the performance of certain duties, a theme that runs through the Magna Charta. The notion of the crown, as Ullman put it, was in fact an abstraction: 'The Crown was to all intents and purposes the kingdom itself. Seen thus, the corporeal diadem, the crown, symbolized the incorporeal, legal bond which united king and kingdom. . . . The Crown did not consist of the community alone nor of the king alone, but of both' (1975, p. 153). Feudal government was thus seen in far more limited and collective terms. This is not to say that kings did not try to assert their authority, although, especially in England, such a policy was contested vigorously. It was also difficult for feudal kings to dominate, with little or no standing armed forces, relying on groups such as the nobility and the Church and underneath them a vast sub-life of semi-independent towns, colleges, universities and guilds of varying size. Many of these groups spoke, understandably, in terms of consent and representation in decisions which affected their lives. Such a feudal perspective was intrinsically hostile to the centralization of authority. The king was seen as one among many. As Ullman has commented 'feudal government proved itself an important harbinger and incubator of ideas which later could be developed on the basis of a theoretically conceived populist or ascending theory of government' (1975, p. 148).

Conciliarism must be viewed in a similar perspective to feudalism. It was a product of the fifteenth-century schism in the Catholic church. Between 1378 and 1410 three Popes existed: Clement VI, Urban VI and Alexander V. None would resign their office. In 1414 the Council of Constance met to try to resolve the matter. The cardinalate asserted that if the council of the Church had to resolve who was to be Pope, then, in a sense, the council must be superior in some way to the Pope. Sovereign authority rested in the representatives of the congregations. As early as 1352 the council formulated the idea of electoral pacts with Popes. Elections would be dependent on fulfilling certain duties. Such ideas flourished during the schism controversy. The council acted rather like a feudal representative assembly.

Conciliarism – whose key writers were Gerson, Ockham, Nicholas of Cusa, Mair and Almain – was essentially a way of coping with the claims of papal sovereignty. Its emphasis was pluralistic. Bishops and the Pope held authority as officers of the Church. The plenitude of power was embodied, therefore, in the Church. It is interesting to note here that Luther, during his disputes with the papal authorities, appealed twice to the council of the Church as against the Pope. In practice the council was a short-lived phenomenon, being quickly quashed at the Council of Basel. Yet it remained a powerful theoretical influence. Its arguments on limited sovereignty, the dispersion of power to the council and the Church as a whole, its claim to be able to seek co-operation in government, to rectify papal abuses and ultimately judge the Pope, were used by later Huguenot and Royalist critics such as Althusius. As Tierney remarks: 'At many points Althusius's state seems like a mirror image of Nicholas [of Cusa's] church. A cluster of communities forms a universal association; authority resides inalienably with the whole people; legitimate government at every level is based on consent' (1982, p. 76). In many ways the pursuit of constitutional liberties in the seventeenth and eighteenth centuries was the result of such ecclesiastical animosites and infighting.

Constitutionalism in France in the early 1500s was overtly monarchocentric. The most famous writer was Claude de Seyssel, whose *La Monarchie de France* (1515) was presented to Francis I. Seyssel did not utilize the word constitutional. He was a convinced monarchist who at the time represented the mainstream of what we would now call constitutional thought. One must realize here that even vigorous Huguenot critics such as Hotman were monarchists. Seyssel maintained that hereditary kingship was the best form of government and that it was good that it elicited awe and obedience. The king was authorized by God and had absolute power, yet within a specific area, similar to Bracton's distinction between jurisdiction and government. Seyssel suggested that there were certain limitations within the office of kingship. He called these the three bridles: *la religion*, *la justice* and *la police*. They were not fixed legal constraints, but flexible controls implicit within kingship. In *la religion*, since both the people and the king were brought up on the Christian religion, Seyssel suggested that devout obedience by the population necessarily implied a pious king. If the king commands something impious he will undermine the religion and devout obedience of his subjects. Therefore, for his own and the kingdom's stability, he ought to work on Christian precepts. In *la justice* Seyssel argued that the courts and Parlement upheld the law. Thus, as Seyssel put it, 'they effectively restrain the absolute power our kings desire to use' (quoted in Keohane, 1980, p. 37). Finally, *la police*, which is difficult to translate precisely, referred to ordinances and rules conferred by time and long usage which 'provide the procedural patterns for the government of the realm' (see Keohane, 1980, p. 37). Seyssel is here referring to the customary fundamental law, as in the rules relating to succession. Bodin also relied on the idea of customary law, but again, like Seyssel, he maintained that such customs were not so much external restraints, as internal parts of the king's authority. This particular argument was one of the crucial planks of the French constitutional tradition.

The category of religio-political controversy during and after the Reformation covers an extremely broad field. Luther, Calvin and their followers, like the proponents of Roman law, have both constitutional and absolutist faces. Luther's destruction of the united Church, his praise for secular over religious authority, his singling out the Church as only a community of the faithful, and his initial arguments for passive obedience to secular rulers, are often connected to absolutist theory. Yet in 1530 Luther, as other radical groups had already done, experienced a volte-face on resistance and disobedience. Calvinism also had a similar conversion in the 1540s (see Skinner, 1978, Vol. 2, pp. 217ff). We must recall that the origins of the word Protestant derive from the 'protests' against Charles V at the Diet of Speyer in 1529. It was argued that if a prince commits impious acts or undermined true religion, it is just and right to resist. By the 1550s many Calvinist writers developed ideas on popular revolt against unjust rulers. This became a standard idea in constitutional theory in the sixteenth century, namely that a people had an ultimate right to depose or resist a king. Protestant writers could in fact find support for some of their arguments in conciliarist writers such as Ockham, Almain and Mair, who, although not arguing for tyrannicide, did provide a groundwork for popular theories of sovereignty and the consequent resistance to absolute rule.

Theories of the right to resistance were developed over the 1560s and 1570s by Huguenot writers such as François Hotman in *Francogallia*, Theodore Beza in *De Juri Magistratum*, and Du Plessis Mornay in *Vindiciae Contra Tyrannos*. These writers – often known as monarchomachs – utilized, eclectically, ideas drawn from conciliarism, Calvinism, Lutheranism, Roman law, historical scholarship, Catholic scholasticism and popular sovereignty theory. They represent a watershed in the development of constitutional theory. As Quentin Skinner has argued, in the monarchomachs we see a gradual but decisive shift in emphasis from constitutional argument based on the religious *duty* to resist toward the *right* to resistance. This was an argument which prepared the ground for later writers such as Locke. For Skinner, some later monarchomachs, for example Buchanan and Althusius, were not talking theology but politics – 'about the concept of rights, not religious duties' (Skinner, 1978, Vol. 2, p. 341).

Hotman, in his *Francogallia*, written during the French Wars of Religion, argued that the problems of France were due to the fact that Louis XI had undermined the ancient Frankish or Gothic constitution, which Hotman claimed had been the customary law of the Gauls before the Roman invasions. The Gauls had been a freedom-loving people who had elected their kings, insisted on coronation oaths and believed in a consultative relation to their monarch. The royal domain ultimately belonged to the people who, through their representative assemblies, could depose, if necessary, their monarch. Hotman displays a wealth of historical citation to try to support this claim. He maintained that if consultation was not taking place then the prince was becoming tyrannical. Hotman focused his attention on the Estates-General in France, which he considered to have been of great antiquity. The Estates-General, with the Parlement, in his view had been part of the governing process. They had enforced the unwritten customary laws of the ancient constitution which were outside the control and ordinances of the king. Hotman, in one sense, was expanding on Seyssel's ideas, but with added historical emphasis.

Hotman's theories were used fairly extensively in the seventeenth century. In England, during the civil wars, William Prynne's *Soveraigne Power of Parliaments and Kingdoms* (1643) employed Hotman's arguments on the Estates-General to demonstrate the authority of the Long Parliament. One scholar has remarked on this point that 'It became common practice among critics of Stuart monarchy in the 1640s to quote Tacitus in reference to the political institutions of the Saxon conquerors of England, and even to suggest parallels between English parliament, French estates and German diets' (Salmon, 1959, pp.120–1; see also Giesey, 1973). Despite attacks from Royalists, the ideas of the Gothic constitution were slowly assimilated into the old Whig school of the eighteenth century. This was specifically the case in figures such as Viscount Molesworth, who was a great admirer of John Locke and Algernon Sidney. Molesworth edited the first English translation of *Francogallia* in 1705. In the 1721 edition Molesworth remarked in his introduction that 'much had been written to justify the revolution of 1688 as a return to the solid foundation of our *Constitution*: Which, in truth, is not ours only, but that of almost all *Europe* besides; so wisely restored and established . . . by the *Goths* and *Franks*, whose descendants we are' (quoted in Giesey and Salmon, 1972, p. 124). Molesworth later maintained that the Whig is one 'who is exactly for keeping up the strictness of the true old *Gothik* Constitution' (quoted Giesey and Salmon. 1972, p. 125).

Beza's and Mornay's emphasis was less historical than Hotman and more towards a radical interpretation of Roman law (combined with Old Testament themes on contracts and covenants). Resistance, as with Hotman, although being apparently situated with the people, was always to be carried through by magistrates and representatives on the Estates-General. Other theorists used ideas of natural law from the counter-Reformation scholastics to support their arguments. The Huguenot writer Althusius is also interesting for being the first to realize that Bodin's arguments could be turned against absolutism. Bodin had thrown a number of hostages to fortune with, for example, his demands for consent to taxation from the Estates-General and that king's should abide by fundamental law. He had also indicated that if an immature king was incapable of ruling, a regency could be appointed by the Estates-General on behalf of the whole community. Althusius interpreted Bodin as saying that sovereignty lay in the whole community and that magistrates were sanctioned by the people not the king. All the marks of sovereignty previously reserved for the monarch were in consequence transferred to the whole people, again though, acting through their representatives.

Thomist counter-Reformation scholastics such as Francisco Suárez, Domingo de Soto, Francisco de Vitoria and Juan de Mariana had far more in common with the subjects of their criticism than they realized. They reaffirmed natural law arguments, spoke seriously of the idea of a state of nature, utilized ideas of consent and contract, opposed absolutism and advocated popular sovereignty. As one scholar has put it, they 'developed and crystallised the doctrine of popular sovereignty and thus served as a bridge between the medieval and modern world' (Lewy, 1960, p. 153). John Locke was later to utilize most of the ideas and assumptions of these Jesuit and Dominican writers, specifically on the theme of natural law and rights. The Counter-Reformation theorists themselves, like the Huguenot monarchomachs, had taken over some of their ideas from conciliarists. Juan de Mariana pushed his argument to the extremes of his Protestant opponents by advocating tyrannicide as a preventive measure in his book *De Rege* (see Lewy, 1960, p. 75). Such a device was only advocated where a king consistently rejected all advice and consultation. In discussing these Jesuit and Dominican writers it is tempting to overstate their constitutional role. Whereas Mariana argued for popular resistance, limited monarchy and extensive power for the Spanish parliament (the Cortes), Suárez seemed to return to ideas of kings as more absolute. Undoubtedly they believed in notions of natural law and rights and restraints on political power, but by no stretch of the imagination could they be called full constitutionalists, let alone democrats.

There is a certain irony here which Figgis comments on, namely that 'The two religious bodies which have done most to secure "the rights of man" are those which really cared least about individual liberty, and made the largest inroads upon private life wherever they attained supremacy – the Roman Catholic Church and the Presbyterians' (1956. p. 118). Ruthlessly maintaining their own independence, often in a hostile enviroment, and searching for arguments to justify and explain this, they paradoxically were driven into ideas which, although providing grounds for checking central power and maintaining independence, also 'put forth a theory of political liberty, which was the direct parent of the doctrines triumphant in 1688, and through Locke the ancestor of those in 1789' (1956, p. 118).[1]

The final category influencing the growth of constitutional theory were the debates on sovereignty during and after the English civil war. These debates took place against a background of theorizing that has already been examined in this section. To discuss it in detail would be to repeat points already made. The period of the civil war was also dense in theorizing and it would be impossible to do it justice in so short a space. Yet it must be appreciated that in a situation where a king was being resisted by a Parliamentary body, all the complex argumentation on the people's right to question, limit or depose a monarch, through their constituted representatives, came into sharp focus. Could a people remove and/or execute a king? Could a constituted body of representatives legislate without a king? Was the office of kingship distinct from the actual person of the king? Thus even if Charles I refused to sign a Bill, since the office of kingship must be coeval with the whole community and its representatives, the *person* Charles can be ignored and it could be assumed that the *office* consents to the Bill. Was the king's power fiduciary, as Henry Parker argued in his *Observations upon Some of his Majesties Late Answers and Expresses* (probably one of the first statements of Parliamentary sovereignty in England)? Was there an immemorial law in England? Between 1621 and 1688 a new constitutional theory of government was worked out. The king remained to a large degree *legibus solutus*, but this was construed within a framework of law and a balanced constitution, which in practice increasingly limited the scope of the royal prerogative. The constitutional history from here onwards became an oscillation between the development of the theory of private rights and liberties of individuals, set against the desire for order. At this point we are into the actual practice of the constitutional theory of the State in the eighteenth and nineteenth centuries.

THEORIES OF LIMITATION AND DIVERSIFICATION OF AUTHORITY

This section deals with the most important element of the constitutional theory of the State. Constitutionalists have placed their primary emphasis on limiting and diversifying authority and power. This is not to argue that other theories have not been concerned to limit or diversify, but this has not been their primary emphasis. Inevitably, because of the comparative longevity of constitutional practice, the character and nature of the limitations have changed and mutated and we are faced with a diversity of such attempts. A rough and ready distinction between types of limitation would be that constitutionalism used to rely more on religious and quasi-historical claims, whereas later constitutional thought has relied on more rationalist, moral and philosophical arguments. For the sake of clarity the limitations are broken down on the basis of this distinction.

Historical and legal limitations

The ancient constitution and the common law   The oldest constitutional device for limiting authority was the doctrine of the ancient constitution. There are two closely related ideas which are often taken as part of the ancient constitution, namely fundamental and customary law. All shared certain common themes in argument and can be treated as coeval. Customary law, as in the old English 'law of the land' and later common-law tradition, was treated as fundamental in the sense that it could not be simply altered by statute or ordinary legislative practice. Admittedly not all regarded such customary law as part of an ancient constitution, but part of the major prop of fundamental law was its very antiquity or long-established usage.

The common themes that one finds in these ideas are that the ancient constitution, customary law and so on, had been established over generations or since time immemorial. The fact that it was ancient gave it a special prestige and significance, especially when coupled with a myth of virtuous forefathers. The claim behind this has what we might now regard as a distinctively conservative ring. The argument is one that was stated by the Whig Edmund Burke and has since been adopted wholesale by many conservative apologists. It is embodied in Burke's doctrine of prescription which maintains that we should always have a presumption in favour of the established institution, laws and practices – the entailed inheritance – because they embody the collective wisdom of past generations. For Burke we should always have 'a presumption in favour of any settled scheme of government against any untried project'. The constitution in Burke's terms is 'wisdom without reflection', because it was 'out of mind', it could not be examined via the canons of critical reason or changed at whim. It was tried and tested by years of experience. The constitution was not the result of philosophical thought or a monarch's passing fancy, but rather of an accretion of decisions over a long period. Thus if a philosopher or absolute monarch claims to be able to create law, the doctrine of the ancient constitution inevitably makes us sceptical. Burke did not take his argument quite as far as this. One cannot question the origin of the constitution because its origin cannot be known, but none the less it is the source of authority. The ancient constitution is also at one with the whole community. It is embodied in the customary life of the whole people.

In France, as discussed in the previous section, François Hotman was the key exponent of the ancient constitution. He traced it back to the fifth-century Gothic constitution. Hotman concentrated on the constitutional role of the public assemblies, for example the Estates-General, in restraining the king. To Hotman, the signs of tyranny were lack of consultation and the presence of foreign bodyguards around the monarch. For Hotman, the Gothic constitution implied 'that the community as a whole retained the "real" or ultimate sovereignty, that government . . . was prevented from abusing the purpose for which it was instituted by the balance of the constitution between King and Estates' (Salmon, 1959, p. 168). In England some took up the theme of the Gothic constitution, others looked to a Saxon constitution. The seventeenth-century Levellers, as well as Tom Paine in the next century, referred to the Norman usurpation of the old constitution. The Magna Charta and the Saxon constitution were discussed by Levellers such as Overton, Lilburne and Wildman. As Woodhouse comments, 'A wave of Anti-Normanism swept through the ranks [of the New Model Army], and Edward the Confessor became a Puritan hero. The Normans had destroyed the primitive English state and enslaved a nation; all the long struggle with kings had been in effect to regain its lost rights; Magna Charta and the other concessions wrung from them were so many fragments of recovered freedom' (1966, p. 96). Some suggested that there was an Arthurian or Trojan constitution of even more ancient heritage. During the Exclusion crisis many pamphlets employed the idea of the ancient constitution to defend the antiquity of Parliament over the monarchy, tracing it back to the Danes and Saxons.[2]

In England the other main plank of argument, which linked closely to the ancient constitution, was the common-law tradition (see Maitland, 1908, pp. 22–3). For French thinkers such as Du Moulin and Seyssel, and later Bodin, this fundamental law, as Figgis remarked, was 'invested with a halo of dignity, peculiar to the embodiment of the deepest principles and the highest expression of human reason and of the law of nature implanted by God in the heart of man' (1956, p. 228). In England the common law was regarded as deeply significant. It was constituted by basic customs as interpreted and used by the courts. Statute law was seen as declaratory of established custom. McIlwain argued in his *The High Court of Parliament and its Supremacy* (1910) that in the late middle ages Parliament was not primarily a legislative body but a court, statute being the affirmation of existing practices. For McIlwain, it was not till sovereignty was focused on Parliament, during the Long Parliament era, that it assumed a more legislative role and even then it was not properly understood. Others have doubted as to how far fifteenth-century judges would have tried to nullify statute in favour of the common law (see Chrimes, 1936, p. 291). Although again it has been argued that where the liberties and rights of the subject were concerned, specifically in relation to property and personal freedom, it was often presumed in judicial interpretation that statute law would protect these (Gough, 1955, p. 23).

The common law came thus to have authority from long usage and virtually a supernatural wisdom. This sometimes brought it into conflict with the crown. The most famous example on this point was Sir Edward Coke's judgment of the Bonham case where the common law was upheld against Parliament. Coke himself came into personal conflict with James I on this judgment. In England this common-law perspective nurtured generations of lawyers who saw it as *jus non scripta* – an immemorial ground of reference (see Pocock, 1957). Thus, as Pocock argues in a later essay, 'It therefore became possible to believe that the whole framework of English law and (when that term came into use) the "constitution" – meaning the distribution by law of powers of declaring and applying the law – existed from the obscure beginnings of English history. . . . Legal history, read upon such assumptions, became a series of declarations that the law was immemorial' (Pocock, 1972, p. 209). Such ideas on the common law came to form part of the cult of the ancient constitution in Stuart England. It also formed the basis later of Burke's ideas, although as Pocock points out, there was some considerable dispute as to whether or not the origins could be known (1972, p. 229). Whereas Burke emphasized the unknowableness of the origins, others thought that the first principles could be discerned and worked out by 'right reason', in order to show where events may have gone wrong. Apart from this dispute, the authority of the ancient principles, embodied in the common law, was unquestioned. As the Leveller John Wildman stated in his 1650 pamphlet, *London's Liberties or a Learned Argument of Law and Reason*: 'I think a man may assert that what is founded upon the true common law of England, as Sir Edward Coke saith, which is right reason, no authority ought to alter . . . for if we should aver that, we should aver contradictions in the very terms and say that right reason of right may be altered by right reason' (quoted in Woodhouse 1966, p. 371). The common law thus embodied the essence of 'right reason'.

Conventions Another closely related device to the ancient constitution and common-law tradition is one which appears during the eighteenth century. The idea of a convention is a rather elusive notion. Its use and importance varies with successive administrations. The royal assent to a Bill in the United Kingdom is a fairly consistent, formal and established convention which is more or less universally recognized. Other conventions gain importance at particular points in time and may be formalized as law, as in the removal of the power of the House of Lords over money bills.[3] Some conventions, such as ministerial or collective responsibility, are subject to diverse intepretations, others have simply dropped out of use altogether. A convention may be defined as a 'binding rule, a rule of behaviour accepted as obligatory by those concerned in the work of the constitution' (Wheare, 1958, p. 179). It implies a usual way of doing things, a *modus operandi*, one which has been practised over time and consequently becomes the accepted norm. Wheare in fact distinguished between two type of non-legal rules: 'conventions', which were obligatory, and 'usages', which were descriptions of usual practices that were not obligatory. Conventional rules would thus prescribe obligations, usage would simply describe certain practices (see also Marshall and Moodie, 1967, pp. 27–9). However, the distinction is not particularly convincing. The line between obligatory rules and descriptions is not clear; there is considerable overlap and lack of clarity. Many apparent conventions, such as collective responsibility, lack an obligatory character. Conventions are obviously not enforceable by law, although legal difficulties can arise if some are not carried through; for example, if Parliament were not summoned at least once in a year illegal expenditure would result. The similarity of conventions to the common law and ancient constitution lie in the arguments justifying authority. All of them rely on long-established functional usage to justify themselves. In this sense conventions are parallel to customary law, although in the case of conventions they explicitly apply to Parliamentary practice; the common law has a wider ambit. It is claimed that the fact of long established usage means that they serve a definite function in the process of government. As opposed to the idea of ancient constitution, conventions have no religious or mystical implication. Although conventions can arise in any political arrangement, within constitutional theory they are used to extend, supplement and operationalize political and legal processes. In this sense they are not very effective limitations since they can too easily be changed by politicians according to their own interests. This is true to a certain extent, but it can also be true of written constitutions. In fact conventions can develop because of shortcomings in a written constitution.

The written document One of the problems envisaged with the ancient constitution, fundamental law and the like, is that because of their vagueness and somewhat mystical quality they could be employed in all manner of ways. Charles I and Louis XIV both paid lip-service to fundamental law. The ancient constitution, in other words, could quite easily be transformed into the interests of an arbitrary ruler. The same point holds for many conventions. The convention of collective cabinet responsibility in Britain today could be said to work solely in the interests of the executive by ensuring cabinet cohesion on possibly unpopular measures. The supposed virtue of the convention is its flexibility, something that A. V. Dicey drew attention to (1902). Yet this very virtue has been seen as a vice by a recent writer reflecting on the British constitution who remarks that flexibility is fine in its own way, yet it can 'serve chiefly to justify the relentless extension of public power and the erosion of such notions as may survive of the limits within which it may properly be exercised' (Johnson, 1980, p. 33). Parliament, Johnson complains, has become a mime show of procedure, opposition an institutionalized Mephistopheles. We are in fact victims of an unwritten constitution; Britain, he argues, has become a constitutionalized wasteland. Characteristically, in such circumstances, Johnson directs our attention to the virtues of some kind of written constitution. Conventions can thus be viewed as a prop to an executive and not a check or limitation. These potential weaknesses in the doctrines of the ancient constitution and conventions led many in the eighteenth century to opt for the written constitution.

The virtue of the written constitution or document to its proponents was that it supplied a definite point of reference which was beyond purely arbitrary interpretation. It could be either a single document, the first classic example being the American constitution of 1787, or a series of historical documents. Both are supplemented by conventions and amendments. The single document tended to be the dominant model in the eighteenth and nineteenth centuries. It was difficult to emulate the British example of the unwritten constitution, although many anglophiles obviously devoutly wished to do this. As Benjamin Constant pointed out, it took generations to a build up such a constitutional tradition. It was far quicker and simpler to write a document or code; whether it would be obeyed was another matter. The heyday of such constitutional documents was the eighteenth and nineteenth centuries, although they are still being written in the twentieth century. The Covenant of the League of Nations, the United Nations' Charter and the European Charter of Human Rights (which some argue should be embodied into English law) are products of this constitutional tradition on a more international level. Other States, for example India, have established their own constitutions in the post-war era.

The precedent for such written documents derives originally from seventeenth-century England during the civil war. The first constitutional attempts were the three Agreements of the People of 1647, 1648 and 1649, constructed by the Leveller group in the New Model Army. In part these were were offered as serious alternatives to more compromising schemes such as The Heads of the Proposals (1647) produced by the Grandees in the Army. The Levellers, by the time of the third Agreement, were worried, not just by royalist or Parliamentary claims, but also by Cromwell's autocratic potential, specifically after he had crushed a Leveller rising at Burford in May 1649. The Leveller Agreements did not make any headway and oddly it was Cromwell who moved the next attempt at a written constitution – the Instrument of Government (1653). These attempts were followed later in the century, after the deposition of James II, by partial constitutional documents such as the 1689 Bill of Rights and the Triennial Act of 1694. These various bills and proposals began to constitute a gradual accretion of constitutional documents and ideas which have subsequently characterized the British constitutional tradition. The first single constitutional documents to be fully implemented were written in North America in the next century. The constitutional tradition began with the Pennsylvania Constitution (1776), Virginia (1776), Massachusetts (1780), and the full American Constitution (1787). France followed suit with her constitutions of 1791, 1793 and 1795 with an accompanying Declaration of the Rights of Man. Some other European States followed – Sweden declaring a constitution in 1809 and Holland in 1815. In this century even the Soviet Union has felt it necessary to join the throng with constitutions in 1936, 1965 and 1977. The 1977 document is more honest, declaring that rights must tie in with the ends of the Communist Party of the Soviet Union.

Essentially the written document is initially a statement of intent to follow certain stipulated rules. The collection of basically regulative rules are laid down to provide the parameters within which government operates. They entail certain basic restraints, details of the organization of government and methods of amending the basic rules. As well as detailing such powers and their limits it will usually always include some statement or declaration on the rights of individual citizens. This holds true up to the present. It is a tradition which dates back to the initiative of writers such as Tom Paine in *The Rights of Man* to enshrine human (or natural) rights in a codified form. It is still being argued today in Britain by figures such as Lord Scarman, amongst others, that we need such a Bill of Rights, or alternatively that we should incorporate the European convention into our own legal system.

Many eighteenth- and nineteenth-century constitutionalists insisted that a constitution had to be written. C. J. Friedrich remarked on this that 'superficial though this may seem to us today, it was widely held during the age of constitution makers in the past century and a half' (1968, p. 124). Such an idea was often challenged by nineteenth-century British constitutional writers such as James Bryce, on the ground that the written document is too rigid and inflexible. On the other hand, as proponents of the written constitution noted, conventions and the like could be too flexible or simply ignored (Johnson, 1980). In Britain, for example, the actual legal doctrine of Parliamentary sovereignty, in practice the sovereignty of the executive, does not rest at all easily with the idea of convention. As McIlwain observed, with some prescience, 'A popular despotism must result [in Britain] . . . if Parliament ever becomes in practice what it now is in law' (1940, p. 20). Convention is not a very effective barrier to such a possibility. Conventions are acceptable if they work, but in Britain they are a poor substitute for genuine limitations, which is the essence of constitutional government. Parliamentary sovereignty exercised via a dominant executive, ministerial responsibility and a strong party discipline, is not a comfortable bedfellow for constitutional rule. Britain stands out from practically all developed industrialized societies in having no formalized or written constitution to limit government (see Johnson 1980, p. 31). It is questionable now as to whether Britain could be characterized as a constitutional State even though the disposition for constitutional government still exists.

Institutional devices for limitation

The other main procedure for limiting and diversifying authority has been the institutional devices, for example, the mixed constitution, balanced constitution, checks and balances and the separation of powers. Each of these will be briefly examined.[4]

The idea of the mixed constitution has in fact an ancient heritage going back to the Greeks. Plato, for example, in the *Laws*, argues that unrestricted power in one person has a corrupting effect on the whole regime. He used the Persian monarchy as an example, since it had been defeated by the much smaller Greek city-states because of its internal corruption. On the other hand Plato disapproved of an excess of liberty as in Athenian democracy. The ideal was Sparta, and the secret of its success was its balance of ruling elements – power shared between kings, ephors and elders. In the section 'The Reasons for Sparta's Success' (Plato, 1970, Book 3, pp. 139–42), Plato remarks, through his Athenian character in the dialogue, 'If you neglect the rule of proportion and fit excessively large sails to small ships . . . or too high authority to a soul that doesn't measure up to it, the result is always disastrous.' Proportion in Sparta meant splitting up authority. Thus the Athenian maintains that 'This is the formula that turned your kingship into a mixture of the right elements' (Plato, 1970, Book 3, pp. 139–40).

Aristotle in his *Politics* also discussed the idea of a mixed constitution in the form of the Polity – a combination of oligarchic and democratic features. The basic idea was that greater stability could be maintained if there was a degree of proportionality or a judicious mixture between various kinds of rule such as democracy and aristocracy. If different groups are involved they will automatically limit and balance each others tendency to excess. The argument had some parallel with the division in England between king, Lords and Commons (see Maitland, 1908, p. 20). As Charles I stated in 1642: 'The experience and wisdom of your Ancestors hath so moulded this government out of a mixture of these monarchy, aristocracy, and democracy, as to give this Kingdom the conveniences of all three, without the inconveniences of any one' (quoted in Richter, 1977, p. 87). Many took up this theme in the seventeenth century as a description of England; something that the royalist writer Sir Robert Filmer complained about. However it is important to remember that it was not premised on any conception of separate functions of government. This is especially true of the Greeks. It also had no overt connection with constitutional theory. The link with constitutional theory began in the late seventeenth century and continued in the eighteenth.

The balanced constitution evolved from the mixed constitution as a description of England; power being restrained by a judicious balance of elements rather than a mixture. The doctrine of checks and balances is also closely related to the idea of the balanced constitution. As Melvin Richter observes, the two doctrines were at times virtually indistinguishable – 'Much depended upon whether the balance was said to exist between different parts of the society or parts of the government or functions of government' (1977, p. 88). The checks were needed to prevent abuse of power, the balance of elements was maintained to ensure such checks could exist. A typical statement on the balanced constitution can be found in William Blackstone's *Commentaries on the Laws of England* (1765–9). It must, however, be pointed out that there is an element of artificiality in rigidly dividing up checks and balances, the separation of powers and the balanced constitution. Much of the time these doctrines were integrated.

The separation of powers is the most well-known of these devices. Blackstone, for example, greatly admired Montesquieu and the theory of the separation of powers, and combined it with the doctrine of checks and balances and the balanced constitution. The distinctive feature of the separation of powers is that it focuses on the abstract notion of separate powers, agencies and functions of government. Before the idea of the separation of powers could be formulated, it was necessary that there should be some conceptual grasp of the idea of separate spheres, powers and functions of government. This is something that was not available to Greek thought. If law was a relatively static phenomenon what need was there for any concept of a flexible legislative or executive power? Judicial power also was not in any way separate from the ruling process. The mixed constitution was not a conception of separate powers of government being mixed, but rather a way of integrating classes or groups into government. Still, in the medieval period the concept of law as an ancient unchanging pattern was widely accepted. The doctrines of fundamental law, the ancient constitution and the common law made Parliament and the like into declaratory rather than legislative bodies. As Vile remarks, in the medieval mind 'The modern notion of an executive power distinct from the machinery of law enforcement through the courts, could hardly be envisaged in an age when almost the only impact of government upon the ordinary citizens was through the courts and the law-enforcement offices' (1967, pp. 28–9).

It was from the introduction of the idea that law could be the result of human agency that the beginning of separate functions arises. Already from Aristotle there was a distinction between the existence of a general rule and applying it in particular instances, or the making of law and its application; when the making of general rules was seen to arise in the agency of government it was possible to see it as distinct from its actual execution. In England, Bracton had separated government from jurisdiction. Conscious of the growing power of the agency of kingship, lawyers still wanted to conceive of jurisdictional parameters to that power. The guarantee of jurisdiction also 'provided the basis for the evolution of "legislative power" independent of the will of an executive power of the king' (Vile, 1967, p. 26). This notion combined with the idea that separate agencies had different functions. Thus the initial twofold distinction, which emerged slowly in the seventeenth century, was between legislative and executive powers, identified in countries such as England with separate functions and to an extent agencies. However, executive power still included judicial functions. It was not until the eighteenth century that a threefold classification appears between legislative, executive and judicial powers; even Montesquieu's famous exposition of the separation of powers in *The Spirit of the Laws* (1748) hovers between a two- and a threefold classification. It should be noted, however, that arguments for the independence of judges had been put forward over the sixteenth and seventeenth centuries. The emergence of the judicial function as separate was a product of the eighteenth century, although in Britain the doctrine of the Crown in Parliament and the dominance of the executive and legislative branches still lessens the significance of the role of the judiciary in a constitutional sense. British courts still give way too readily to the executive and legislative branches.

Even John Locke, who was an influence on Montesquieu, was not too concerned to distinguish functions, although the early formulation of the doctrine can be found in embryo in his writings. The main functions of the State were still juridical. For Locke, executive power incorporated federative power, which dealt with foreign affairs. Legislative power in its widest sense incorporated the executive, namely the king in Parliament; the executive (king) for Locke could not legislate. Parliament supervised the execution of law but must not itself execute it. This was basically a doctrine of a balanced constitution. Over the seventeenth and eighteenth centuries the separation of powers was discussed in tandem with the mixed and balanced constitution, particularly after the Restoration of Charles II. The installation of William and Mary was also a clear demonstration of the power of the legislative branch.

Montesquieu did not invent the term separation of powers; he took it from English writers such as Locke. Montesquieu provides, though, the most well-known exposition of the doctrine in his *Spirit of the Laws*, specifically in his discussion of England in Book XI, chapter 6. *Spirit of the Laws* is a very wide-ranging work involving legal, political and moral philosophy, comparative government and sociology. The theory of the separation of powers in fact only occupies a very small portion of the work. Montesquieu does not offer a description of England, which was if anything more of a mixed or balanced constitution. Rather he discusses an ideal type. Most English writers, for example Blackstone, who picked up the idea of the separation of powers, domesticated and anglicized it within the notion of the balanced constitution. It is also questionable as to how far Montesquieu offers a pure separation doctrine. The purer sense is that there are three powers: the legislative which makes and passes laws, the judiciary which interprets the law and the executive which enforces the law. Essentially these are rule-making, rule-settling and rule-enforcing branches of government. The aim of this separation is to uphold liberty. Each branch should have totally separate powers, functions and personnel, thus they act to check each other.

Montesquieu does not seem to give equal weight to the various agencies. He also gives different accounts of the various powers. In Book XI, chapter 6, political power is subdivided into legislative and executive. Executive power is again subdivided into executive power in foreign affairs (as in Locke) and judicial power, which deals with domestic laws. In his second account the power of judging crimes is raised almost to the same level as executive and legislative power. This is the basis to the trinity which is the most familiar doctrine. His third account of political power is made while discussing the British constitution where 'the legislative body is made up of two parts, each is made dependent on the other by their mutual power to reject legislation. Both will be connected by the executive power, which itself will be connected to the legislature' (quoted in Richter 1977, p. 91). This is really the theory of the mixed constitution. 'Such a notion', as Richter remarks, 'is no part of the theory of the separation of powers' (1977, p. 91). Further, Montesquieu does not indicate in any of these accounts the actual nature of the powers and whether personnel could overlap, as was the case with the mixed and balanced constitution. In the case of the third account of political power, he explicitly links himself to these latter doctrines. Montesquieu was in fact represented by some thinkers such as Benjamin Constant as arguing only for a partial separation of powers, combined with blended powers and checks and balances. In this sense it would be hard to make out a case that Montesquieu was a clear exponent of the pure doctrine of the separation of powers. However, like Locke,

Montesquieu provided the intellectual tools for later constitutional writers, specifically in the USA. Montesquieu himself does not rest so easily in the constitutionalist mode; he was not a democrat or proto-liberal. Monarchy was still the best form of government, but the spirit of the law was determined by traditional constraints. In this sense he was still very much of a traditional constitutionalist despite his apparent modernity.

Moral and philosophical limitations

The other broad area of limitation lies in the realm of philosophical and moral argument. Again this is an extremely broad area. Many of the arguments form the substance of much contemporary political theory. The topics which will be discussed are natural law, natural and human rights, contractual theories of obligation, consent theory, popular sovereignty and democracy. Like the legal and historical limitations, these points claim some kind of rational priority in order to limit authority. However, they are none the less *intrinsic* to a particular view of the State. Taken independently there is nothing necessarily constitutionalist in any of these arguments. Consent, popular sovereignty and contract theory were employed by absolutist writers to great effect. By the eighteenth century most of these had become characteristics of the constitutional approach.

Natural law   One of the oldest philosophical and theological devices to limit and control the behaviour of both individuals and governments was the idea of natural law. Natural law must be distinguished from the law of nature – the regularities and patterns which have been the concern of the natural sciences. Natural law was characteristically seen as a normative order, either legitimated and created by some kind of deity or embodied in objective reasoning powers. For Greek thinkers there were unwritten codes implicit in nature and more importantly in human nature. Nature was harmonious and purposive. Humans were social creatures by nature. To develop they needed sociality and the ideal sociality could be clearly specified; Aristotle and Plato tried to perform this task in their political writings. The notion of this inner harmony and purpose in nature was taken up by the Stoics and through this school moved into Roman thought with philosophers such as Cicero. The Stoics offered a universalist doctrine: all humans possess the capacity to reason, and the divine spark of reason in each enabled the perception of an unchangeable moral order. With the spread of these ideas it would have been odd if they did not have have some import for government. No Roman jurist ever asserted that natural law ought in any way to override positive law, but undoubtedly it could not be disregarded in the formulation of law. Early Christian thought took on board many of these ideas (see Armstrong and Markus, 1964). Natural law shifted easily into the promptings of the Christian conscience.

The difficulty that the early Church fathers had with natural law was simply that 'nature' was not wholly trusted. The Gnostic sentiment that nature was basically corrupt and sinful, as against spirit, impinged on Church doctrine. The Christian must deny the flesh. In the development of medieval philosophy, specifically in Thomas Aquinas, rational natural law was drawn into the very substance and structure of the church. Aquinas synthesized Christian and Greek thought and provided the basis of canon law, the law of the church, which was dominant until comparatively recently. Natural law, which complemented revelation, was seen as the rational ordering of the universe, including the State, for the common good. The whole process had been advanced under the Emperor Justinian, whose lawyers had constructed the *Institutes* and *Digest*. These books of law integrated Christian and Roman natural law thinking into positive legal codes. They formed the basis for subsequent reflections on natural law by both canon and civil lawyers during the renaissance of Roman law in the eleventh century. As a result of reflection on these codes, natural law ideas diffused throughout Europe.

Most recent commentators on natural law, for example A. P. D'Entrèves or Leo Strauss, have noted the gradual change in its character from the 1500s onward till its partial decline in the 1800s. The older medieval notions of natural law, which at times became inextricably connected to Roman law doctrine, as well as customary law, were tied in closely to theological concerns. God was definitely the architect of the principles of natural law. It was also closely bound up with the hierarchical structure of medieval society. Like fundamental law, it was not a radical theory. Burke was still an exponent of this version of natural law in the eighteenth century. Natural law tended to justify and sanctify the existing order. Very gradually it began to lose some of its theological aspect and the focus fell on the objectivity of rules of reason – which even God had to obey. Also natural law began to link up with natural rights which, with their universal and egalitarian character, began to have a radicalizing effect on politics. Instead of binding rules of reason propounding duties to Christians, natural law became a series of rights claimed by individuals. D'Entreves calls this a change in 'accent' (1970, p. 58). Natural law lost part of its objective character and became associated with subjective judgement. Some, like Hobbes, had a particularly idiosyncratic use of the term, where natural law virtually functions as a set of prudential maxims. However, the rational individual now becomes the starting point, not the ordered universe. Thinkers such as Locke, Pufendorf, Grotius, Vattel and Blackstone provided a theory which placed sovereignty in natural law, which in turn validated natural rights and consequently acted to restrain governments.

The basic claim of natural law, in the classical sense, is that there are certain basic principles which are ahistorical, unchangeable and rational, which provide intelligible norms for the human will and for government. These norms are morally obligatory and any reasonable creature should be able to discern them, since they are the prerequisite for being fully human. These moral principles help us to evaluate our own and others' conduct and they can find full expression in legal and political structures. Human nature and the substantive ability to reason are of course deemed to be consistent throughout time.

Natural and human rights Connected to the whole thesis of natural law is the idea of natural and human rights. Natural and human rights are recognized as justified claims held by humans *qua* being human, attributed to all human beings on account of their common human nature and underpinned by asocial values, that is to say not originating in social or political claims. The notion of rights is in fact comparatively recent. The concept *jus* is not really translatable from Roman law as a modern right, rather *jus* implies something which is right or correct in a given situation. It was closer in fact to our modern usage of justice. Property was never described as a *jus* in Roman law. Claimants in a dispute each took an oath on the righteousness of their case. The favourable verdict was a *jus*. It thus implied objective righteousness or a just state of affairs (see Tuck, 1979, pp. 7–8).

Some writers, for example the Catholic philosopher J. Maritain, have traced the idea of natural rights back to the medieval period, or in fact to the first principles of a Christian life. As he stated, 'natural law deals with the rights and duties which follow from the first principle "do good and avoid evil"' (1958, p. 39). On the other hand, D'Entreves has remarked on Aquinas that 'St Thomas nowhere committed himself to anything which many be said to approach even remotely the idea of "original" or natural right' (1939, p. 32). Aquinas was more concerned with duties than rights. Natural rights took precedence in the seventeenth-century writings of Locke and others. Rights derived from natural law were conceived as moral constraints on individuals and governments. They were individualistic, pre-social and intrinsic to humans.[5] They could not be acquired, relinquished, transferred or alienated. For the Lockean specifically, government was set up with the express purpose of maintaining such rights as life, liberty and property. Civil rights were seen as founded on fundamental natural rights. They form the ground for all other social claims. Essentially the older natural rights are the same as the more secular equivalent of human rights. It is this tradition of fundamental rights which became eventually enshrined in the various constitutional bills of rights which proliferated during the eighteenth century. The original prototype model for this was the 1689 Bill of Rights in England. Initially the American colonists had appealed to English constitutional rights before shifting to the 'immutable' truths of natural rights. This century also has seen a continuation of this traditon with the United Nations' 'Universal Declaration of Human Rights' (1948) amongst others. After the Second World War, western States, in Winston Churchill's words, attempted 'to enthrone human rights' (Cranston, 1962, p. 5). Natural and human rights, whether enshrined in a bill of rights, constitutional document or simply asserted, acted as definite limitations to governmental activity. The best State is thus the constitutional one which tries to incorporate and codify these rights.

Contractualism The contractual theory of obligation, often coupled with natural law and rights, was an important tool of limitation. Admittedly it did not always function in this manner. Hobbes is probably the clearest example of a thinker using the contract/natural right tradition for absolutist purposes. Contractualism was and is usually used to explain the *nature* rather than the origin of political rule and authority. The state of nature was not usually seen as an actual but rather as a hypothetical condition. Contractual theories in the seventeenth century arose in the context of centralized power. They were designed for the protection of the privileges and liberties of groups and later individuals against centralized encroachment.

One can find elementary contractual notions in Plato's *Republic*, and also in the Old Testament. In fact the covenants and contracts between the kings of Israel and God became crucially important in later Calvinist and Puritan political thought in the sixteenth and seventeenth centuries. Theodore Beza, for example, argued that David and Solomon had been *made* kings by the people and had certain contractual duties. For other Huguenot theorists such as Philip Mornay, fundamental questions arose from the Old Testament: are subjects bound to obey a prince whose commands are contrary to the laws of God? If a prince has broken his contract with the people and/or God, can the people resist him (see Oestreich, 1982, p. 145)? Roman law had strong contractual elements, while some medieval philosophers, such as Aquinas, argued that governments had contractual duties and obligations giving rise to Lord Acton's comment that 'Aquinas not the Devil was the first Whig' (Figgis, 1956, p. 7). Another important root of contractual theory was feudalism. Many scholars have noted that the feudal system up to the fourteenth century involved a complex hierarchy of mutual contractual obligations. Kingship itself was regarded by many as an elective office, the coronation ceremony incorporating promises. Medieval contracts were often concerned with the autonomy of traditional privileges and rights in perpetuity – the Magna Charta (1215), The Golden Bull of Hungary (1222), the Aragonese Privileges (1285–7), were examples of such a demand. Often such documents were referred back to by seventeenth-century constitutionalists who saw a definite continuity. As Figgis remarked, 'The contractual theory is . . . the last phase of that juristic concept of politics which is largely medieval, but remained an influence through the eighteenth century' (1956, p. 11).

Contractual theory developed firstly in Huguenot circles, specifically in the monarchomachs such as Beza and Mornay, although its first major systematic exponent was Althusius. Paradoxically, it was the Catholic Counter-Reformation critics of the Huguenots who produced very explicit arguments on the state of nature and contractual theory, figures such as Mariana, De Soto and Vitoria, who were deeply influential on the great exponents of contract theory such as John Locke. The great age of contractual thought is represented by writers like Locke, Grotius, Pufenforf and later Rousseau. Contractual language became part of popular political discourse in the seventeenth century and was taken on board by the English Whigs in the eighteenth century, although with modifications.

The key values and assumptions behind contract theory are that there is some notion of a rational, asocial individual, who, whether in a hypothetical or actual state of nature, is capable of rationally assessing and evaluating decisions. The contractual method is a way of both evaluating political institutions and establishing the basis of their legitimacy. Usually contractual theory was tied to natural rights and sometimes natural law, specifically in the great age of contract theory. Government was seen to exist for specific ends, mainly the guarantee of individual rights. Its function was to serve the interests of the aggregate of individual citizens and to maximize their liberty. The major elements of contractual arguments were firstly, some kind of 'state of nature' (hypothetical or actual), which formed the platform from which individuals moved into society. In the state of nature, individuals possessed natural rights and were aware of natural law. Within these parameters the individual seeks a way out of the state of nature by contracting with his fellow beings to form a society. Contract theorists varied considerably not only in their interpretation of natural law and rights, but also in how and in what manner contracts were made and also how many were made. Locke, for example, conceived of a contract to establish society but a trust relationship behind the setting up of a government. Hobbes, on the other hand, saw contracts taking individuals out of a very unpleasant state of nature, but being totally without substance unless reinforced by an absolute sovereign with whom no contract is made.

Contracts have been viewed in two ways: historically and hypothetically. The dominant motif has been the hypothetical one which is concerned with the logic of obligations rather than the historical chronology. The arguments tend to be somewhat juristic, *a priori* and mechanistic. The person or persons who are supposed to be contracting have also varied. Contractual theorists explored contracts in the field of God and the people; God and the king; God, the king and the people; the king and the people; and the government and each individual citizen. The two most well-known contracts are the contract of society, taking individuals out of the state of nature, and the contract of government, which actually establishes government. It is, however, worth emphasizing again that not all contract theorists adhere to this structure.

Contract theory has been subject to vigorous criticism in the last two centuries from various quarters, not least because of its association with the natural right perspective. The development of the historical school of law, legal positivism and sociological theories, uniformly rejected contractual ideas; although it is still a very active form of argument, as in the work of the American philosopher John Rawls. However, the fate of contractual theory was to become slowly absorbed into the constitutional tradition. The desire to confirm rights, contracts and the like led, in the same vein as natural rights, to the attempt to embody contracts in documents, though Oestreich remarks on this process, 'the transition from ruling contracts to constitutional instruments is one of bewildering variety' (1982, p. 181). Thus, certain writers, such as E. Barker and J. W. Gough, have maintained that constitutionalism is a modern substitute for contractualism, which avoids many of the intellectual difficulties of contractual theorizing. Barker, for example, regards the constitution as 'the articles of a contract which constitutes the State' (see Gough, 1955, pp. 250–55; Barker, 1948, p. xv).

Consent Closely related to the contract and natural right tradition is the concept of consent. Often the history of this word is treated as coterminous with that of contract. It would be true to say that contract arguments embody the notion of consent, although conversely it is not necessarily the case that all consent arguments require the idea of contract. The essence of the consent argument is that 'no man is obligated to support or comply with any political power unless he has personally consented to its authority' (Simmons, 1979, p. 57). All obligations to authority are therefore grounded in voluntary acts. Someone authorizes or accords someone a right to act. The assumptions that lie behind this view are also largely shared by contract theory. Individuals are all naturally free to choose, any alienation of that liberty will be through a deliberate voluntary choise. Consent is a way of protecting the individual from the government, since the government is set up to defend the interests of all citizens. Consent theory is the attempt, within the parameters of society, to maximize individual liberty. As one commentator has observed, in consent theory 'The State is an instrument for serving the interests of its citizens' (Simmons, 1979, p. 68).

Although there is some debate on the issue, John Locke is most often cited as one of the first theorists to utilize more systematically the idea of consent. He drew, however, a distinction between tacit and express consent which gave rise to a number of difficulties (see Pateman, 1979). Consent in recent years has been analysed as a form of promising, wishing to grant permission, granting a right, authorizing and attempting to induce reliance in others. Despite the considerable ambiguity of the idea the concept has been crucial in the constitutional tradition.

Popular sovereignty There is a lot of sense in a recent remark that 'the theory and practice of constitutionalism ignore the logical niceties of absolutism, opting instead for the contradictions of popular sovereignty' (Schochet, 1979, p. 12). The roots of popular sovereignty lie deep in European thought. Roman law anticipated some of the ideas in the doctrine of *lex regia*. The people were seen to confer authority on the prince. Canonist teaching in the Catholic Church, reinforced later by conciliarist debates, argued that the 'whole' Church embodied the authority. The independent life of many thirteenth-century Italian cities fostered the image of sovereign units independent of the prince. The idea of popular sovereignty is present in such writers as Hotman, Althusius and Buchanan and also the Counter-Reformation scholastics. In these early writers it had no connection whatsoever with democracy and no necessary theoretical link with contractual and natural right theorizing. The most famous theorist to link up many of these ideas with popular sovereignty was J. J. Rousseau. Sovereignty was expressed in the general will, which incorporated the whole people. The people came to decisions in the public assembly via participatory democracy. Such ideas became more common currency through the 1780s and 1790s specifically in the so-called *sans cullotte* phase of the French Revolution.

There were a number of unresolved questions in the idea of popular sovereignty. Did the people concede or just transfer power to the governors? As A. J. Carlyle and A. W. Carlyle remarked, 'It would seem . . . to be clear that as late as the middle of the thirteenth century the civil or Roman lawyers were unanimous in holding that the *populus* was the ultimate source of all political authority, that they recognised no other source of all political authority than the will of the whole community' (1936, Vol. 2, p. 66). The point at issue here was – did the people give up that power and was it something that could be resumed by the *populus*? How could the people be the source and subject of law? This was a dilemma also facing monarchic exponents of sovereignty who recognized fundamental or natural law. Rousseau provided one solution to it through his idea of the self-legislated general will. If the individual wills the law, then logically he wills his own subjection. This was an idea later taken up by theorists such as Hegel. An important problem for the idea of popular sovereignty is who is to count as the *populus*. It could mean, in the doctrine of the general will, the whole people; on the other hand, it could mean a body of representatives or an electorate. If we look over the last century and a half at the history of the electorate we can see marked changes in its nature. In other words the definition of the *populus* has been continually changing.

Popular sovereignty on its own has no necessary connection with constitutionalism or democracy. Otto von Gierke in fact argued that popular sovereignty 'never played any serious part in the theory of constitutionalism' (1934, p. 152). From the thirteenth to the seventeenth centuries it was a device which needed to be supplemented by what Tierney called 'auxiliary precautions' (1982, p. 54). This idea is markedly close to that of James Madison in the *Federalist* – 'you must first enable the government to control the governed; and in the next place oblige it to control itself. A dependence on the people is, no doubt, the primary control of the government; but experience has taught mankind the necessity of auxiliary precaution' (quoted in Schochet, 1979, pp. 9–10). Popular sovereignty, like participatory democracy in the eighteenth century, was seen as a dangerous principle and practice. Ironically, the idea of popular sovereignty and participatory democracy did act as a bridge between absolute sovereignty and nation State sovereignty. The popular will, although acting as a restraint on the central will of the prince, was as potentially absolutist in its implication if it acquired dominance. Thus popular sovereignty was intrinsically as much in need of constraint and limitation as absolute sovereignty, unless, that is, it could be supplemented by auxiliary precautions.

Democracy   Democracy is in a similar position to popular sovereignty. There are certain elements of it which constitutionalists have wished to take on board and others that they have not. Broadly speaking there have been two dominant lines of thought on classical democracy: the participatory and representative models.

Participatory democracy which originated in Athens (800–500 BC) incorporated the idea of total involvement in the policy-making process. Democracy was an education for the citizen. Offices were open to all and continually rotated. The ideal was only to be realized, however, in a small-scale homogeneous community. Representative democracy, with certain restrictions on the definition of the electorate, demanded far less involvement by citizens. It could be realized on a much larger scale and implied less disruption to everyday life. Constitutionalism found that representative democracy, within limits, was again a useful tool for limiting and controlling authority. Each individual representative had to theoretically take cognizance of the wishes of the electors. This entailed notions of responsibility and accountability, but again within limits.

The idea of mass participation has never appealed to the constitutionalists. In the 1800s specifically it smacked too much of Jacobinism, Rousseauism and the excesses of the French Revolution. Writers such as Benjamin Constant and Madame de Staël in France, Jeremy Bentham and James Mill in England and James Madison in

America wanted to use democracy as an instrumental device to prevent the dominance of any one group, whether the masses or aristocracy. They did not regard democracy as in any way an intrinsic good or value in itself. In Britain, J. S. Mill came closest to the idea of democracy as an intrinsic good, but even here Mill never abandoned the idea of representative democracy as an instrumental device controlling either the 'mediocre majority' or the 'sinister interests' of the aristocracy. His advocacy of proportional representation, based on the scheme of Thomas Hare, was precisely to balance out proportional interest and prevent any one particular group dominating. Despite this protective fear on Mill's part, he had also seen democracy as an educative practice to enable citizens to broaden their horizons. The paradox of Mill's ideas was that democracy was seen as a means to the education of citizens, but it could not function adequately without intelligent, perceptive, educated voters. Mill's fear of the simple majority voting system was that it allowed the dominance of a ignorant majority over minorities. Liberals who adopted constitutionalism thought that democracy was a useful device but needed limitations itself − in other words, auxiliary precautions. The elective chambers needed to be checked and balanced with non-elected chambers, a separate judiciary and possibly a monarchy, set in the context of a written constitution. Mill was thinking in the same vein as this when he argued for legislation to be structured by a non-elective body of experts appointed by the Crown. The elective chamber would only have a power to accept or refuse to pass laws.

In the nineteenth century the term 'liberal democracy', as distinct from either just liberalism or democracy, came into use. It indicated that democracy had become one of the key limiting tools. Liberals, who by the nineteenth century were the key exponents of constitutionalism, institutionalized democratic practices and norms as a way of both controlling and legitimating government. It also helped to integrate an increasingly literate and active body of citizens by channelling their energies in formal institutional procedures within a Parliamentary framework. Democracy thus helped to incorporate and control large sectors of the population.

Civil society   Another of the tools employed in the constitutional theory of the State for limiting authority was the separation between the public and private realms, often conventionally termed State and society. This has involved many in the defence of what has come to be known as 'civil society'. The terminology is not however crystal clear since some eighteenth-century writers used the term civil society to refer to a particular type of State. Hegel is one example of this and he only follows a tradition. The defence of civil society coincided with the development of ideas on individualism, individual rights to liberty and property. By the late 1200s mercantile capitalism was beginning to develop in northern Italy and Flanders. Some have thus found the embryo of civil society ideas in thirteenth-century Europe, although the ideas did not develop for several centuries. The idea of property rights and rights to privacy had also been explored by some Roman lawyers. Civil society culture, however, was alien to that of the medieval Guild which tended to monopolize and collectivize economic and social affairs, controlling prices, wages, conditions and the quality of goods produced within a single unit. It was not fortuitous that early exponents of the values of individualism and civil society, for example, Adam Smith, should have gone out of their way to repudiate Guilds. The more collective Guild strands of thought never quite gave way to the advocates of civil society. Trade unionism carried on some of the Guild mentality. In western industrialized societies it has, however, taken a more subordinate role since the late seventeenth century. Yet, as Anthony Black points out, civil society represents only half of the European tradition: 'If, for example, there are no limits to what some may acquire and others may lose in the market place, then legal equality and personal independence themselves slip away' (1984, p. 240).

From the sixteenth century the mercantile groups began to regard themselves no longer as just another medieval estate, or a useful tool for absolutist control, but rather as a separate and powerful interest. Some tried to integrate themselves with absolutism, others resisted. Increasingly many began to criticize traditional sources of authority. Through ideas of the independence of property rights, they asserted the right of personal privacy, security, freedom from arbitrary intervention and consequently rejected the ideas of aristocratic privilege. The legal order was seen to exist as upholding equal legal rights. The administration was peopled by such exponents of civil society ideas, which in Black's terms were shorthand for liberal values or 'bourgeois ideology' (1984, p. 32). The central theme of such an ideology was 'personal independence, and its central imperative of respect for persons' (1984, p. 43). This entailed a fairly clear separation between the realm of the individual and the realm of the the public legal process. Law should be a safeguard of the liberties and rights of civil society. Although, once again, it should be stressed that this separation exists *within* the constitutional State. It is not in reality, as it might appear, a separation between the State and civil society. It is the constitutional State which constitutes, in itself, a separation between public authority and private liberty. There is no sanctified area around individuals unless the State defines it as such. Accordingly at various points of economic, political or military crisis constitutional States have simply ignored or redefined this liberty. The constitutional State *decides* that individuals will possess a certain area of liberty. This is an intrinsic constitutive value of the theory itself.

The theme of civil society also connects up with the principle of the rule of law. The rule of law is a regulative principle which attempts to characterize the nature of law and the condition of a citizen's life. Laws, for the constitutionalist, should be a framework of known, standing and settled rules which do not single out any individual or group on the grounds of birth, status or any other special privilege for special exemption. They must be general, equally applicable to all and applied without fear or favour. The ultimate aim of a such a rule of law is to uphold or defend maximum equal liberty. Laws must be fully consonant with individual freedoms in civil society. It is this sense that it has become and remained a central principle for liberal thinkers, although not all have argued like Hayek that it must be fully consonant with a free market economy. Laws, under the rule of law, are the conditions for a moral life. They do not lay down what the individual ought to do but rather provide the opportunities for individuals to choose. In this sense they are relative to morality since they must be seen to be worthwhile and beneficial. The rule of law embodies a form of procedural fairness and rightness. It is not arbitrary in its treatment of individuals. It might also be added that the rule of law perspective also implies that laws will neither be retrospective nor retroactive, individuals should be able to know and understand them before they act. They should be open, consistent with each other, constant over time and thus possess a degree of finality in human affairs. Finally legal rules should be, by and large, predictable. This is a very different conception of law than one finds in the absolutists where the prince is regarded as 'living law'.

ORDERLY CHANGE AND THE MAINTENANCE OF VALUES

The constitutional theory of the State tries to overcome one of the intrinsic problems of absolute sovereignty, namely the transition and continuity between sovereigns. It maintains structures of rules and principles which allows for change and places a heavy emphasis on institutionalizing power relations, creating offices and positions with rights and duties operating within specific rules. Finally, it is concerned to establish how fundamental rules are to be modified.

Central to the constitutional theory is the value of individual persons. C. J. Friedrich gives this particular point a distinctly religious reading. In his book *Transcendent Justice* he argues, 'The constitution is meant to protect the *self* in its dignity and worth; for the self is believed to be primary and of penultimate value. The preoccupation with the self, rooted in Christian beliefs . . . eventually gave rise to the notion of rights [which] were thought to be natural' (1964, p. 17). This is an extension of his earlier definition of constitutionalism as 'the technique of establishing and maintaining effective restraints on political and government action'. With the idea of personality at the centre of constitutional theory the 'rights' of the person become a central preoccupation. For most constitutionalists these rights are recognized claims which are antecedent and morally prior to other positive laws of the State. One of the key rights, often tied to the right to property, is that of liberty. For most constitutionalist writers liberty was understood in a negative sense. This liberty was seen in terms of freedom from obstacles to the expression of opinion, free speech, association, economic activity and so forth. The implication was that constraint was incompatible with liberty, thus the less constraint the more liberty. Carried into the sphere of law, if law implied restraint then the less law, the greater liberty. Yet individuals had to be protected from incursions from others exercising their liberty, as well as from the public authorities. The right to equal liberty was therefore a fundamental value and right of the constitutional State. For Friedrich, these basic rights were seen to derive from the value of the person. The centrality of the person also gave rise to the assertion of the values of autonomy and privacy. An individual should only be interfered with if consent had been acquired, thus liberty was guaranteed as far as possible within the State. The liberty of individuals and their rights to freedom of conscience and the like had in fact developed from a paradoxical heritage. Many of the most vigorous early proponents of limitations implicit in the State for the end of liberty were religious groups such as the Jesuits and Presbyterians who, when in positions of authority, showed little interest in the ideas, specifically in their application to other denominations.

CONCLUSION

Modern constitutionalism, with the emerging liberalism whose
ideology it shares, predicates natural free, political, and right-
bearing individuals who *need* and therefore establish government
that can, may and should control.

Schochet, Constitutionalism

By the end of the nineteenth century, and especially in the twentieth,
the fate of constitutionalism and liberalism have been intertwined. A
critique of liberalism usually entails, if only by implication, a critique
of constitutionalism. Most constitutional States, as opposed to those
which simply have a constitution, are liberal or more often
liberal–democratic.

Liberalism has, however, changed in character over the nineteenth
and twentieth centuries. The classical liberals from the 1820s and
1830s were concerned with the liberty of the independent private
individual. Civil association was viewed as a minimal framework,
checking and balancing powers, so that individuals could pursue
their own economic, social or cultural interests. Later in the
nineteenth century, liberals, starting with the utilitarian school,
began to see a wider function for State action. They did not accept
the purely negative understanding of freedom. Freedom might be
about the development of persons and their ability to pursue certain
goals. In this sense a State, through law, could act so as to maximize
the conditions for an individual's liberty. They also did not accept
the rather rigid and false separation between the State and the
individual. Humans were intrinsically social or communal creatures.
The rights and freedoms of individuals could not be so clearly
separated from the State. This process of transformation within
liberalism was even more marked in liberal thinkers such as T. H.
Green, L. T. Hobhouse, J. A. Hobson, John Dewey, and more
recently John Rawls. They have all tended to emphasize communal
values, mutual dependence and a more positive view of liberty (see
Gaus, 1983). They have also seen a much more active role for the
State, integrating and promoting the lives of individuals. This has
caused the survivors of classical liberalism to cry out in horror at
such Statism being associated with liberalism. Hayek has even
doubted as to whether the 1908 New Liberal government under
Asquith should be called liberal at all. The oddity of such criticism is
that it is premised on the idea that the State somehow stands apart

from individuals or society. Such an idea, although promulgated within liberalism, has to be looked at carefully. The distinction between the State and society is made *by* the constitutional theorists within a particular theory of the State. A clearer way of putting the point would be that within the constitutional State a separation is observed between the governing institutions and society, society being constituted by right-bearing individuals. In other words the liberal constitutional State is self-limiting or subject to auto-limitation.

The beginnings of the unity of liberalism and constitutionalism date back to the 1680s. Even though the word 'liberal' did not exist until the early 1800s, many have seen John Locke as a primary liberal thinker (see Skinner, 1978, Vol. 2, p. 239). Locke is usually regarded as crucially important for two reasons. First, he differentiated rational constitutionalism from the ancient constitution tradition. Underlying Locke's whole philosophical position is the view of humans as rational, autonomous agents capable of making choices and acting responsibly. There were no wise ancients for Locke but rather primitive unsophisticated men. This view changed the tenor of constitutional argument. Secondly, Locke prepared the ground for the vigorous discussion of notions such as the separation of powers, constitutional monarchy and majority rule, although it is clear that he was not interested in the slightest in any form of mass equal suffrage, periodic elections, democracy or even Parliamentary supremacy.

Locke adopted many of the conventional modes of constitutional argument that we have already encountered, utilizing notions of natural law, natural rights, contract and consent theory. His vision of the State does not possess the grandeur of vision of the absolutists, but it does detail some the main characteristics of the constitutional understanding of the State. Locke's State was 'a voluntary society constituted for mutual protection' (Parry, 1978, p. 110). The extent of political life in the Lockean State was delimited by the original contract and the 'right-claims' of the mass of individual citizens. Essentially the State was envisaged as a minimalist civil association regulating the general conditions whereby individuals could exercise their liberty to the full in pursuing their individual interests. The magistrate was conceived of as virtually equivalent to an umpire. As Locke put it, 'It is the duty of the civil magistrate, by impartially enacted equal laws, to preserve and secure for all the people in general and for everyone of his subjects ... the just things that belong to his life' (quoted in Parry, 1978, p. 115). The elementary division of powers, the consensual basis of authority and the ultimate right to the dissolution of government provided grounds for the limitation of civil government in order to maximize individual liberty. As Parry argues 'The theory of civil government – limited and conducting itself according to the rule of law – has had a long history as one of the main contributory strands in liberalism. . . . Liberalism began, in the hands of such as Locke, as a theory aimed at discovering constitutional defences for the rights of self-direction' (1978, p. 156). He goes on to argue that the 1980s have seen a return to the Lockean ideas in the work of the American political philosopher Robert Nozick.

The pattern of thought that we find in Locke became characteristic of the later liberal and liberal-democratic tradition. Humans were viewed as a rational agents with interests and right-claims. Society was an aggregate of such competitive independent agents. Each needed a guaranteed sphere of liberty and therefore each should accord others respect for their sphere of liberty. Only a State conceived of as a civil association, providing a general framework of over-arching rules (a rule of law), and restrained in its conduct, could guarantee such conditions. As argued earlier, liberalism has changed in character especially in this century. Liberals such as T. H. Green and New Liberals such as L. T. Hobhouse and J. A. Hobson, accepted a very much broader notion of the State going well beyond the idea of a civil association (see Vincent and Plant, 1984 and Vincent, 1986). This initiated a rift within the liberal tradition which in many ways has still not been resolved, namely the extent and limits of State activity especially in relation to economic life. It is wise to remember that some of the most far-reaching ideas on economic and social reform adopted this century within liberal–democratic States were introduced by liberals, for example, in Britain by J. M. Keynes and W. H. Beveridge. In Britain, the ideas of Green and the New Liberal theorists provided the underpinning for a social democratic or social–liberal view of the State which was taken on board by the British Labour party and some elements of post-war Conservativism. This vision of the State has submerged. Neither Labour Party nor Conservative theorists have really attempted to articulate a theory of the State. The old latent distrust of the State has crept into both ideological traditions. We are now left with the inevitable crudity and ignorance of those, who, within the confines of a powerful State, call for 'something' to be rolled back. What that is is anybody's guess. It is clear, however, that the fate of liberalism and constitutionalism are inextricably intertwined.

4

The Ethical Theory of the State

> Hegel's main endeavour as a political thinker was to develop and
> to formulate a theory of the modern state.
>
> Ilting, *Hegel's Political Philosophy: Problems and Perspectives*

INTRODUCTION

The ethical theory of the State was constructed against the
theoretical background that we have been reviewing in the previous
two chapters. It developed in the context of German idealist
philosophy just after the era of the French Revolution. Subsequently
it had a considerable impact on the whole European tradition of
thought in this century. The key figure in the formulation of this
theory was G. W. F. Hegel (1770–1831), although reference will be
made at points to other thinkers influenced by the Hegelian
perspective.

The proponents of the ethical theory tried to say something
significant about the idea and practice of the State in the present
historical epoch. Hegel particularly maintained that it was the
destiny of humans, for the foreseeable future, to develop within States.
State-living was thus inevitable for the majority of humans in
advanced societies. We are not just social creatures but State-
creatures. The State does not exist by accident. It is the culmination
of a long historical development from the Greeks. Hegel constructed
a theory of history to show how the present epoch has gradually
developed from previous stages of human culture. The State,
however, was not just a system of laws, a sovereign-ruler or
institutional arrangement. The ethical theory was an extraordinarily
ambitious attempt to make something far more significant out of the
State. It was seen to have an inner as well as an outer sense. It is the

destiny of humans to develop in States not because the State is an ineluctable power, but rather because it develops out of the nature of human beings or rather out of the inner nature of human beings as rational creatures. The State and individuals share a common substance and purpose. In this sense the ethical State is an example of what Michael Oakeshott calls an 'enterprise', or Hayek, a 'teleocratic' association. Oakeshott defines it in the following terms, as something 'composed of persons related in terms of a specified purpose or interest and who recognise one another in terms of their common engagement to pursue or promote it. Each associate knows himself as the servant of the purpose pursued. . . . A state understood in terms of purposive association is, then, identified in terms of a purpose and of the persons joined in pursuing it' (1975, p. 315).

The other point to note about the ethical theory of the State is that it is rooted in a profound, if at times baffling, metaphysics. In order to link the inner and outer senses of the State, Hegel tries to show how the objective world of institutions and law is rooted in the subjective world of the human consciousness. In attempting to achieve this identity, encapsulating differences, Hegel develops a metaphysical thesis based on the idea of *Geist* (Mind or Spirit). The notion of *Geist* has given rise to a host of interpretations and will be discussed later. Very basically though, *Geist* is the metaphysical principle linking together human history and human consciousness. It can be secularized into the collective mind of humanity. On the other hand, it is sometimes identified with God. There are also many more subtle variations between these two views. The State, in Hegel's thought, is part of the unfolding character of *Geist* and thus has a strong normative and historical significance. As Hegel put it, in his somewhat grandiose terms, 'The State is the divine will, in the sense that it is mind present on earth, unfolding itself' (Hegel, 1967 section 242, *Zusatz*, p. 166).

The ethical theory, in Hegel's work, was shaped to some extent by history. In fact it is characteristic of Hegel to give a particularly philosophical significance to certain historical events. Since history is to a large extent the history of human consciousness, particular events can reveal something profound about the nature and direction of that consciousness. As a young man Hegel lived through the tremendous upheavals of the French Revolution, the rise and fall of Napoleon Bonaparte and the collapse of the *ancien régime* and Prussia. For Hegel, the French Revolution manifested a total 'radical freedom' – where the human will claimed an absolute freedom for itself. The revolutionaries had cast off all the older forms of authority and claimed to be able to rebuild France out of their own subjective wills and reason. Hegel describes this state of consciousness as an 'unrestricted possibility of abstraction from every determinate state of mind' or 'pure indeterminateness' (1967, section 5; *Zusatz* pp. 21–2). This form of 'negative freedom', as Hegel puts it, can take many forms but 'it takes shape in religion and politics alike in the fanaticism of destruction – the destruction of the whole subsisting social order' (Hegel 1967, section 5, *Zusatz*, p. 22). This 'unrooted' concept of negative freedom could only end in terror and confusion. Such an empty notion could not in fact build anything since it lived in a void of destruction. Its *raison d'être* was 'negation', namely to demolish reality. As Charles Taylor states, 'Faced with existing society, the *ancien régime*, the aspiration to absolute freedom was driven to destroy institutions. . . . But since it could not produce anything in its place, absolute freedom was stuck in this negative moment' (1979, p. 118).

Hegel was no advocate of the *ancien régime*, although he did recognize, in a Burkean sense, that humans are creatures of traditional customs and habits.[1] He was also mildly contemptuous of the traditional Holy Roman Empire of German States. For Hegel, in his early essay on *The German Constitution*, Germany was not a State. Like many intellectuals at that time, Hegel looked with some despair on German disunity. For Germany to be a State it needed a consistent, strong uniting bond, to be able and willing to defend itself and to be united around a strong public authority. As Hegel argued, 'The State requires a universal centre, a monarch, and Estates, wherein the various powers, foreign affairs, the armed forces, finance relevant thereto etc. would be united, a centre which would not merely direct but would have in addition the power necessary for asserting itself and its decrees, and for keeping the individual parts dependent on itself' (1964, p. 150). Only such a strong State could tolerate and protect the free activity of individuals. Freedom cannot subsist in an indeterminate sense, as in the French Revolution. It must develop within a strong framework of rules. We can find even in this early essay one of the main innovative ideas in Hegel's theory of the State, namely that human freedom is not gained without a strong, centralized State. The individual cannot be truly free in an indeterminate negative sense. Humans develop in the context of rules and customs and only the strong State has the flexibility and sensitivity to allow maximal play to human freedom.

The major influences on Hegel's thought are a matter of considerable debate. Undoubtedly one of the key influences was the

German idealist tradition of philosophy in Kant, Herder, Schiller, Fichte and Schelling. Greek thought also played a crucial role, specifically the idea of the *polis*. Hegel, like many of his fellow German intellectuals, tended to idolize Greece somewhat. The young Hegel followed in the tracks of Goethe, Winckelmann and Hölderlin in seeing Greece as a 'paradise of the spirit'. Finally, the classical political economy of Adam Smith and Adam Ferguson stimulated Hegel to think seriously about the effects of industrialization and the market economy on human culture and history. All of these concerns will arise in the following account of Hegel's vision of the State.

Hegel's theory of the State is not easy to categorize. Despite embodying his view of the State in a complex metaphysics, he insisted that philosophical, moral and political principles were to be found in the concrete customs and habits of the community. Also, although critical of feudalism, his ideas on the 'Corporation' and 'estates' in the *Philosophy of Right*, embody a form of feudal pluralism, which existed to limit the possibility of caprice in central government. He was also deeply critical of bourgeois individualism and negative freedom, which are characteristic of liberal constitutional thought. Such individualistic ideas were shot through with contradictions as well as being dangerous in political practice. Yet Hegel also incorporates bourgeois individualism as a necessary element of his vision of the State. In Hegel's terminology, it was a necessary 'moment', something that the modern State could not do without. Hegel was also critical of democratic theory, in its participatory form in revolutionary France and in its representative form in Britain. Yet he also argues for a complex mediation of public opinion through the estates assembly. He believed that such opinion acted as a valuable corrective and source of information to the bureaucracy. Hegel was also critical of the notion of a written constitution. A constitution, for Hegel, was something which developed and grew slowly over the life of a State. This was a definitely Burkean motif. However, the constitution also acts as a check on the behaviour of central authority. As Hegel argued, 'The constitution must in and by itself be the fixed and recognised ground on which the legislative stands, and for this reason it must not first be constructed. Thus the constitution *is*, but just as essentially it *becomes*, i.e. it advances and matures' (1967, section 298, addition 176, p. 291). Hegel's peculiar synthesis of ideas cannot be fitted into any other perspective. It is a distinctive and unique theory of the State in its own right.

Hegel's theory of the ethical State must be viewed primarily through his metaphysics. The central category, as stated, in his metaphysics is the notion of *Geist*. Spirit or Mind is a self-realizing entity developing in the self-consciousness of human beings through their activities as individuals in States. The human subject and State are inextricably tied up with the metaphysical theory. As one writer has put it 'the institution of the state offered the possibility of developing the self-consciousness of human members within a more universal objective framework' (Dyson, 1980, p. 144). World history is the gradual growth and decline of political communities viewed in the context of Spirit. The modern State, which Hegel tries to articulate in his *Philosophy of Right,* is therefore the culmination of a long process. It 'is what makes possible both the maximum satisfaction of the individual's particular wants and needs and the realisation of his essential nature and true freedom' (Schacht, 1972, p. 322).

In this chapter the metaphysical basis of Hegel's thought and complex vision of the State will be reviewed, concluding with some critical remarks.

METAPHYSICS AND THE SYSTEM OF PHILOSOPHY

One of the most distinctive aspects of Hegel's philosophy of politics is that he is looking for a way of overcoming the alien, impersonal character of political and social institutions. One of the most significant questions we are faced with in political philosophy is the relationship between the individual and the State. Hegel does not offer us a naïve organicist or holistic theory to integrate these elements, rather he tries to show, by an extremely subtle argument, that the individual and social world of institutions have essentially the same substance. This overcomes the alien quality of institutions, in philosophical terms, the division between subject and object. This substance is not a simple identity. Hegel tries developmentally to show, through an analysis of the concept of the human mind, how mind basically presupposes the institutional structure of the social world. Presupposed in the notion of Mind is also a complex series of categories explained in his *Logic* and *Philosophy of Nature.* The work of the social theorist and philosopher are often kept distinct in contemporary thought; either the philosopher will investigate the concept of mind, or the sociologist will examine the nature of the social world. The tendency of much recent philosophy has been to ignore or pay very little attention to the historical and social setting of ideas. Sociologists, on the other hand, have tended to explain ideas, not understand them – in other words, to see them as the result of certain antecendent causal conditions. As Nigel Harris comments in his book *Beliefs in Society*: 'Inevitably, ideas treated in isolation seem to be ritual, only accidently related to what men do. Thus, explanations have to be offered suggesting that ideas are decorative features of an on-going process, or concealments of *real* drives' (1968, p. 29). Hegel tries to link these two lines of investigation, which is one of his great virtues as a theorist.

Hegel's concept of Mind (or Spirit) does not fit very easily into any contemporary discussion of the philosophy of mind. This is primarily because he is not thinking of individual minds. Individual minds are part of, or instances of, some kind of universal Mind, which is the essence of what we call reality. This universal Mind is embodied in or immanent in the world. In individual minds it becomes conscious of itself in the world and its own development through history. In this sense the philosopher is an instance of the self-consciousness of Mind-in-general. The task of the philosopher is to apprehend the course of this development. As Hegel put it 'Mind is . . . in its very act only apprehending itself, and the aim of all genuine science is just this, that Mind shall recognize itself in everything in heaven and earth. An out-and-out Other does not exist for Mind' (Hegel, 1971, section 377, *Zusatz*, p. 1). The essential presupposition to grasp here is that reality is the development of Mind. This ontological presupposition immediately rules Hegel out of court for many contemporary philosophers, although it can be read in a number of different ways. There is, on the one hand, the more cosmic-religious reading of Hegel. As one recent commentator argued, 'The very possibility of accepting the Hegelian definition of the Absolute as spirit . . . depends on the acceptance of the pan-psychist romantic philosophy of nature which Hegel took over from Schelling' (Butler, 1977, p. 65). Also Richard Kroner notes, in his introducton to Hegel's early theological writings, that 'Hegel's philosophy is in itself a speculative religion – Christianity spelt by dialectic' (1948, p. 53). In contrast there are those who wish to read Hegel in a non-theological sense. The first of these was the young Hegelian Ludwig Feuerbach. Hegel is viewed as a philosopher of human praxis. All theology, to use Feuerbach's phrase, is really anthropology (see J. M. Bernstein, 1984, p. 39). Community and history provide the true grounds for knowledge. Individuals realize themselves and their own natures. Mind is human rationality through and through.

Whether Mind is viewed in the more cosmic or anthopological senses, it was still seen by Hegel as self-creative. Mind *is* its own act (see Hegel, 1971, sections 441 and 442). All categories are Mind-dependent, including nature. The implication of this, put very crassly, is that when we say something is 'finite', it is Mind in one of the stages of its development which has assumed the character of finiteness. Mind as a whole is a massive self-producing, self-justifying and self-correcting system, an eternal activity of self-alienation, self-discovery and self-union. As Hegel stated in the famous preface to his *Phenomenology of Spirit*: 'the whole is only the essence perfecting itself through its development' (1966, p. 32). The process of movement, which Hegel calls 'mediation', is a 'self-identity that moves itself'. Having differentiated itself from itself, Mind seeks to reunify itself. Thus H. S. Harris remarked that Hegel, from his early years, 'became more and more consciously convinced that "truth is the whole", and at the same time that the wholeness of truth was essentially a process of development' (1972, p. 29). Speculative idealism for Hegel is the philosophy that assumes that the world can with great efforts be intellectually and practically mastered. Absolute Spirit or Mind is *not* the goal of the enterprise, it is the very process itself of self-discovery. It is indistinguishable from the process. In this sense all rational human beings are moving along this path of discovery. Individual persons are a process of self-consciousness and self-realization in a concrete context. Consciousness, therefore, changes according to the context. As Hegel argued, 'Consciousness appears differently modified according to the difference of the given object and the gradual specification of consciousness appears as a variation on the characteristics of its objects' (quoted in Plant, 1973, p. 205). A new situation demands a new form of conceptual grasp. This is the essence of what the Germans term *Bildung*, in its broadest sense.

The role of philosophy is as a systematic exposition of categories and forms of consciousness. In one sense this is an infinite extension of the Kantian scheme of categories. Each category is examined as an existential possibility and slotted into its particular position in the development of human consciousness. Hegel thus takes our familiar experiences to pieces and tries to place them before us with their complete conditions in systematic form. As the British Hegelian Bernard Bosanquet argued, philosophy 'tells you . . . the significant connection of what you already know' (1898, p. 7). Hegel's philosophy is equivalent to Aristotle's self-thinking thought. In other words, we see in Hegel's philosophy a systematic morphology of the way thought works. As has been remarked, 'It was [Hegel's] peculiar gift to be able to project himself into the minds of other people and of other periods, penetrating into the core of alien souls and strangers' lives . . . he used this ability to make intellectual worlds intelligible by illuminating them, as it were, from within' (Kroner, 1948, p. 9).

Dialectic is the actual inner movement of this intellectual process. When a particular category is examined internally its limitations will be identified and a more adequate idea will arise to overcome the difficulties. The initial category is not totally abandoned but overcome and preserved in the higher category. It is *not* abolished. Thus 'The more adequate forms of thought and the more adequate modes of being *include* within them what has been surpassed. It is precisely this which makes them more adequate, more rich. A Dialectical advance is one in which what has been surpassed is also preserved' (Plant, 1973, p. 142). Dialectic is thus a form of what J. N. Findlay once called a 'higher-order-comment' (1972).

The overall structure of the system is outlined in full in his *Encyclopaedia of the Philosophical Sciences*. The largest of his dialectical structures encapsulates the whole system of philosophy, namely, logic, nature and spirit. Logic is the science of pure thought. It deals with forms of knowledge. It is a realm essentially of necessary abstractions or abstract universals. Hegel maintained that he was elucidating the basic structural categories necessary and conditional to all thinking. He was not considering how these categories might be realized in the world. Thinking structures our experience in terms of universal categories such as quality, quantity, measure, appearance and so on. The science of logic systematically examines these. In this sense Hegel *was* expanding and completing the Kantian scheme of categories of the *Critique of Pure Reason*. The logic can thus be viewed as a systematic grammar of the conditions of thought. For Hegel, the categories were not invented. He thought that he was articulating the deep-rooted implicit principles of thought. Logic was therefore not discovering new facts but showing us in detail what we already possess. Through the study of logic we become aware and master the categories already implicit in our rational thought. Reality is revealed in the rich content of the sciences in their abstract and later concrete form.

Whereas the logic deals with the essential elements of thought, the philosophy of nature examines external existence. Thought provides certain abstract categories but the content of representations are taken from something apparently external. In this sense nature appears as outside thought. The existent idea is nature. The philosophy of nature deals with the varieties of existence which correspond to our ideas. The material world is the cradle out of which consciousness and spirit develop. It is thus, for Hegel, an essential preliminary to any account of human consciousness or social development. The apparent external character of nature is viewed by Hegel as only a stage in the development of Mind. In the philosophy of nature, Mind treats nature as an external object. After reviewing such ideas as matter, motion, space, time and the development of organic life in plants and animals, the philosophy of nature arrives at consciousness. In the moment of consciousness, Mind realizes that *it* has posited the separate existence of nature. Ultimately, nature has no independence from Mind. Its apparent externality was a phase in the development of Mind.

The philosophy of Mind is premised on the idea that in reviewing nature Mind is revealing its own structures. The self-conscious knower is the ultimate fact to which all else is relative. Consciousness is the self-active, self-revealing universal. Hegel works through three crucial phases in the philosophy of Mind: Subjective Mind, which deals with the growth of consciousness and self-consciousness. Hegel develops his argument through the stages of anthropology, phenomenology and psychology. The second moment is Objective Mind. Objective Mind encapsulates all the insights of Subjective Mind. Psychology is given a deeper and richer sense when discussed through social life in the State. Mind is rooted in social, political, moral and legal structures. The structure of Objective Mind is spelt out in detail in Hegel's *Philosophy of Right*. This is the area where Hegel develops his theory of the State. The final moment of Objective Mind deals with the history and relationship between States. This is also dealt with in detail in Hegel's *Philosophy of History*. The final moment of the system is Absolute Mind when consciousness grasps itself, or Mind makes itself fully known to itself, as mediated through art, religion and finally philosophy. This is the highest realization of Mind. Philosophy is Mind which totally comprehends itself. The ability to grasp the dialectical interconnections of the whole is what Hegel terms Reason (*Vernunft*). Reason is distinct from understanding which only grasps ideas as disconnected entities. For Hegel, the understanding stands for 'separating and remaining fixed in its separations' (quoted in Plant, 1973, p. 140). Reason apprehends the unity in the vast array of differences facing it in its perception of the world.

THE INDIVIDUAL AND THE SOCIAL WORLD

> The basis of right is, in general mind; its precise place and point
> of origin is the will. The will is free, so that . . . the system of
> right is the realm of freedom made actual, the world of mind
> brought forth out of itself like a second nature.
>
> Hegel, *The Philosophy of Right*

The link that Hegel wishes to establish between the individual and
the State can be examined in the important transition from
Subjective to Objective Mind. The transition is built up in the
psychology section of Subjective Mind. Hegel works through three
stages in this section: Theoretical Mind, Practical Mind and Free
Mind. The latter is the high-watermark of the consideration of the
individual subjective mind. All of these broad stages attempt to
elucidate the faculties of the human mind.

Theoretical Mind examines the development of Mind to the stage
of formal thinking. Hegel works through the phases of direct,
intuitive acquaintance, an unanalysed awareness of the world similar
to Kant's idea of *Anschauung*. He moves on to the development of
imagination, recollection, memory and finally to the stage of
conceptual thought and judgement. Objects in the world are taken
up into the rational thought processes of individuals. The individual
begins to possess the world intellectually in the form of conceptual
knowledge. The private intuitions that we had, presumably at a
younger age, are transformed into a series of concepts. This analysis
is a familiar enterprise which philosophers have always addressed
themselves to – namely, the elucidation of faculties such as intuition,
memory and thought. For Hegel, the elucidation of these faculties is
not enough. Thought can only grasp objects when it has *made* the
objects fit its requirements. The individual does not passively observe
the world but actually manipulates it. Hegel moves at this point to
Practical Mind. The individual confronts a world moulded by human
practice. The individual will also transform the world according to
personal impulses and motivations. It is here that Hegel discusses the
the idea of will. Will is thought translating itself into existence (see
Hegel, 1971, p. 226). 'As will', Hegel argues, 'the mind is aware that
it is the author of its own conclusions' (1971, p. 228). This
description of will is close to Kant's idea of *Willkür*, which refers to
the arbitrary preferences of individuals. The individual disciplines
himself according to his own capricious interests.

In a few rather obscure paragraphs Hegel tries to show the dialectical mediation of Theoretical and Practical Mind into Free Mind (1971, sections 479 and 480). In contemporary terminology Hegel is advancing an agency thesis. Explanations of human activity are given in terms of the agent's reasons and intentions, not in terms of antecedent causes. Individuals have total responsibility for their own actions. The actual transition to Free Mind is a demonstraton that thought implies practice and practice implies thought. Thus the practical transformation of the world implies that it has been intellectually assimilated, but the intellectual assimilation implies that the individual has transformed it. Self-conscious free will is acquired when agents can fully articulate and explain their activity to themselves and others. Free will is therefore attained when individuals realize that they are radically autonomous. Human thought and intentions are embodied in their actions. Individuals can determine the content of their own action. For Hegel, Free Mind has infinite possibilities 'because its object is itself and so is not in its eyes an "other" or "barrier"' (1967, sect. 22, p. 30). In willing the individual is its own object.

It is at this point that Hegel links his discussion of Subjective to Objective Mind. He tries to show that the faculties of the human mind are integrally connected to certain forms of social order, and that these types of social order contribute to the development of these faculties. Hegel stresses that rationality is intersubjective and social in character. In the final paragraph of the section on Free Mind, he argues that individuals becomes aware of their own creative capacity to determine their own actions. Individuals control their diverse desires and impulses and structure them within certain specific ends or goals. Hegel maintains that if each individual only sought their own totally individual ends, the social world would be torn apart by caprice. He was arguing here neither for conformity with some pre-estabished ends nor the abandonment of harmless goals. He was arguing, however, that there must be some agreed normative ends upon which social life is based – for example, respect for persons and their right to self-development. Concrete freedom exists where individuals control their impulses through such socially established norms. Individuals must recognize others' rights to self-development in order for their own claims to be recognized. This argument encapsulates the move towards a positive notion of freedom, which can be defined as self-determination within the parameters of social norms. The subjective interests are not destroyed, but brought into the rule-governed framework of the social world. The arbitrary quality of the individual will is structured by what Hegel calls the concrete universal of social rules. These social rules embody rationality. Rationality is not something the individual invents, rather it is derived *from* the social world as a rational practice or norm.

Hegel therefore takes a 'positive liberty' perspective, arguing that free will is dependent on the object willed. There must be a reconciliation between the 'objects of will', namely the individual's interests, and the 'objects of reason', the social norms and rules. Freedom is the will determined by an object of reason, or more strictly when individuals determine themselves by an object of reason. The objects of reason are derived from the rules embodied in social institutions such as the family, corporation, neighbourhood and so on. 'By their existence', Hegel argues, 'the moral temper comes to be indwelling in the individual, so that in this sphere of particular existence . . . he is actually free' (1971, sect. 482, p. 240). Hegel calls these institutions, which are imbued with reason, 'Objective Mind'. Bosanquet adopts the same position in his *Philosophical Theory of the State* in a chapter significantly titled 'Institutions considered as Ethical Ideas'. Thus the argument is that individuals participate in common institutions. In the mundane sense they share institutions and norms characteristic of them. These norms embody rationality and 'solidified' human will. Therefore individuals who participate in these institutions come to share a common rationality and will. Since rational institutions should embody the means to encourage citizens to be free and ethical, it follows that in developing within such institutions the individual assimilates the common norms of society and in so doing develops characteristics of free will. Institutions, as the result of human practice, embody substantively the same content as rational individual minds. They embody past and present generations of thought. Idealists, such as Hegel, therefore thought of them as externalized concepts or social mind. The argument is advancing here, in a somewhat convoluted form, a socialization thesis, although it is also a very traditional argument deriving from Greek thought, namely where the identification and understanding of rational autonomous individuals entails a close study of the rule-governed framework of the social-world.

Therefore individuals determine themselves autonomously, yet subjective freedom must collapse into caprice and disorder. Freedom, properly understood, must be consonant with the development of the person. Freedom is concerned with increasing self-control over one's impulses and consequently accepting the norms which further this end. The end of political association for Hegel, following directly on Aristotle, is aimed at the attainment of the highest forms of human excellence and virtue. This could not be achieved in a situation of rampant individualism. The rule-governed framework of ethical institutions is based on the ideal of self-development and freedom. The philosophy of institutions is therefore designed to show their implicit teleology. Human practice has established the institutions, yet the rules form the substance to rational human practice. Although the individual comes into a world of given meanings and rules, none the less these rules are the *result* of reflective human agency. By maturing within institutions the individual can rise from pupillage to participation. Individuals, for Hegel, do not necessarily accept the status quo, but also criticize it. Bad States, for example, do exist for Hegel and should be criticized. In fact, he argues that some have no 'genuine actuality' (1967, section 270, addition, p. 283; see also section 258, addition, p. 279).

For Hegel, salvation, theologically and secularly, lies in a deeper understanding of this world and not another. The individual acquires the most fundamental rational norms by participating in social life, since it expresses the ontological structure of human nature. To deny one's citizenship was in essence to deny one's humanity. The social world thus embodied the structure of human will.

FORMS OF STATE

The philosophical premises that we have been have been outlining above are characteristic of Hegel's more mature views. His early views on the State expressed in the *German Constitution* essay see it primarily as a strong legal and political framework. In reviewing the disunity of Germany and the ineffectiveness of the Holy Roman Empire of German States, Hegel argued for the necessity of strong central control: without it effective freedom could not exist. In Jena, while writing his *Phenomenology of Spirit*, his views began to change. He was deeply impressed by the Greek *polis*. Religion in the Greek city-state was not other worldly, rather it tied into the whole customary life of the Greek citizen. Hegel, for a time, toyed with the idea of a German equivalent to Greek religion, a Germanic 'folk-religion' which would would unify all Germans. However he soon realised that the size and complexity of the modern State could not be fitted into the Greek perspective. The development of the conception of the separate individual possessing rights, specifically from the Reformation, the notion of a free market economy, the specialized nature of government, were all completely alien to the Greek world. Hegel's mature view of the State developed against the metaphysical and philosophical background, yet he did not abandon his previous views, rather they were assimilated into his later perspective.

The problem, and also the uniqueness, of Hegel's mature conception of the State is that he overloads it with a number of developing senses. He is not always clear in distinguishing these senses. They appear to be ways in which the State can be viewed, presumably equivalent to the developing consciousness of individuals. The mature, educated individual will view the State in the most complete ethical sense. There are, however, three senses in which Hegel employs the idea of the State. The conventional wisdom on Hegel is usually that there are two. However this does not do justice to the complexity of Hegel's views. The three senses are: (1) the State in the context of civil society, something Hegel calls the 'external state'; (2) the political State; and finally (3) the ethical State. The last of these is the most complete and rounded sense of the term and preserves aspects of the other views.

The notion of the State in the first sense is ultimately identified as a codified system of law over and above the mêlée of the market. This is the sense of the State which lurks in the phases of 'Abstract Right','Morality' and 'Civil Society' in the *Philosophy of Right*. Abstract Right refers to external rules governing personal rights and liberties. The individual, with certain specific rights and autonomy, faces the State as a system of external rules. Hegel realised that, specifically after the French Revolution, individualism, the principle of subjectivity, had to be given a place in the modern State, as he put it 'The principle of modern states has prodigious strength and depth because it allows the principle of subjectivity to progress to its culmination' (1967, section 260, p. 161). This is the basic thesis of the bourgeois liberal individualist State. Ultimately, Hegel envisages the supersession of this view, although from the perspective of one in the midst of civil society, the State is still a system of laws standing over and against them. Thus the inhabitant of this region will often see the State as an enemy or dangerous entity which should be controlled or 'rolled back'. The classical liberal and anarchist share a common idea here.

A more developed, if still narrow, conception of the State, is one we find discussed by Hegel in the section entitled 'The Constitution (on its Internal Side)' in the *Philosophy of Right*. This is the Political State. In this conception Hegel examines the State in terms of specific institutions of government. Hegel discusses the nature of the constitution (in its older more descriptive sense) as embodying the Crown (Monarch), the executive and legislative bodies. Hegel is here looking at the system of political authorities and powers. This is the closest to the themes of his earlier *German Constitution* essay. The structural description of the Political State is a fairly conventional view of the State which some find an anticlimax after the metaphysical build-up (see Pelczynski, 1984, p. 62).

The third sense of the State, which is drawn distinct by Hegel from the Political State, is the Ethical State (see Hegel, 1967, sect. 267, p. 163). This is the stage where the citizen finds ethical import in the institutional structures of the State. Hegel indicated that in the modern State we reach a culmination of human and historical development. The State is neither just a domain of codified laws, independent of the citizen's actual interests, nor is it to be regarded as a political structure reflecting aggregated interests. Rather, formally speaking, it is an ethical institution which embodies, in its laws and political structures, the real ethical interests of its members. There is, or should be, no discontinuity between the individual's will and the will or purpose embodied in the laws. This allows Hegel to claim that the truly subjective, the intrinsic desires and needs of the individual citizens, is rooted in the objective world of institutions. It is clear from these formal features that Hegel, in defining the State, is not thinking of *any* political institution or structure. He is laying down fairly stringent criteria on a formal level for a State to be a State. In one sense Hegel has taken the more liberal constitutional vision of the State and woven into it certain complex ethical themes which changes its character. As K. H. Ilting argues 'Although [Hegel] starts from the liberal principle of the autonomy of the individual, Hegel (unlike Kant) is not a theoretician of the liberal state . . . he does not think that liberal principles alone are sufficient for a comprehensive theory of the modern state' (see 1971, p. 95). The primary interpretation and function of the State is ethical. The initial stimulus for these views was Hegel's admiration for the Greek *polis*; however, his own conception is markedly different. It is the Ethical State which embodies the rational ontological structure of human nature and will.

One final point to note in Hegel's view of the State is that it implies a system of States on an international level. The final two moments in the *Philosophy of Right* discuss the relation of States and world history. When Hegel defines the State, part of that definition logically requires the existence of other States. This is an external definition of sovereignty. Unless other States existed and recognized each other as States, the whole enterprise of speaking of States would be pointless. Hegel in fact makes the same point about individual persons. To define oneself as a person is to do so in relation to other persons, who recognize that personhood. Hegel put it thus, 'Existence as determinate being is in essence being for another' (1967, section 71, p. 57). He is expressing a typical Hegelian paradox. To define oneself is to express one's separateness and individuality, also one's reliance on others. It is through others that I acquire individuality. The same point applies to the State. Each autonomous determinate State defines itself in relation to other States. As Hegel unequivocally says 'A state is as little an actual individual without relation to other states as an individual [person] is actually a person without *rapport* with other persons' (1967, section 331, *Zusatz*, p. 212). Thus part of the very definition of the State and the nature of its sovereign quality presupposes the separate existence of other States. Therefore, whether one approaches the State via international relations, or whether one approaches international relations via the State, each presupposes a multiplicity or system of States. It is a logically necessary feature of the world.[2]

THE EXTERNAL STATE

If the state is represented as a unity of different persons, as a unity which is only a partnership, then what is really meant is civil society. Many modern constitutional lawyers have been able to bring within their purview no theory of the state but this.

Hegel, *The Philosophy of Right*

Hegel's discussion of civil society involves the description of a basically market-based society. His intellectual source for this description is the Scottish school of classical political economy, specificallly Adam Smith and Adam Ferguson. Before Tocqueville or Marx, Hegel had identified the bourgeoisie as bearers of the new individualism. Civil society embodies the ideas which subsequently acquired the title liberal individualism. The liberal individualist understanding of the political community is an area in which individuals can pursue their self-chosen conceptions of the good life. The State is envisaged as a minimal constitutional order acting as a neutral arbiter. It exists fundamentally to maintain a formal rule of law behind the flux and flow of individual actions. It does not exist to inculcate a moral outlook. The individual's liberty is sovereign. Hegel speaks of the individual's freedom of conscience as a 'sanctuary which it would be sacrilige to violate' (1967, section 137, *Zusatz*, p. 91). The duty of the citizen *vis à vis* the State, is not to support it as pursuing a common good but rather as a nomocratic order, providing a rule-of-law framework in which individuals pursue their private goods.

For Hegel participation in the market and the civil society mentality was a necessary moment in human development. As Knox observed, 'Civil society is not only a kind of State, the kind about which the Understanding's political theories are true enough, it is a moment in the State proper. It grows up into the State, because the educative influence of civil life . . . makes men realise that they are by nature not self-seeking individuals but creatures of reason' (1967, section 5, p. xi). The individual cannot leap over this atomistic stage (see Hegel, 1971, section 253, pp. 256–7). In civil society the individual, unknowingly, develops a universality of thought. Civil society demands, on a very practical level, that citizens, when faced with arbitrary necessities – such as the satisfaction of their basic needs and wants – have to *think*. They must recast their *desires* in *thought*. Economic necessities demand certain courses of action. For Hegel this process raises the individual to 'formal freedom'. The necessity for work, labour and production entails an intelligent concern for temporal interest – as Hegel put it – without being aware of it 'a man is no longer wrapped up in his particular impulses . . . on the contrary, he has plunged into the Reason of the actual world' (1971, section 396, addition, p. 62). The cunning of reason becomes here the invisible hand of the market. It is also, however, part of the *Bildung* of the individual. Hegel explicitly speaks of individual's in civil society being 'educated up to subjectivity' (1967, section 187, p. 125). New situations demand new conceptual forms, thus the individual develops.

The kind of assumptions that we find traditionally in this position are that the individual is naturally free, giving up that freedom only by voluntary consent and possibly contract. Consent protects individuals from the State and guarantees the rule of law. The State exists to protect the diverse individual interests of its members. Hegel's recognition of individual rights, the value of subjectivity, personal opinion, freedom of conscience and expression, and tolerance, embody his qualified acceptance of the 'external State' as a necessary, if inadequate, vision of the State. He was deeply critical of the Greeks for not recognizing the value of individuality. 'Particularity', as Hegel put it, '. . . given rein in every direction to satisfy its needs, accidental caprices, and subjective desires' (1967, section 185, p. 123). In Greek thinkers such as Plato 'The principle of the self-subsistent inherently infinite personality of the individual . . . is denied its right' (1967, section 185; *Zusatz*, p. 124).

Civil society, which embodies an early conception of the self-regulating free market economy, presumably summarizes for Hegel the mentality of a large proportion of the population. Most individuals have to labour to satisfy their needs. In fact, since this is the wealth-producing element, it is a practical necessity for it to be present as a mode of thought. If this is so then a large number of the population in business and agriculture must be committed to this conception of the State. It would be difficult for these groups to adopt other views otherwise they would not have the cognitive perspective to engage in civil society. The sole end must be to satisfy selfish wants, each is guided by their 'petty selves and particular interests'. Individuals do not feel obligated to the State because it embodies their rational will but rather that contractually it upholds and protects them in the pursuit of their varying interests and plans of life, defending legal rights to property, life and liberty.

This conception of the State is characteristically a liberal and constitutional one, at least at the stage when constitutionalism was coming to be identified with liberalism. In fact the term civil society in the eighteenth century was often used as an equivalent to the State (see Knox, 1942, p. x). It is clear though, if we look in more detail at the civil society conception, that it also includes other elements, some of which moderate the effects of the market mentality; for example, Hegel incorporates corporations, public authorities and regulatory agencies. In the words of Bosanquet, Hegel's conception is a 'relative individualism': individualism 'represents an element which seems essential in that self, and which, from its nature, could be represented in no other way. But this moment, like all others, is only rendered possible by the whole within which it subsists' (1898, p. 9).

THE POLITICAL STATE

Hegel explicitly identifies the State as an objective organization. He calls this in two places the 'political state' (see Hegel, 1967, sections 273 and 276). This is still not what Hegel calls the 'State proper', although again it is not the same as the 'external State' idea. The fundamental character of the Political State is that it is clearly the objective structure of a constitutional monarchy, embodying a qualified separation of powers. Hegel somewhat ambiguously calls this Political State a 'substantial unity' in which specific powers are 'dissolved and yet retained'. What Hegel means here is that the powers and institutions of the crown, executive and legislature are moments of the organization of the State (politically considered). On one level they appear and are separate. They guarantee 'public freedom'. But to regard them as standing against each other or against the State is false and denies the living unity of the State, which incorporates all three elements. As Hegel maintains 'they are its flexible limbs while it [the State] is their single self' (1967, section 276, p. 179). The State is the identity in the different powers and functions (see also 1967, section 269, p. 164). Hegel gives here an overtly dialectical reading to the separation of powers doctrine. This dialectical reading includes the actual powers themselves. The legislature is seen laying down the *universal* general lines of policy and legislation. The executive carries out the *particular* applications of the general legislation. The crown represents the unity of the universal and particular in the *individual* ultimate decision of the monarch or crown. The monarch gives the aspect of individual volition to the acts of State. Each of these spheres will be examined in reverse order.

The State is personified in the monarch; however, it is important for Hegel that the monarch is neither identified with State (in the absolutist sense) nor that the physical person is in any way significant. The monarch is one moment in a broader unity. The monarchy is a purely ideal unity within the overall internal constitution. In the monarch, though, the State becomes real. Decisions are made by an identifiable figure. Hegel envisaged the monarchy to be hereditary since this sets internal sovereignty beyond the reach of external caprice suffered by elected monarchy. Birth is an unconditional entitlement. Hegel introduces the notion of internal sovereignty in the crown, symbolized in the monarchy, to indicate that the State's laws and powers are neither simply abstractions nor wholly embodied in functionaries. This is another way of saying that the law is neither something alien to the individual's interests and needs, nor simply the whim of the State bureaucrats and officials in the executive branch. It is embodied in offices which themselves embody rational concerns, like that of monarchy. Hegel, as pointed out, was thinking of a constitutional monarchy.

The executive is composed of civil servants and advisory officials who are organized into a network of committees, usually under a supreme civil servant, who is in direct contact with the monarch (see Hegel, 1967 section 289, p. 189). Hegel does also say that the executive includes the judiciary and police, although not much more is said on this point (1967, section 287, p. 189). The executive applies the principle established by the legislature which Hegel calls 'subsuming the particular under the universal' (1967, section 287, pp. 188–9). Ideally they should, through co-operation with corporations and members of civil society, be able to keep in contact with both public and private interests. The membership of the executive should be open to all and solely based on skill and ability, although ultimately the judgement should lie with the crown. The task of the civil service should be clearly laid down and tenure was to be conditional on fulfilling assigned duties. They must be paid enough not to be subject to bribery and should be individuals who are educated and rational enough to be able to 'forgo the selfish and capricious satisfaction of their subjective ends' (1967, section 294, *Zusatz*, p. 191). In this sense the demeanour of civil servants should be 'dispassionate, upright and polite'. It is hardly suprising that the civil service are envisaged as being mainly constituted by the middle class. Hegel's discussion here of bureaucracy is reminiscent of Max Weber's ideas later in the century.

The legislature includes the monarch as the ultimate decision-maker, the executive as an advisory body and finally the Estates. The function of the legislature was to establish universal principles of law and to demand services such as taxation. The final moment of the legislature, the Estates, incorporates an upper and lower house representing the two main interests of civil society – namely the business and agricultural groups. Hegel did *not* accept the idea or need for universal suffrage. Complex mediations of public opinion already existed. One did not need the added factor of suffrage. The upper house of the agricultural estate and the business and corporation interests of the lower house have insights into the specific functions of civil society and thus can advise and check specific officials of the executive. This keeps the executive on their mettle. The representation of groups prevents the dangers of unorganized mobs and encourages the co-operation of groups in the process of government. In this sense the Estates' role is that of pluralistic integration with the State. Even the observation of this long deliberative process is educative. As Hegel stated 'Estates Assemblies open to the public, are a great spectacle and an excellent education for the citizens' (1967, section 315, addition, p. 294). The two houses act to increase the overall efficiency of government, keeping it in contact with civil society, educating the populace and checking on the executive (see Hegel, 1967 section 300, p. 195).

THE ETHICAL STATE

Hegel explicitly differentiates the 'State proper', as he calls it, from the political State and the external State, although they are still seen as moments of the Idea of the State proper. In section 267 of *The Philosophy of Right* he draws distinct the inner ethical sense of the State from the political form (see Knox, 1967, note 9, p. 364). In the *Zusatz* to section 258 he draws the 'State proper' distinct from civil society. He remarks in the latter that 'If the state is confused with civil society, and if its specific end is laid down as the security of property and personal freedom, then the interest of the individuals as such becomes the ultimate end of their association.'

The ethical vision of the State represents the 'State proper', the most rounded and complete sense of the term. Hegel is not altogether systematic in differentiating it from the other senses, but it is clear that the ethical understanding *is* Hegel's distinctive contribution to State theory. The communal sense of the ethical understanding is prefaced in the earlier discussions of the family, which he in fact calls the first ethical root of the State. The family is a primitive model of the State proper; like the corporation it serves a communal function counter-weighting the subjectivity, individualism and self-centredness implicit in civil society. The family embodies group values, norms and aspirations and provides the substance of individual conscious-ness. Unlike civil society it is not a contractual entity, rather it is linked by love, trust, mutual service and concern for the whole. The actual function of the family is, for Hegel, to transform the natural egoistic caprice and sexual desire into rational form. Love raises the individual above immediate interest and the ethico-legal form of marriage lifts the couple out of caprice and contingency. Natural acquisitiveness in the individual becomes transformed into family property functioning in the interests of the whole unit. The child becomes the visible embodiment of the whole process. Hegel's rather laboured point here is that by participating in the institution of the family, the customs and purposes implicit in the institution become constitutive of the parent's consciousness. The individual and institution thus have the same substance. It is thus that Bosanquet used to speak, somewhat extravagantly, of the family meal being a sacrament to the 'larger Mind'.

The corporation for Hegel was another moderating factor within civil society. Hegel thinks of it virtually as a second family – a fraternal whole caring for its members. Anthony Black, in a recent study, places Hegel's discussion of corporations into a long-running tradition developing from medieval pluralist thought. He remarks that 'Hegel's view of corporations was the first explicit attempt by a modern philosopher to give guild values and aspirations a central place in political theory', an achievement which, apart from Durkheim, has 'not been significantly improved upon since' (1984, p. 202). The corporation is a voluntary group which socializes individuals and allows them, through the Estates Assembly, to participate in governing. The corporation can also act as a collective check on the executive. One of the key roles of the corporation is, however, to provide certain welfare functions, caring for the poor, regulating conditions of work, wages and prices as in the older medieval tradition. Again the customs and purposes embodied in the institution of the corporation become constitutive of the members' consciousness. Corporations and the family become part of the *Bildung* or development of individuals. Thus the individual's consciousness, despite what individualist writers might argue, cannot be separated from the social whole to which they belong.

The summation of the more communal process, where the substance of the individual's consciousness and will is objectified in the institutions, is the Ethical State. As is well known, Hegel calls the State, at this stage, 'The actuality of the ethical idea'. This is the stage when real freedom is acquired. The objects of individual will and the objects of reason coincide. In this sense the customs and rules not only exist within the institutional structures but are also self-consciously willed by individual citizens. The ethical life is the operative mode of human conduct. The rules become internalized. Institutions in the Ethical State embody social purpose, which forms the substantive character of the citizens' will. The criterion for evaluating institutions would be whether they embodied social purpose, the constitutive factor of human will. The rule-governed framework of such institutions is based upon the ideal of self-development and freedom. The fully rounded, harmonious individuals are those who have disciplined their subjective impulses through common public rules. These rules are not the creation or property of any one individual but are embodied in the whole community. As Charles Taylor has argued:

'*Sittlichkeit*' refers to the moral obligation I have to an ongoing community of which I am part. These obligations are based on established norms and uses, and that is why the etymological root in 'Sitten' is important to Hegel's use. The crucial characteristic of *Sittlichkeit* is that it enjoins us to bring about what already is. This is a paradoxical way of putting it, but in fact the common life which is the basis of my *Sittlich* obligation is already their in existence. It is in virtue of its being an ongoing affair that I have these obligations; and my fulfillment of these obligations is what sustains it and keeps it in being. (1975, p. 376)

The individual cannot be separated from the social whole without distortion. The ultimate end of both is substantially the same. The State incorporates the totality of citizens and institutional forms united by communal bonds and directed to ethical ends. The truly subjective is rooted in the objective world of institutions.

There is some debate on the actual nature of the ethical community. It revolves around the question as to whether Hegel really develops beyond the Greek idea of community. As mentioned earlier, while at Jena, Hegel – like many of his contemporaries – was deeply impressed by the Greek world. Greece represented a harmony of personal experience with the norms of the close-knit community. The Greek *polis* was the substance, the individual citizens were the accidents. The Greek citizen's identification with communal norms was unconscious. The question 'Why obey the law?' would not, in Hegel's reading, have occurred to the *polis* dweller. For Hegel, modern European humanity seemed divided and fragmented by comparison, perhaps too fond of asking 'Why obey?'. This was not just a division in the person, as argued in Schiller's *On the Aesthetic Education of Man*, but also in the social fabric. Institutions were not alien to the Greeks. They shared a conception of a common life and simply 'read off' their duties from their social life. Greeks could not conceive of an alternative to this life. Religion, politics, art and ethics were all linked.

This nostalgia for Greece led Hegel (as stated earlier) to toy with the idea of a German 'folk-religion'. This would be a common, non-divisive set of beliefs providing Germans with 'a cultural form which could unite the powers of the human mind and unite divided and fragmented men into one society' (Plant, 1973, p. 42). Some recent commentators on Hegel have argued that he was trapped in this 'antique' conception of the Greek *polis*. As Ilting has argued 'The idea of the ethical life, the subject of the third part of Hegel's theory of the modern state, is nothing else but the idea of good which lies at the basis of Plato's theory of the political community' (1971, p. 100). Z. A. Pelczynski has also commented that 'In the *Philosophy of Right* it is the narrower concept of the ethical life (*Sittlichkeit*) derived from Plato and Aristotle, and Greek experience generally, which underlies his theory of political community' (1984, p. 56). Pelczynski sees a wider concept of the ethical community in other writings, where Hegel speaks of a 'national spirit'. This idea, which may have been derived from Montesquieu, is seen as the more modern notion. Pelczynski argues that the 'State . . . is a political community because it is a cultural community because its constitution is grounded in a national culture, because its political institutions are deeply inter-woven and interdependent with all other aspects of culture' (1984, pp. 56–7).

Contrary to these views it is clear from the *Philosophy of Right*, amongst other writings, that Hegel was critical of the Greek view for lacking an adequate concept of individuality and free subjectivity. The Greeks' ethical life was unconscious, not rationally understood or articulated. Early on in his 'folk-religion' phase he had realized that any purely religious transformation was inadequate. The modern State was bigger, more complex and specialized than any ancient city. Individuals were virtually enslaved to the Greek *polis*, unacquainted with private rights, knowing no concept of private property, which in Hegel's view was essential for the growth of personality. In this area Hegel comes close to calling Plato a totalitarian (if only the concept had been available). He remarks that 'The lack of subjectivity is really the defect of the Greek ethical idea . . . Plato has not recognised knowledge, wishes, and resolutions of the individual, nor his self-reliance' (1892–6, Vol. 2, pp. 114–15). Hegel does not slavishly follow the Greek notion of ethical life. The Greeks did lack notions of subjectivity and a fully self-conscious ethical life. Hegel was equally critical, in his early theological writings, of Christianity which encouraged individuals to see God as transcendent. Christian citizens tend to look beyond the political community for their political ideals. Morality, within Christianity, was obedience to a remote transcendent God. This, for Hegel, had a fragmenting effect on social life. Moral fulfilment lay outside political life. Christianity encouraged this private religion and relationship to God. It entailed a religion of private conscience and devotion. The social equivalent of this fragmented individualism is found in modern society in the form of atomistic individualism and free subjectivity.

Thus, in the same way as the communal collective sense of Greek religion and politics needed to be tempered by free subjectivity and individualism, so also the individualism and subjectivity of Christian culture (and civil society) needed to be tempered by communal goals. In theological terms God, for Hegel, was not transcendent but immanent in historical and political forms. Political institutions were epiphanies of God. When individuals participate in them they participate in God's self-realization. If Greek life represented the *universal* and Christianity *particularity*, then the Ethical State represented the unity of the universal and particular. This State embodies the self-conscious rational *Sittlichkeit*. It is the rational resolution to community and individuality. It is not simply aping the Greek experience. The intellectual sources of this idea lie deep in Hegel's system.

CONCLUSION

There are many criticisms of Hegel's theory of the Ethical State. The most traditional arguments are that Hegel situates all ethics and freedom within the confines of the nation State. Therefore freedom and ethical value become relative to the nation State; thus it follows that there are no moral codes to mediate between States. Individuals are identified only through membership of the nation State and can relate to each other only as members of States. The separate States are also seemingly given a divine sanction by Hegel. Hegel's comment that the State is 'the March of God in the world' is usually brought out at this point. It is the quotation which is used to signify that the nation States, with their relative moral codes and conceptions of freedom, have a divine legitimacy. This has particular impact when conjoined with the idea of war. The argument usually proceeds that the victor in any war has some kind of divine approval. Thus it is said that Hegel maintained that the real is rational and the rational real, the State which triumphs is the healthiest, and that ultimately might is right. Friedrich Meinecke specifically argues that Hegel deifies the State making it into a 'power State'. Hegel, with Machiavelli and Frederick the Great, is made into an exponent of *raison d'état* (Meinecke, 1957, pp. 364–6). This interpretation falls in line with those who portray Hegel as a servile Prussian nationalist and a forerunner of fascism. As many might be tempted to add, it was the Italian Hegelian Giovanni Gentile who had tied his State theory to Mussolini's fascist ideology. Hegel is sometimes portrayed as the evil genius behind this, the arrogant megalomaniac who offers the world the culminating philosophy towards which all previous thought had been aiming. In this interpretation Hegel's name is sometimes linked to German aggression in the two world wars (see Hobhouse, 1918; Popper, 1950; McGovern, 1940; Kaufmann, 1970).

It is difficult to answer these criticisms with brevity, but it must be pointed out that Hegel was not thinking of just any political structure. He does lay down stringent conditions for a State to be a State and he draws a clear distinction between good and bad States (1967, section 270, addition, p. 283). The modern State, as argued, is a constitutional monarchy with a separation of powers and a plurality of mediating groups. A State must possess, within parameters, a stable civil society and free market economy. Separate plural corporations must have a relatively independent role to play in providing for their members' needs. Laws, for Hegel, should be codified and jury systems established. The State should respect the institution of monogomous marriage and also have some responsibility for children in terms of formal schooling and vaccination. Hegel is equally insistent that there must be respect, again within limits, for freedom of speech, conscience and opinion, especially in relation to the various estates.

The State is grounded on the development and freedom of its membership. A State, for Hegel, could not be based on slavery, which he described as an 'outrage on the conception of man' (1967, section 2, p. 15). It is also clear that Hegel is thinking in terms of the ethics of Protestant Christianity. Protestant Christianity is the Absolute 'revealed religion', which enshrines the importance and value of the individual. Even in some of his earliest essays, for example, on the *Würtemburg Estates*, Hegel took for granted certain fundamental rights of individuals. Protestant Christianity as the revealed religion, fused with morality, is progressively realized in history and human society. This is the substance to the ethical life, although it should be pointed out that this is Hegel's somewhat idiosyncratic immanentist intepretation of Christianity. It is this common value system found in genuine 'actual' States, which leads Hegel to say that 'The European peoples form a family in accordance with the universal principles underlying their legal codes, their customs and their civilisation' (1967, section 335, addition p. 297). Thus although all individuals are members of separate States they can relate to common moral codes. The supposed divine sanction of the State is ambiguous partly because of Hegel's view of religion. When Hegel sees the State as divine, all he means by this is that the

State is explicable as a product of Mind or Spirit. He is not saying either that the State has some kind of divine mission from a transcendent God or that might is right. It is also far from clear that Hegel glorifies war or is an exponent of *raison d'état*.

Hegel's philosophic method must be grasped. In one sense it was partially descriptive. He shows us the relationship between war and human consciousness at that time. Yet he is by no means exalting war. War in fact should not really exist between properly constituted States. It is a negative event which shows the individual the instability of life and the imperfection of States. In a Christian sense it fits in with providence: do not store up your riches where the moth and Napoleonic soldiers can get to them. Finally, Hegel cannot be called a servile nationalist. The Germanic realm which he describes in the *Philosophy of Right* and *Philosophy of History* is a way of referring to an attitude, or more accurately a reflective disposition, which has nothing intrinsically to do with Prussians. It is a disposition characteristic, in its most limited form, of the European peoples. It is also prudent to recall that Hegel's thought was repudiated by the Nazis in the 1930s.

More recently criticism of Hegel has taken a different tack. Hegel is disarmingly honest on some of the insoluble problems of the State. One of these was poverty. Civil society and the market economy creates what Hegel calls a 'Pauperized rabble'. It is endemic to modern society. The poor have no property to protect. Their view of the State cannot be that of an ethical institution. They cannot be integrated into the State with any ease, and yet Hegel's State is premised on such integration. Hegel does suggest a number of ways to deal with the poor including emigration and public works, but overall he presents a rather half-hearted picture. As stressed, Hegel's central task, however, is to integrate the free subject into the Ethical State. It has been argued by some recent exponents of the 'legitimation crisis' that the values of civil society are incompatible and antithetical to the communal ends of the State. The acquisitiveness and self-centredness implicit in the civil society perspective implies a particular view of human nature and action. Large sections of the population must exist in this practical and cognitive domain. It is highly questionable whether Hegel is correct in thinking that this domain can be simply assimilated with a 'higher' ethical, communal perspective. The two views of human nature are not simply to be joined by dialectical virtuousity.

Part of the novelty and interest of the ethical theory of the State is also at the root of its ambiguity. Hegel attempts to bridge a number of diverse traditions in the understanding of humanity and social existence. He tries to link notions of community, plural group life and pure individualism. He also tries to link up these complex sociological forms with a philosophy of mind. Individualism is viewed in the context of civil society, plural group life in the corporations and estates, community in the family and the Ethical State. It is important to realize that the Ethical State is as much a cognitive disposition as a concrete institutional structure. The development of the individual from family life, through civil society and into 'State consciousness' is seen as a process of self-development. During this process, the State will be seen initially as an external system of laws and rights. It will then be identified with the political institutions characteristic of a constitutional monarchy. Individuals, as they develop in business or agriculture, will wish to participate in government, for example though the Estates Assembly. Finally, the State will be seen as the totality of an individual's development, an ethical order implicit in the subjective consciousness and embodied in external laws and concrete institutions. It is questionable as to how far Hegel was successful in bridging these diverse traditions and as to whether *all* individuals progress though the process of self-development. Some seemed doomed to a static condition. What, however, is undoubtedly the case is Hegel's relevance to the problems of modernity and the State. Many of his particular answers may appear antiquated or just downright odd, but the problems he faced are still deeply relevant to our present society.

---------------------------- 5 ----------------------------

The Class Theory of
the State

INTRODUCTION

It is paradoxical that the most popular modern interpretation of the State, which permeates much of the contemporary social scientific literature, is not really a theory of the State at all, except in a very weak sense of the term. The theory referred to here is associated with Marx and Engels and the subsequent tradition which has evolved from their writings. It is necessary to deal with this interpretation not because of its intrinsic merits but rather because of its predominance (although it is not being argued that we should not thereby take it seriously). Marx is one of the most profound theorists of recent times and what he has to say *about* the State is of great interest. Yet he was not a great theorist *of* the State.

There are a number of problems intrinsic to any account of the class theory of the State. First, it is difficult to acquire any clear unitary theory of the State, not only from the Marxist tradition, but also from the diverse writings of Marx and Engels themselves. One important reason for this is that Marxism is a *praxis* philosophy which, even in the case of Marx, prides itself on responding to immediate events and issues. From the eleventh of the early *Theses on Feuerbach*, Marx made it clear that the point is not to contemplate or interpret the world, or the State, but to change it. Philosophy is of no use if it remains abstract and inaccessible. It has to be realized or grasped by the masses and so forth. This, of course, did not stop Marx speculating and writing abstract works of interpretation, but theoretically it was not the done thing.

Second, the actual theoretical approach of Marxism *tends* towards political economy. Much of human activity, thought and practice is regarded as the epiphenomenon or result of certain antecedent conditions. In other words the emphasis of Marxism, whether consciously or not, has not been to understand the State in itself, but rather to explain it as a result of a more fundamental reality. This more 'fundamental reality' is usually economic in character. It is the functional role of the State within the economy, rather than its constitutional or institutional form, which is significant.

Third, nowhere do Marx and Engels systematically address themselves to the State. They certainly do not in any way offer a normative theory of the State as an institutional structure. Institutions are rather seen as the result of deep-rooted objective structural laws. The closest Marx ever comes to a systematic treatment of the State is in his early *Introduction to a Critique of Hegel's Philosophy of Right*, which will be reviewed briefly in this chapter. The problem with this early work is that it engages in mainly negative criticism which is variable in quality and obviously not designed for publication as it stood.

The final and most intractable problem in dealing with the class theory is the theoretical ambivalence of the phrase 'the Marxist theory of the State'. This chapter will use the phrase 'class theory'. This is a problem which will be returned to later. It is clear, however, that much Marxist writing has been directed to the fact that the ultimate end of history and class struggle is communism, which appears to be a Stateless condition. It is at this juncture that Marxists try desperately to differentiate themselves from anarchists. The important point which needs to be emphasized here is that the State is seen as a universal but temporary phenomenon, which it is the ultimate aim of humanity to abandon or do away with. The paradox intensifies when we are told that Marxist–Leninist States *exist* in the world. In fact some would tell us that the State can help to do away with itself by being stronger than ever. At this point certain Marxists wheel in other doctrines (on the basis on Marx's and Engels's writings) such as 'the dictatorship of the proletariat', or the Trotskyist 'decayed workers' State' to explain this arcane material. Opponents and critics of Marxism also bring in time-honoured, if somewhat moth-eaten, accounts of totalitarianism to explain what is really going on. Yet it is difficult simply to dismiss the intrinsic paradox of, on the one hand, the theoretical denigration of the State and, on the other, its continued existence in practice in powerful entities calling themselves Marxist–Leninist States.

Despite considerable variation in Marxist theorizing there is one central concept which informs Marxist accounts of the State – the idea of class. The State is seen as the expression or condensation of class relations. For Marx this implies a pattern of domination. The State is not a representation of any collective or consensual good or public impartiality. It is, rather, integral to certain specific interests in society. This gives rise to other general elements of Marxist theory, namely oppression and domination. These can be exercised covertly or overtly. A class interest is seen to manage the State apparatus in the interests of that class alone. This involves the exercise of power over other groups or classes. The history of States can therefore be subsumed under the history of such class domination and therefore class struggle. As Engels argued, 'It was . . . Marx who had first discovered the great law of motion of history, the law according to which all historical struggles, whether they proceed in the political, religious, philosophical or some other ideological domain, are in fact only the more or less clear expression of struggles of social classes' (Marx and Engels, 1968, p. 96). Admittedly the notion of class links up with human labour and a particular theory about human nature and history; however, it is class which is the key to the State. Another point to bear in mind here is that it is clear that the Marxist tradition has built up immensely more sophisticated and subtle theories of class, human labour and so on this century. A selection of these will be reviewed in this chapter, although the discussion will not enter into the intricate dialogues (and one suspects occasional monologues) of Marxist theoreticians. The aim is to clarify the basic outlines of the arguments.

One final point to note in dealing with the class theory of the State is that even within Marx's and Engels's writings there is a certain ambivalence on the idea of class itself. It is clear that despite its centrality in Marxist theory, nowhere does Marx or Engels offer a systematic account of the concept. The ambiguity of the concept can be revealed through four basic questions, although these alone are not exhaustive.

The first question is: what is class? This would appear to be an unproblematic question for Marxists. It is obviously a crucially influential concept in European thought, specifically in the socio-logical tradition. It offers an account of social stratification and the organizational dynamics of modern States, often countering other theories such as ideas on equal citizenship or national identity. The basic ideas behind class are as follows. It refers to a large social group linked together in certain economic relations within a mode of production. Each group or class receives differential rewards, power and status. Relations *between* classes tend to be exploitative. A dominant class will have interests which it will pursue usually to the detriment of another class. All individuals are connected and defined by their class position. One's work, property ownership, sense of one's own worth and personality are objectively determined by it. A class to be a class must be, at least potentially, conscious of itself. A loose entity with no hope of any consciousness of identity could not constitute a class. Thus there is a sense of a collective persona to a class, although again Marx does not really elaborate on this. Individuals do not relate as individuals but as members of a class. Their social relations are predetermined. The nature of society and State are determined also by the nature of class and the character of the struggle, whether it be feudal noble and serf, or bourgeois capitalist and proletarian. These features of class are never argued for systematically but can be picked up from various writings.

Further questions remain to be answered here. Are all social groups equally classes? This point remains deeply problematic. It is clear that at some points Marx, for example, did not regard the peasantary as a class (see Marx and Engels, 1968, p. 172); although if one carefully examines his prose on the previous page he refers to them in passing as a class. Also, presumably groups which are not directly linked to an objective mode of production are not classes; how Marx fits the class of lumpenproletariat into this scenario is left open. At best they are only marginal to a prevailing mode of production. This question is closely linked to another: what classes are there in modern States? The mystery deepens here since Marx produces a number of social groups in his various writings which sometimes do and sometimes don't appear as classes. In Volume 3 of *Capital*, there are three key classes mentioned: the landowners, the capitalists and the wage-labourers. Although again Marx is not clear as to whether they appear in Britain at the time. Britain, we must recall, was the most advanced industrial State in the world, thus presumably being the best example of Marx's overall theses on capitalism. In *The Communist Manifesto* two main classes appear: the proletariat, those who own no means of production and can only sell their labour as a commodity for wages; and the capitalists, who own the means of production and live by exploiting wage-labour.

Despite the more simpler vision of classes in the *Manifesto* we do encounter other groups who are referred to as classes. We mentioned the peasantry earlier. Marx is rather ambivalent on this question partly because they do not, whatever anarchists like Bakunin said, possess class consciousness in the same way as industrial workers. They also tend, for Marx, to have reactionary instincts. Marx also mentions the lumpenproletariat, who come in for some acid comment from Marx in the *18th Brumaire*. At various points Marx also refers to the petty bourgeoisie, tenant farmers, the middle class and the intelligentsia as classes. The latter class is occasionally slotted in as paid wage-labourers for the bourgeoisie, although he is not always so clear as to their relation to this bourgeois class. Presumably, in speaking of intellectuals, Marx had to give some room for himself and Engels, as separate from bourgeois interests. Marx also distinguishes at points the financial capitalists from the industrial capitalists – a prescient distinction, since it is clear that the two groups often have different interests. It is not quite so clear though whether he regards them as separate classes. Potentially then one has, approximately, up to ten possible classes mentioned here in the writings of Marx and Engels. A careful investigation might possibly reveal more. In this context, it is quite obvious that this adds difficulties to interpreting Marx. One might argue that there is a difference between classes which are central to a prevailing mode of production and those which are marginal. This might explain the character and existence of certain classes, for example, the lumpen-proletariat, but it is doubtful that it provides a satisfactory overall account.

Further questions arise here: is there a clear relation or link between property ownership, class and political power in the State? Nowhere does Marx establish a clear theoretical or empirical link between ownership and any single class. Also he does not establish any precise connection between class and political power, except possibly in the overly simplistic *The Communist Manifesto*. Thus it is not surprising to find a recent synoptic work on Marxist theorizing arguing that in contemporary Marxism 'The State is not regarded simply as an instrument of the ruling class. . . . Who rules the State *is* an important issue, but few, if any, current writers claim that the ruling class controls the State directly' (Carnoy, 1984, p. 250). Before Marx could have analysed the State *simpliciter* as a condensation of class interest he should have analysed which class, the concept of class itself, the relation between the multifarious classes, and what is their relation to property ownership and the mode of production. Clearly he does not do this.

Putting these criticisms to one side for the moment; in this chapter the traditional class theory of the State will be examined, focusing briefly on the intellectual and historical context in which it was formulated. The question whether there is *one* traditional theory of the State will also be looked at. The chapter will then turn to review selectively certain attempts to develop the original Marxist theory, which, in some cases, try to rectify some of the problems and contradictions of the older theory. Finally, the question of the future and destiny of the State under Marxism will be discussed, namely, is it something that simply withers away?

THE TRADITIONAL CLASS THEORY OF THE STATE

Many of Marx's ideas were a response to particular events and theories. As one recent commentator observed, in Marx and Engels 'Most of their political writings were produced to describe specific political events and to situate them in a specific historical context; and/or to provide a theoretical basis for the identification of political class interests and an appropriate mode of intervention in the class struggle' (Jessop, 1983, p. 29). The growth of Marx's ideas relate to a complex of intellectual sources. The most prominent of these was, first, a radical Enlightenment tradition, represented in the work of the French Utopian socialists such as Saint-Simon and Charles Fourier. Reason could be used creatively to restructure society. The French anarchist tradition, specifically P. J. Proudhon and his work *What is Property?*, was also significant. Humans were regarded as essentially rational and good by nature, social ills could be cured by adjusting social conditions rationally. A second potent influence on Marx's thought was the philosophy of Hegel and the school of thought which emanated from him. The key figure in this latter school with respect to Marx was Ludwig Feuerbach. Many of Marx's fundamental motifs and views of the economy were derived from his philosophical studies. As one writer has stated, 'Marx's doctrine of world revolution and communism has its origins in the movement of modern German philosophy from Immanuel Kant to Ludwig Feuerbach' (Tucker, 1961, p. 26). A third influence on Marx's thought was classical political economy. It was the study of this area, from Adam Smith onwards, which occupied the major part of his intellectual work from 1844 until his death in 1883. This was not simply for the sake of academic interest. As Terrell Carver has pointed out, Marx 'took it that political economy incorporated the presuppositions of bourgeois society as well as certain hypotheses ... about the workings of the contemporary economy. He was approaching the economy in an entirely practical way – through works of economic theory which he took to have an intrinsic, rather than merely academic relationship to contemporary social reality' (1982, p. 20).

Apart from these theoretical influences, Marx derived a great deal from practical work as a journalist and editor working on the

Rheinische Zeitung. He was brought into direct contact with social issues which stimulated his reflections (see Carver, 1982, pp. 5–7). Marx's own ideas developed over this period from a theory of republican democracy towards full-blown communism. His early journalistic articles and critical reflections on Hegelian thought still speak in terms of radically reforming the State. Thus Marx's early work, the *Introduction to the Critique of Hegel's Philosophy of Right*, has been referred to as pre-communistic. The notion of class is also not very prominent in his writings up to 1843/4. In fact it is sometimes argued that Engels developed class analysis before Marx. Through his appreciation of Feuerbach's writings, as well as those of Moses Hess and Lorenz von Stein, coupled with his experiences as a journalist, Marx's ideas began to change. By 1844, with the construction of his *Economic and Philosophical Manuscripts*, Marx was quite definitely converted to a particular form of communism.[1] By the time his (and Engels's) work *The German Ideology* was written, class, communism and philosophical materialism had been fully taken on board. From approximately 1845 onward Marx began to examine political economy in detail as the groundwork to any explanation of history and the fate of capitalist societies. This is the mature Marx of the *Communist Manifesto* and *Capital*.

The key to Marx's ideas lies in his response to Hegel and the young Hegelian school. Together with Bruno and Edgar Bauer, Arnold Ruge, Max Stirner and Ludwig Feuerbach, Marx studied Hegel's works assiduously over the 1830s and early 1840s. Feuerbach was the most influential figure in the group. He had started initially as a clear disciple of Hegel's absolute idealism. In fact in one sense he never abandoned Hegel; as Marx Wartofsky has observed, 'In an important sense, Feuerbach remained a Hegelian all his life. The unifying theme of his work was the progress of human consciousness, the unfolding self-awareness. And it is Feuerbach himself who recognises that Hegelian philosophy establishes the form of this development, and suggests the mode of its progress' (1977, p. 141). Feuerbach engaged in a dialectical critique of Hegel. The definition of man through his thinking abilities, specifically through the notion of Spirit (*Geist*), is one step short of reality. Humans were explained through Mind; however, for Feuerbach, it is humans who think, not Mind. The transcendental ego of Kant, the absolute ego of Fichte's philosophy and Hegel's idea of Spirit, were seen by Feuerbach as human creations. Thus the basis of Feuerbach's critique of Hegel is that he was offering an esoteric theology or rational theism. Humans are not vehicles for Spirit, rather it is the sensuous human being which has created notions of Spirit or God. Reality is still, for Feuerbach, the unfolding process of self-consciousness and self-understanding, but it is rooted in ordinary human sensibility. In Hegel 'What was a logic of Being becomes a psychology of human concept formation' (Wartofsky, 1977, p. 193). Philosophy reflects human wants and needs. Hegel in this sense becomes another part of the history of philosophy and not the summation of philosophy. As Feuerbach argued, 'Hegel was led to take representation which expressed merely subjective needs, as objective truths, because he failed to go back to the origins, to the needs which gave rise to the representation' (quoted in Wartofsky, 1977, p. 192). The highest object of philosophy for Feuerbach was therefore the human essence.

Feuerbach's critique of Hegel is directly related to his critique of religion in *The Essence of Christianity*. Hegel's Spirit is the last speculative outpost of God. Speculative philosophy and religion need to be led from the realm of Spirit into that of humanity. The essence of Feuerbach's critique is that 'all theology is anthropology'. The object of religion is not God but really idealized humanity. Religion deals with human essence idealized; it is the alienated form of the individual's recognition of its own nature. God is a creation of the human imagination unknowingly idealizing itself. Thus a radical demythologizing or demystification is needed. This process profoundly affected subsequent theology into this century. Love of God is really love of humanity in symbolic form. Theology is therefore a kind of 'psychic pathology' (see Wartofsky, 1977, p. 258). The dichotomy between God and humanity is really a dichotomy *within* humans. Religion is a form of alienation or self-estrangement. This process of criticism became more conventionally known as the 'transformative criticism', namely the subject and predicate are interchanged in any proposition about the world. For example, it is not God that is the key to understanding humanity, conversely it is humanity which is the real subject and God the predicate.

This criticism affected the thinking of the young Hegelians. Feuerbach himself was not exempt from this criticism, even his own transformative criticism. Max Stirner, taking his own idiosyncratic angle, argued that Feuerbach's idea of sensuous humanity and 'species being' was unsatisfactory. Species being also needed transformation into a predicate. It was the single ego which was the true subject. For the ego, species being was a predicate. For Stirner this solipsistic ego was the creator of all value in the world – an argument which was not lost on the young Nietzsche. Marx took a different tack again. In his *Theses on Feuerbach*, amongst other writings, he argued that Feuerbach's great achievement had been to bring holy ideas down to earth. However, he had remained with a philosophical and abstract vision of humanity, a theoretical humanism and materialism. What was needed for Marx was a practical humanism and a new materialism which took into account the reality of social and economic relations. For Marx, Feuerbach had ignored the true subject, which is practical, labouring, historical humanity. Philosophy must be moved away from mental abstraction and contemplation into the realm of social, political and economic realities. This critique forms the basis for Marx's studies of Hegel in the early 1840s. It was this line of philosophical argument which led Marx to the study of political economy.

On a positive note Marx saw considerable value in many of Hegel's ideas. He adopted a central theme, immanent in Hegel and brought to the surface by Feuerbach, that philosophy is about unbinding humanity. As one writer has argued, 'Hegelianism was the philosophy whose very own confession was that of Prometheus. Its epochal significance lay in the revelation of "human self-consciousness" as the supreme divinity' (Tucker, 1961, p. 75); or as Marx stated, 'The criticism of religion ends with the doctrine that man is the highest being for man' (Marx, 1971, p. 123). History was imbued with teleological significance as the growing possibility of freedom for humanity. Philosophy had a definite role in this process. The development of humanity was dialectical, although for Marx it was a dialectic of human labour and production. Humans, as Hegel had grasped, were self-producing creatures. Hegel grasped the centrality of labour but only in its mental form. Thus Marx refers to Hegel's thought as 'concealed criticism that is still obscure to itself' (Marx, 1971, p. 163). Hegel had suggested that humans produce themselves and the world in their self-consciousness. For Marx humans produce themselves by actual labour and the ensuing social relations in the world. Thus, although initially regarding Hegelianism as an esoteric psychology, Marx gradually came to regard it as an esoteric economics. Finally, Hegel had seen that the State was a definite stage in the development and secular emancipation of humanity. Marx argued the same point in his early essay *On the Jewish Question.* Hegel's mistake, for Marx, was to interpret the State as a product of Mind or Spirit, rather than sensuous labouring humanity. What was needed was a transformative criticism of Hegel, specifically Hegel's political philosophy.

For Marx, Hegel's *Geist* (Spirit) was really about humanity. Hegel's philosophy mystifies reality. As Marx put it, Hegel makes the 'exoteric esoteric' (Marx, 1974, p. 47). Alienation existed for Hegel, but as an intellectual or mental problem. For Marx alienation was in the actual world of work and production. Thus Hegel's fundamental error was that he 'made the subject of the idea into the product and predicate of the *Idea*'. Feuerbach was right to make alienation a problem for humans but he did not carry his theory into the realm of politics. As Marx stated in Thesis VI, 'Feuerbach resolves the religious essence into the human essence. But the human essence is no abstraction inherent in each single individual. In its reality it is the ensemble of the social relations' (Marx and Engels 1968, p. 29). Marx summarizes this whole development with great precision when he remarked that 'The first task of philosophy, which is in the service of history, once the holy form of self-alienation has been discovered, is to discover alienation in its unholy forms. The criticism of heaven is thus transformed into the criticism of earth, the criticism of religion into the criticism of law, and the criticism of theology into the criticism of politics' (1971, p. 116). For Marx, both Hegel and Feuerbach had a positive dialectic but a negative subject.

Marx's actual critique of Hegel's *Philosophy of Right* is really his only systematic treatment of the State and even then, as pointed out, it is mainly negative criticism. In the same way it is a misnomer to call it a critique either of Hegel's work or his theory of the State. The actual manuscript was a rough unedited work of thirty-nine sheets dealing with sections 261–313 of Hegel's work. It was first published in 1927 and was never intended by Marx for publication. The oddity of the work is that it *only* deals with the 'Political State' in Hegel – although there is a strong sense that he wishes to collapse it into the 'external State' of civil society. Marx does not deal with the metaphysical underpinning, the logic and so forth. Most importantly he does not deal either with Hegel's attempt to discuss the authority structure and nature of civil society or with the ethical sense of the State. Thus Marx's work is radically incomplete and flawed since he does not deal with Hegel's notion of the State in its completed form. In fact, as has now been shown in subsequent scholarship, Hegel does anticipate much of what Marx has to say about markets and civil society. Hegel was deeply cognisant of the problem of poverty in market society, although he treated labour and economic production as but one determinant of human existence. They are not the sole motive of human conduct. In fact Marx, in his more reflective moments, seemed to agree with Hegel on this particular point.

Even more strange, and yet deeply complementary in another sense, Marx treats Hegel's version of the State as summing up

German reality at that time. To criticize Hegel's State was to criticize the actual State. As Marx put it, 'The criticism of German philosophy of the state and of law which was given its most consistent, richest and final version by Hegel, is ... the critical analysis of the modern state and the reality that depends upon it' (1971, p. 122). In this manner Marx was idealistic enough (in the philosophical sense) to see the important role of ideas in determining reality. One could from this comment reverse later statements to the effect that it is not man's social being which determines his consciousness but conversely his consciousness which determines his social being. Such an idea is of course difficult to reconcile with the later popular image of 'Marx the materialist', seeing consciousness as epiphenomenal.

The root idea behind his critique of the Political State, which is developed on its economic side in the *Economic and Philosophical Manuscripts*, is that the State is supposedly above civil society and the market order. In fact the State for Marx is based *on* the defence of particular property interests in civil society. Humanity becomes the predicate of private property and the State reinforces this. Hegel couples his position with further mystification by seeing the State as prior to human beings; as Marx comments, 'Instead of recognising that persons attain their actuality in and through such species-forms as the family, a particular community, etc. – Hegel makes it seem as if all actuality of personality developed out of the abstract concept of the state' (1974, p. 56). The State is also sanctified by the idea of Spirit, or as Engels put it 'A philosophical benediction [is] bestowed upon despotism, police government, star chamber proceeding and censorship' (Marx and Engels 1968, p. 597). In fact Marx is not quite correct here. Hegel does see persons as developing and growing in the family and community. If he had taken the trouble to grasp the complexity of Hegel's ideas on the Ethical State, he might not have made so crass an assertion. What, however, Marx wished to argue, in essence, is that the State in Hegel, despite all theorizing, reflects particular property interests in civil society.

In his commentary Marx examines the particular institutions discussed by Hegel. Monarchy, he takes as a symbolic upside-down way of saying that the State is really about private persons and their particular interests. In this sense the monarch is taken by Marx as a symbol of the individualist ethos of civil society. This judgment in itself is rather odd, symbolic for whom? The executive is formalized into the bureaucracy – the incarnation of the so-called universal interests of the State. In Marx's view, bureaucracy does not safeguard any universal interests, but formalizes the protection of particular private property interests. As Marx stated ' "Bureaucracy" is the "State formalism" of civil society' (1971, p. 68). It is not the bureaucracy who are the universal class for Marx but rather what he was to call the proletariat. It is they, not the bureaucracy, who stand for the whole of society. 'Modern man', for Marx, 'especially since the French Revolution, has been separated from his universal social nature (which has been objectified in the formal organization of the *bureaucracy*), and has been left with nothing but the atomization of social life which is found in the classes of civil society' (1974, p. 69). Thus it is through the abolition of bureaucracy (the abstract universal) that true liberation can be realized by the proletariat (the concrete universal). The legislature, comprising specifically the Estates, is purely superfluous for Marx. Even in Hegel their relation to the bureaucracy is only theoretical. Once the people (proletariat) 'repossess their natural right to give *themselves* their constitution, questions about "whether the legislative determines the constitution or vica versa" will become superfluous' (1974, pp. 66–7).

In summary, therefore, the State and civil society cannot be mediated as Hegel suggested. Abstract property rights are embodied in the State (see Avineri, 1968, p. 31). The State exists to maintain this interest. Thus Marx, in his *Economic and Philosophical Manuscripts*, argues that his aim, specifically in the section on 'Alienated Labour', is to grasp 'the subtle connections between private property, selfishness, the division of labour, capital and landed property . . . and the consequent degradation of man. As man alienated his essence into God so the worker is now seen to alienate his essence into the production of goods' (quoted in Tucker, 1961, p. 146). The worker is seen as a wage slave. The solution envisaged, in this situation, in his early critical work, is a version of Jacobin, egalitarian, republican democracy involving the abolition of private property and classes (Avineri, 1968, p. 38). In later works the solution is very specifically communism, which Marx describes in dialectical terms as 'the positive negation of the negation' (1971, p. 157). Private property is the negation of man, therefore communism – being the overcoming of private property – is the negation of that negation. The oddity of both Marx's solutions is that they abandon the bourgeois notions of privacy and private rights, which signals virtually a return to the Greek *polis*, as in the early Hegel. Marx scorned the values of subjectivity and subjective rights, but one is tempted to argue that he does not thereby face the problem of subjectivity and modernity, but simply retreats into an antique community idea. The ambiguity in Marx is compounded in that communism is not explicitly analysed anywhere in his writings, therefore it is difficult to say with any precision whether any elements of the State remain.

From the above discussion it is relatively easy to see why Marx reflected on what he called his 'leading thread' in his semi-autobiographical *Preface to the Critique of Political Economy*. As he stated:

> My investigations led to the result that legal relations as well as forms of state are to be grasped neither from themselves nor from the so-called general development of the human mind, but rather have their roots in the material conditions of life, the sum total of which Hegel . . . combines under the name 'civil society'; the anatomy of civil society is to be sought in political economy. The investigation of the latter, which I began in Paris, I continued in Brussels . . . The general result at which I arrived and which, once won, served as the leading thread in my studies, may be briefly formulated as follows: in the social production of their life, men enter into definite relations that are indispensible and independent of their will, relations of production which correspond to a definite stage of development of their material powers of production. The sum total of these relations of production constitutes the economic structures of society, the real foundation, on which rises a legal and political superstructure and to which correspond definite forms of consciousness. The mode of production of material life conditions the the social, political, and intellectual life process in general. It is not the consciousness of men that determines their being, but, on the contrary, their social being determines their consciousness. (Marx and Engels, 1968, p. 182).

Marx does not fill in the complex philosophical reasons as to how or why he adopted this leading thread of political economy. Possibly he wished to overshadow this aspect of his past. He was obviously unwilling to dredge up his philosophical past. After Marx's death Engels also refused to countenance the publication of the early philosophical work, *The German Ideology*.[2]

Within the political economy perspective the fundamental motifs of traditional Marxism were formed. These can be summarized as follows. It is the material conditions of life which form the basis of all social and political structures, as well as of human consciousness. Relations of production are the real foundation from which arise the legal and political superstructure. The State, in other words, is not to be understood as arising from human conscious intention. The State reflects the intrinsic class struggle which takes place at the economic base of society. The political struggles on the surface of the State are only reflections of the real class struggle that takes place underneath. The State, despite what many bourgeois theorists will tell us, does not represent any over-arching common good, but is rather a condensation of the property interests of the dominant expropriating class. In this sense, with the more simplified scheme of classes put forward, the State becomes 'the executive committee to manage the affairs of the bourgeoisie'. It acts as its oppressive agent in civil society, suppressing proletarian interests in favour of capital. The key to understanding the State is thus to examine 'the direct relationship of the owners of the conditions of production to the direct producers'. The personnel of such a State belong or owe allegiance to one particular class. Intellectuals, for example, in one view would be the paid lackeys of the bourgeoisie. The capitalist class dominate political power completely through their economic power. The form of the State and the way it emerges are shaped by the modes and relations of production. As modes of production change so also does the State – but at 'its heart is always the protection of capitalist interests.

At first sight this would seem to be the conventional or traditional class-based account of the State in later Marxism from 1849/50 onwards. Despite the appeal of the above view, two questions remain. First, what did Marx and Engels mean by the term 'State'? Second, is there *one* unequivocal account of it, as suggested in the foregoing discussion?

It is not easy to answer the first question with any great clarity. It seems that Marx intended to write about the State at some point as part of a larger project; although it would, presumably, still have been seen as an aspect of bourgeois political economy. What he does say about the State, however, remains somewhat fragmentary. In his early critique of Hegel's *Philosophy of Right*, Marx seems to be identifying the State with definite political institutions. This would include the executive, legislature, crown and judiciary and the various personnel involved. This squares with his later stray remarks which identify the State with the 'government'. How far Marx stretches the term government is left open. There is an implication, specifically in the later writings, that government implies the political institutions, bureaucracy, police and military structures (see Marx and Engels, 1968, p. 289). Marx is not very clear on this point. He sometimes envisages 'administration' being distinct from government. Exactly what the relationship between bureaucracy and administration is not clear, specifically where Marx speaks of administration existing in communism. The lack of clarity exists here simply because Marx does not address himself to the juristic account of the State. One might have expected that he would have tackled this as a preliminary to any negative criticism, if only minimally to grasp *what* is being criticized.

Secondly, it is far from clear, if one looks more closely at the mature writings, whether there is one clear traditional theory. Primarily there is the problem discussed earlier, that Marx does not elucidate either the concept of class or its precise relationship to property ownership. Added to this problem is that there is no clear account of the relation of class to the State itself. The crudest view is that the State is the condensation of the interests of the capitalist class. This is the doctrine found in *The Communist Manifesto*. One implication of this is that if no class existed then presumably no State would exist. Class conflict is the premise to the very existence of the State. This is the idea which can be found clearly expressed as well in Lenin's *The State and Revolution*. The State can be even more stringently seen as a parasite and epiphenomenon – a somewhat superficial reflection of a much more significant economic domination. In this sense the State, from the standpoint of a strict materialism, is a rather insignificant entity, a pale reflection of basic structural forces. Although it still reflects a clear one-to-one relation of class to State. However, there are other writings where this one to one relation is clearly undermined.

In the *18th Brumaire* (1852) and *Class Struggles in France* (1850) there are indications that the State may represent the interests of only a section of a class, like the financiers under Louis Philippe. Furthermore, the State bureaucracy may not reflect immediately the interests of the bourgeoisie: first, because of the very expertise of the bureaucracy; second, the bourgeoisie often have no interest in administration; and finally because there may be divisions within the interests of capital. In addition, Marx explicitly argues in the *18th Brumaire* that in certain situations, like that which existed in France in 1848–50, the State may *not* represent the interests of any class. In the case of Bonaparte it may work directly against the interests of the bourgeoisie (see Marx and Engels, 1968, p. 177). This undermines both the idea of the direct synonymity of class to State and also the necessity of class to the existence of the State. It is this thesis which enabled the development of what is often called in Marxist circles

'State autonomy theory', which has affected a number of contemporary Marxist theories. The theory, in varying degrees, sees the State as a 'factor of cohesion' or an institution regulating class conflict – although most would add regulating it in the interests of capital. This particular theme can be clearly observed in Marx's attitude and comments upon the English Factory Inspectorate in *Capital*. If the State and political power were the instrument of the ruling bourgeois class and the State acted coercively and oppressively, how could Marx remark on State officials such as Leonard Horner of the Factory Inquiry Commission, as rendering 'undying service to the English working class. He carried on a life-long contest, not only with the embittered manufacturers, but also with the Cabinet' (1909, Vol. 1, p. 208 n. 1). It is also worthy of note that Marx, who relied on Factory Inspectorate reports for a lot of the empirical detail for his *Capital*, should have commented that the British manufacturers 'denounced the Factory Inspectors as a kind of revolutionary commissioners like those of the French National Convention ruthlessly sacrificing the unhappy factory workers to their humanitarian crotchet' (1909, Vol. 1, p. 271). It is difficult to reconcile the view of the State as a totally oppressive bourgeois institution helping to further exploitation and thus immiseration of the proletariat with these other views. This ambivalence over the State is also reflected in the tension between the doctrine of the State as a purely coercive class instrument and the doctrine of the proletarian use of the State (under the dictatorship of the proletariat) as an agency of revolutionary change. The latter doctrine gives a rather positive role for the State, the former an extremely negative one. One might try to get round this criticism by drawing a distinction between State power and the State apparatus; however, the distinction appears more casuistical than intellectually helpful.

Before concluding this section I wish to return for a few moments to the meaning of the word State in Marxism. As pointed out, Marx does draw a distinction between government and administration. He remarked, for example, in 1872 that 'once the aim of the proletarian movement, the abolition of classes, is attained, . . . the state power disappears and governmental functions are transformed into simple administrative functions' (quoted in McLellan, 1980, p. 221). This point was also made in his drafts for *The Civil War in France* (1871), where he speaks of 'Doing away with the state hierachy altogether and replacing the haughty masters of the people with always removable servants' (quoted in McLellan, 1980, p. 220). Administration seems to apply here to a post-State situation. There may be echoes of

Saint Simon's 'administered society' here. In this view, presumably, administration is *not* part of the State, or at least not a necessary part of the State. This is odd if we reflect back to Marx's remarks on Hegel's State where the administration *par excellence* represents the '"State formalism" of civil society' (1971, p. 68). It is only by overcoming the abstract universal of the bureaucracy that the true concrete universal of the proletariat can arise. Perhaps the word *Aufhebung* is the problem here. It is often translated as 'abolition' or 'transcendence', but it also implies 'preservation'. The bureaucracy would be preserved and would function in the interests of the proletariat; thus it would not be utterly abolished or transcended.

The only thing apparently wrong with 'administration' in the 1871 writings is not the principle of the institution but rather whether administrators are responsible and democratically removable. Exactly how one has administration without a body of rules, some authoritative guidance, some kind of division of labour, hierarchy and so on, which seem to imply many features associated with authority and Statehood, is not explained.[3] In fact such features are still perfectly compatible with accountability and democratic removal. It is difficult to ascertain here whether or not Marx is arguing for an anarchic federation of communes in the mode of Bakunin or Proudhon. On the other hand, Marx was not clear whether he really did want to abandon some form of central but democratically based control – combined with maximum individual freedom. Such central control was not compatible with early Proudhonism. At points he seemed to be arguing for a more responsive, accountable, less hierarchical and democratic State, even in the later writings of the 1870s. There is some parallel between Marx's call for the abolition of the State and Proudhon's claim that 'all property is theft'. Where Proudhon was paradoxically admitting some form of property (in order for the concept of theft to make sense), so Marx wished to abolish a particular conception of the State in order for a truer, more democratic view to arise. Such an idea, however, remains conjectural since Marx nowhere spells it out and the vague spectre of communism, and thus anti-Statism, haunts his later writings. This only muddies the waters around any possible theory of the State present in Marxism.

GRAMSCI AND THE STATE:
THEORETICIAN OF THE SUPERSTRUCTURE

In the 1890s Marxism entered a period of flux. A number of important developments were taking place. Firstly, a separation occurred between, on the one hand, the interpretation of Marx as the propounder of a revolutionary doctrine, which formed the basis for political activity, and, on the other, the adoption of Marx as an independent social theorist of some academic standing. In the latter many 'had accomplished the essential task of separating out the general social theory from the mass of revolutionary principles . . . Once "decontaminated" in this fashion, Marxism could be absorbed into the mainstream of European social thought' (Stuart-Hughes, 1979, p. 97). Marx became a respected sociological theorist rather than a practical revolutionary. Secondly, a vigorous debate developed as to whether Marxism, purged of its dialectical dross, could be integrated into liberal-democratic parliamentary politics. This was the core of the revisionist controversy. The father figure of such revisionism was Eduard Bernstein. This debate has continued in European Marxist thought. Finally, and most significantly, a split began to occur, later to be reinforced by the publication of Marx's early writings, between, on the one hand, the proponents of a more scientific, objectivist and deterministic Marxism and, on the other, a more humanistic, moralized and voluntarist Marxism. The scientific Marxism, which some have seen as characteristic of Marx's later writings, is connected to the association, by Engels, of Marx with Darwin (see Marx and Engels, 1968, p. 435). As Darwin is supposed to have discovered biological laws, Engels claimed that Marx had discovered laws of history. Engels explicitly identified Marxism as a form of natural science, specifically in such works as the *Anti-Dühring* and *The Dialectics of Nature*. In this view history is seen to be determined by objective dialectical laws. The human self is relatively unimportant. The individual is identified with a class which has a determinate role in the economic process. Economic structures are primary, they determine the superstructure. The older, mature Marx is thus the important area for study, not the younger, philosophical Marx. Recent critics, for example Alvin Gouldner, associate this strand of thinking with more recent writers such as Althusser, Poulantzas, Galvano della Volpe, Godelier and Bettelheim (see Gouldner, 1980). Conversely the humanistic young Marx is seen to be concerned with the human self and voluntary activity. It is human pyschology sensuously considered which is important. Alienation is a moral and philosophical dilemma, not just an economic conundrum. History is not about inevitable objective laws, but rather about 'tendencies' and the redemption of humans from alienation. Consciousness seems to have a definite role in human affairs and is not just an epiphenomenon. In this scenario Marx links up closely with his Hegelian origins. Alvin Gouldner identifies this stream of thought with writers such as Lukács, Marcuse, Habermas and Gramsci. This analysis provides a somewhat over-simplified dichotomy in the Marxist tradition. There are admittedly considerable variations between Gramsci, Lukács and Habermas, as there are between Poulantzas and della Volpe. However, relatively distinct traditions have developed on the question of the State, which can, very roughly, be split up on the grounds discussed above.

There is considerable debate on the interpretation of the writings of Antonio Gramsci. Yet not many would disagree with the judgement of Joseph Femia that, with Karl Korsch and Lukács, Gramsci reformulated Marxist orthodoxy 'in such a way as to allow room for both the influence of ideas and the powerful effect of the human will' (Femia, 1981, p. 1). Gramsci expressed disenchantement with orthodox positivist Marxism and wanted to give a more prominent role to cultural and intellectual ideas within Marxist interpretation. This led him to a re-engagement with some themes in Hegelianism.

Most scholars divide up Gramsci's career into four phases: firstly, his interest in Benedetto Croce's Hegelian thought between 1914 and 1919; secondly, 1919–20, during a time of mass strikes and factory occupations by Italian workers, Gramsci formulated ideas on factory councils. Greater emphasis was placed in this stage on concrete political organization and workers' self-education. The period 1920–6 saw the collapse of the Factory Council movement. Revolution was seen to be a much slower, more complex process than previously anticipated. Finally, after his arrest by the fascist authorities, Gramsci spent virtually the rest of his life in prison up to 1936. He died three days after his release. It was in this final period that he constructed his famous *Prison Notebooks*, approximately 3000 pages in thirty-two notebooks, which attempt 'to re-adapt the Marxian "weapons of criticism", to construct a theoretical strategic paradigm applicable to the conditions of mature capitalism' (see Femia, 1981, pp. 4–6). The notebooks themselves are rather elliptical and occasionally very elusive writings. They were written under prison conditions, without scholarly resources.

In the background of Gramsci's arguments was a much subtler, more complex grasp of materialism than the prevailing crude 'economism'. Gramsci, primarily under the influence of Croce's Hegelianism, emphasized the role of consciousness and human autonomy. He rejected the passive materialism of much orthodox Marxism in favour of a vigorous 'philosophy of praxis' and human will, in line, to an extent, with Marx's early *Economic and Philosophical Manuscripts*; although Gramsci's rejection of crude materialism also fits neatly with Marx's rejection of a similar doctrine in his *Theses on Feuerbach*. Gramsci commented that 'man does not enter into relations with nature just by being himself part of nature, but actively, by means of work and technique. Furthermore these relations are not mechanical. They are active and conscious' (quoted in Femia, 1981, p. 70). In this context he argued that the ideas of Engels should not be confounded with those of Marx and that the vulgarized Marxism of Plekhanov and Bukharin should be rejected. Marxism was a subtle development of Hegelianism. It was a philosophy

> that has been liberated (or is attempting to liberate itself) from any unilateral and fanatical ideological elements; it is conscious-ness full of contradictions, in which the philosopher himself, understood both individually and as an entire social group, not only grasps the contradictions but points himself as an element of the contradiction and elevates this element to a principle of knowledge and therefore action. (Gramsci, 1971, pp. 404–5)

This stress on the independent role of ideas and human consciousness and their effect on the economic base of society, make up Gramsci's distinctive contribution. He was neither saying that the base determines the superstructure nor the opposite. Rather he tried subtly to integrate consciousness with materialism. As Femia comments, 'historical materialism can incorporate a crucial role for consciousness without losing, in the process, the essential economic core that constitutes its uniqueness. It was Gramsci's achievement to fashion just such a synthesis' (1981, p. 66). This is neither crude materialism nor idealism. Rather 'the will . . . moves history but only in so far as it conforms to the needs constituted by extant economic conditions' (1981, p. 121); or as Gramsci argued, in his somewhat elusive form, 'The philosophy of praxis is absolute "historicism", the absolute secularisation and earthliness of thought, an absolute humanism of history' (1971, p. 465). It can be a temptation to read too much into Gramsci and overrate his distinctive contribution

(Dyson, 1980, p. 107). However, it is this autonomy of ideas in one sense which provides Gramsci's distinctive contribution to State theory. This contribution lies in his idea of *hegemony*.

Gramsci's focus on the autonomy of ideas and political activity as distinct from the economic base was systematizing something present in Marx's writings. Marx in both his early and later writings did occasionally appear to be giving a strong role to human consciousness and ideas. This is a mode of argument which can also be found in Lenin, who despite his often crude Engels type arguments on materialism in *Materialism and Empirio-Criticism*, does contend in another work, 'What is to be done?', that socialist ideology must defeat bourgeois ideology in order for socialism to succeed in practice. Gramsci's notion of hegemony is however infinitely more subtle than Lenin's crude voluntarism.

Essentially Gramsci's emphasis is that ideas and ideology play a crucial role in the determination of economic structures and that bourgeois society is not simply controlled by open force, but that its mode of operation is through consent. Hegemony represents a subtle form of cultural domination. Power is redefined in terms of intellectual hegemony. The masses are co-opted and quelled by means of ideational domination. It is bourgeois ideology which not only holds sway in the dominant class but is internalized by the masses through such forms as morality, language and the like, such as to elicit consent and legitimation. The State is, therefore, not just a political or institutional apparatus which coercively dominates one class. It is a vessel of intellectual dominance which actually elicits a response from the masses. It wishes to be legitimate in the eyes of the broad masses. Thus as Gramsci's biographer put it:

> Gramsci's originality as a Marxist lay partly in his conception of the nature of bourgeois rule (and indeed any previous established order), in his argument that the system's real strength does not lie in the violence of the ruling class or the coercive power of its state apparatus, but in the acceptance by the ruled of the "conception of the world" which belongs to the rulers. The philosophy of the ruling class passes through a whole tissue of complex vulgarisations to emerge as "common sense": that is, the philosophy of the masses, who accept the morality, the customs, the institutionalised behaviour of the society they live in. (Fiore, 1970, p. 238)

Thus the very conceptions of life, value, morality, political action, which become part of 'common sense', are subtly formulated by bourgeois theoreticians ultimately in their own interests. Bourgeois hegemony moulds the personal convictions, norms and aspirations of the proletariat. Thus an ideological consensus can be acquired without any force. Such an idea is distinct from simple conspiracy theory. No intellectual sits down and intends to construct such a hegemony. The consent and consensus play a decisive role in Gramsci's notion. They undermine the whole process of class conflict by providing a deep-rooted substratum of agreement. It was in this context that Gramsci saw a crucial role for both intellectuals and the educative process. Each class produces its intellectuals who formulate the self-awareness of that group. Proletarian intellectuals have a decisive role in both education and in combating bourgeois hegemony. The criticism of bourgeois hegemony is an essential preliminary to the rise of proletarian consciousness. There are early echoes of this argument in Lenin's criticism of 'legal Marxism' and so on, in his 'What is to be done?'.

The argument had considerable implications for revolutionary activity since it implied that the realm of ideas in the superstructure was as vital a place for struggle as the base. Class struggle was also manifest in the realm of ideas. The actual disintegration of capitalism hinged, for Gramsci, on the notion of hegemony. The war of ideas was as significant as any class conflict in the factory. Proletarian hegemony would exist in the future for the sake of the whole of society. This produced a consequent change in the role and significance of intellectuals within Marxist thinking. In fact Gramsci developed various complex ideas on revolutionary strategy, such as the 'war of movement' and 'war of manoeuvre'. Without entering into either Gramsci's discussion of revolutionary tactics and crisis or the complex interpretations of the notion of hegemony, Gramsci's view of the State will now be examined.

The State, for Gramsci, is undoubtedly linked to the idea of class but not in the direct way in which it is often considered. As one recent writer has put it, 'Gramsci's theory of the State, although not presented systematically in any of his writings, emerges from the Marxist notion of a superstructure rooted in class and a juridical-political system rooted in the social class struggle' (Carnoy, 1984, pp. 86–7). It is also clear that the State minimally involved the executive, legislative, judiciary, police and military. Gramsci adds to this the ideas connected with hegemony. The State is not simply an organ of class rule. It is rather an area where power is organized, struggled for, debated over, often by 'fractions' of classes. The modern democratic State cannot, for Gramsci, ignore classes. As he argued 'the dominant group is co-ordinated concretely with general interests of the subordinate groups, and the life of the State is conceived of as a continuous process of formation and superseding of unstable equilibria ... between the interests of the fundamental group and those of the subordinate groups – equilibria in which the interests of the dominant group prevail, but only up to a certain point' (1971, p. 182). In this sense, the State is a key area of struggle and possesses a 'relative autonomy' from the economic base. It is also not just a set of institutions but rather a dominant intellectual ethos – an idea which harks back to Hegel.

Gramsci's own account of the State in his *Notebooks* is not, however, crystal clear. The State was 'the entire complex of practical and theoretical activities with which the ruling class not only justifies and maintains its dominance, but manages to win the active consent of those over whom it rules' (1971, p. 244). This would include the education system, teachers and churches, which is a fairly all-inclusive idea. One might ask at this point what has happened to the idea of society or civil society? Gramsci had a rather distinctive understanding of the idea of civil society, which is different from Marx's usage. Civil society did not refer to economic relationships simply but rather to the superstructure – 'The ensemble of organisms commonly called "private" [which] corresponds to the function of hegemony which the dominant group exercises throughout society' (1971, p. 12). Generally it implied the organizations and means by which hegemony is diffused in all domains of culture and thought. Femia remarks on this that Gramsci 'was perhaps inspired by those passages in *The Philosophy of Right* where Hegel included in the realm of civil society the corporations or trade associations, which, through their educative functions, mediate between the anarchic particularism of civil society and the integrated universal aspect of social life embodied in the state' (1981, p. 26).

In other places Gramsci obviously runs together notions of political society and civil society into the State. He noted that 'it should be remarked that the general notion of the State includes elements which need to be referred back to the notion civil society (in the sense that one might say that State = political society + civil society, in other words hegemony protected by the armour of coercion)' (1971, p. 263). In fact, he even says that 'civil society and State are one and the same' (1971, p. 160). The State here seems to represent a synthesis of consent and coercion. Gramsci also identifies the State with political dictatorship. The State, he says, 'is usually understood as political society (or dictatorship; or coercive apparatus . . .) and not as an equilibrium between political society and civil society' (quoted in McLellan, 1979, p. 188).

As Perry Anderson (1977) has pointed out, Gramsci's ideas on hegemony, civil society and the State are far from consistent in their usage. There is also a strong sense that hegemony applies to civil society as a realm of intellectual domination; coercion, however, applies to the State as political society. The State, in this view, is identified with the institutional coercive structures. There is a further sense that the State incorporates political society, the institutional and organizational structure, as well as hegemony and civil society. In this sense the State is an appparatus of hegemony backed up by coercion (see Gramsci, 1971, p. 263). One final sense appears in Gramsci's writings, this is where the State is totally identified with civil society. There is no distinction to be made between them (1971, p. 160). It is arguable that Gramsci, in these circuitous reflections on the nature of the State, may have grasped something of the complexity of the Hegelian view of the State. Hegel, in line with an eighteenth century tradition, identified a form of the State with civil society. He called it the 'external state'. It also has certain dispositional traits which fit Gramsci's hegemonic ideas. In the final analysis, it is not possible to conclude precisely what Gramsci meant by the term State. His reflections are too diverse and frustratingly elusive.

Gramsci's contribution to the class theory of the State lies in the fact that he broadened the whole Marxist perspective. This broadening process can be summarized as follows: (1) the notion of class domination had to be modified and reinterpreted. The State was not simply an instrument for one class to use to coerce another. In modern democracies Gramsci contended that class domination had considerable limitations. (2) Any domination which did exist was far more complex than previously understood. Bourgeois hegemony elicited consent from the masses. Open coercion was not necessarily an overt feature. (3) The State was an arena for intellectual ideas and debate. It possessed a certain relative autonomy and was not simply an epiphenomenon. It could act on the economy and through the medium of ideas it could persuade the masses to support it. This idea gave a more active and creative a role for the State. (4) Revolution did not mean outright confrontation, but rather intellectual manoeuvre. The bourgeois hegemony had to be intellectually challenged by proletarian hegemony. In this sense Marxism became part of the hegemonic aspirations of the proletariat. Gramsci, however, still suffers from overall ambiguity not only on the concept of class but also on the very concept of the juridical State. He had far more grasp than many Marxists of the State, but still within limitations.

STRUCTURALISM AND THE STATE

Structuralism is a mode of explanation which rather than focusing on human subjects, relies instead for explanation on deep-rooted underlying structures. The idea was used in a number of disciplines, for example linguistics, anthropology and psychology, this century. Louis Althusser and Nicos Poulantzas took over the idea for Marxism. Althusser, in fact did not apply himself to studying the State in any systematic way; Poulantzas was the first to use structuralism in analysing the State. It is difficult to do justice to a rather complicated movement in so short a space – also there is a strong suspicion in some quarters that underneath the complex terminology of structuralist Marxism is a rather paltry creature. Undoubtedly, though, Poulantzas specifically has had a lot of attention paid to his work and it would be wise to review some of the major ideas. The same problem arises, however, with this as with other forms of Marxism, namely, it is doubtful that they really advance our knowledge of the normative conception of the State.

Another difficult point is that it is hard to classify the structuralists within the Marxist tradition. There is a tendency to classify them as closer to the more scientific school of Marxist thought. The reasons for this are that Althusser began by rejecting the more humanist Marxism of Lukács and J.-P. Sartre, with its emphasis on the young Marx. The autonomous human subject, suffering alienation and seeking redemption in philosophical communism is of no interest to either Althusser or Poulantzas. History is a history of structures not of autonomous human subjects. Furthermore, Althusser explicitly identifies *Capital* as the key text of Marxist analysis. Even the *German Ideology* is looked upon with moderate suspicion. This argument had led structuralists to reject the more Hegelian reading of Marx which was advanced in Gramsci's account. Subjectivism had to be countered. The social system was, therefore, viewed as an objective process. The human being was the vehicle for certain structural class relations, not an independent subject. This would appear to fit structuralism into the more scientific category. The ambiguity of this judgement is that both Althusser and Poulantzas identified themselves more or less as heirs of Gramsci's ideas. They also both rejected the crude materialism and 'economism' of the scientific strand of the Marxist movement. This would imply some kind of rejection of scientism. Poulantzas specifically argued that the failure of Marxism to cope with the development of fascism in the 1920s and 1930s was due partially to the arid economism of many in the Marxist movement. In fact Poulantzas has argued for the interactive nature of political, ideological and economic structures.

One answer to the above dilemma is that it is questionable whether such a neat distinction does exist in Marxist thought. The distinction drawn between humanistic and scientific Marxism is too simplistic and takes no account of the considerable variations within the whole movement. It is certainly the case that structuralists reject the thesis that the State is simply an instrument of a dominant class. Thus they do not share the somewhat crude analysis of Marxism at the turn of the century. Yet, on the other hand, they regard Marx's major discovery as the fact that societies possessed objective structures which could be studied scientifically. Human thought, politics and State activity may be relatively autonomous from the economic base, but it is far from clear what this means in the final analysis. For example, Althusser thought that Marx's concept of the mode of production involved three levels: economic, political and ideological. The economic structure is always *determinate* or determines. Yet any one of these three elements could be *dominant*, including the ideological (see Althusser and Balibar, 1970, pp. 216–18). The dominant perspective will, however, ultimately be determined by the economic. There is a strong sense here of a highly idiosyncratic interpretation of Gramsci's understanding of the relation between the base and superstructure. Althusser argues that 'ideology is an objective social reality; the ideological struggle is an organic part of the class struggle. On the other hand, I criticized the *theoretical* effects of ideology, which are always a threat or a hindrance to scientific knowledge' (1969, p. 12). What Althusser appears to be arguing here, in an extremely roundabout way, is a covert form of rigid determinism. He is arguing that the State and ideology *appear* to be autonomous, but this autonomy is in reality an objective aspect of the *structure* of ideology. To treat autonomy as really or actually true, namely that it does actually exist in the world, is to be fundamentally misled. The nature of objective ideology is neither false nor wrong. It can be highly complex and logical, but its actual nature is only scientifically revealed by the study of structures. Knowledge about ideology is knowledge about 'the conditions of its necessity' (Althusser, 1969, p. 230). This sounds rather like the logic of the argument that one can be 'forced to be free'. Thus the State, like ideology, is not understood in itself, or even ultimately as a realm of Gramscian hegemony, but rather as determined by deep-rooted economic structures, as studied in *Capital*.

Behind this argument is what structuralists like Althusser see as the 'epistemological break' in Marx in 1845. This describes 'the leap from the pre-scientific world of ideas to the scientific. . . . Althusser applies it to Marx's rejection of the Hegelian and Feuerbachian ideology of his youth and the construction of the basic concepts of dialectical and historical materialism in his later works' (see glossary of terms, Althusser, 1969, p. 248). Marx had, in this view, made a break with his more philosophical past and had seen that society must be studied in terms of wholes and structures. Ideology and politics may be necessary and autonomous but they are actually wholes or structures. It is not conscious activities but the unconscious structures which are of vital interest. Thus, as Althusser argued, an individual's beliefs are his 'material activities inserted into material practices governed by material rituals which are themselves defined by the material ideological apparatus from which derive the ideas of that subject' (1971, p. 170).

In these accounts there is strong implication of 'doublespeak'. Althusser appears neither to want to be allied with any crude sense of economism nor with any humanistic interpretation of Marxism. His solution, if one can get past the language and terminology, is to give an impression of valuing human autonomy, but in the final analysis to make it a 'determinate autonomy'. The deep roots to the discussion of autonomy lie outside the realm of autonomy itself. In other words, human agency is fundamentally to be explained as the result of objective structures. Thus it is no suprise that Althusser sees freedom in terms of necessary submission – as he put it 'There are no subjects except by and for their subjugation' (1971, p. 169).

Nicos Poulantzas is often seen as a more acceptable structuralist, partly because, unlike Althusser, he does address the State directly and also he appears to change and moderate his ideas after his early enthusiasm for Althusser. Many see a marked change between *Political Power and Social Class* (1968) and the later *State, Power and Socialism* (1978). The early work is seen as a straightforwardly structuralist account where the State simply reproduces structural class relations. The State's form and nature is shaped by class. The later work argues that the State is the 'site' of class conflict 'where political power is contested: the State . . . is shaped by struggles in production and *within* the State' (Carnoy, 1984, p. 98). However, these distinctions hardly seem to be dramatic world-shaking shifts in thought.

An early debate between Poulantzas and the British Marxist Ralph Miliband in the 1960s certainly revealed Poulantzas's structuralist views on the State. His later changes seem no more than hair-splitting casuistry. Poulantzas was directly critical of Miliband's book *The State in Capitalist Society*, admitting that 'The theory of the State . . . has, with rare exceptions such as Gramsci, been neglected by Marxist thought' (1972, p. 238). Marxism had been for too long trapped in a crude economism. Miliband is certainly concerned to criticize the bourgeois State, but, for Poulantzas, he did not challenge scientifically the bourgeois terrain of ideas. As Poulantzas states, 'Instead of *displacing* the epistemological terrain and submitting these ideologies to the critique of Marxist science . . . Miliband appears to omit the first step' (1972, p. 241). Concepts, as he puts it, are never 'innocent'. When one utilizes the terminology and concepts of bourgeois theory one risks legitimizing them. Lurking behind this judgement is the 'epistemological break' discussed earlier. This failure in Miliband's account contributes to his inability to comprehend 'social classes and State as *objective structures* and their relations as an *objective system of regular connections*' (Poulantzas, 1972, p. 242). Miliband consequently showed far too much concern for subjects, social actors or agents and interpersonal relations. Social actors are the origin of social actions, thus Miliband is interested in human motivation and intention, and fails to grasp Marx's emphasis on objective structural factors behind the State, human subjects and ideology. No one chooses to be a member of a class, thus 'the relation between the bourgeois class and the State is an *objective relation*' (Poulantzas, 1972, p. 245). The State cannot be reduced to the thought or conduct of its agents. It is rather *'factor of cohesion of a social formation and the factor of reproduction of the conditions of production of a system* that itself determines the domination of one class over the others' (Poulantzas, 1972, p. 246). Miliband does establish that the State apparatus is constituted by the government plus the army, police, judiciary and civil administration, but he does not really examine the objective relations between these branches. Poulantzas gives a vigorous nod to Gramsci at the end of the article, arguing that a State does contain both repressive apparatus (in the traditional Marxist sense) and also ideological apparatuses, such as Churches, educational institutions, and political parties. The ideological apparatuses, for Poulantzas, are not unified like the repressive apparatus and thus possesss a certain degree of autonomy. Although, once again, like Althusser, one must not be misled by this argument. Ultimately the ideological apparatuses belong to the same framework as the repressive apparatus and are determined in the last instance (Poulantzas, 1972, p. 252).

The odd elusive tone of the structuralist argument comes again to the surface here. It is picked out in Miliband's reply to Poulantzas, accusing both Althusser and Poulantzas of being overly theoretical and paying too little attention to empirical detail. More importantly, Miliband maintains that despite Poulantzas's structuralist condemnation of economism, 'his own analysis seems to me to lead straight towards a kind of structural determinism, or rather structural super-determinism, which makes impossible a truly realistic consideration of the dialectical relationship between the state and "the system"' (1972, p. 259). Poulantzas simply substitutes objective structures for a ruling class. As Miliband goes on to say, 'if the state elite is as totally imprisoned in objective structures as is suggested, it follows that there is *really* no difference between a state ruled, say, by bourgeois constitutionalists . . . and one ruled by, say, Fascists' (1972, p. 259).

Miliband's points summarize some of the main objections to structuralism. It is unnecessarily abstract and pretentious in its language. Its supposed novelty really obscures the same old tedious economism and rigid determinism of scientific Marxism earlier this century in writers such as Engels and Plekhanov. In fact it is far more insidious, since it pretends to value human autonomy and agency, while covertly bringing in a new form of super-determinism. Its view of the State thus suffers from the same old flaws as the cruder traditional Marxism, despite its sophisticated appearance. In essence it has little or no theory of the State, only a negative appraisal of its nature.

CONCLUSION

The subsequent history of Marxist theorizing on the State resembles a form of late medieval scholasticism and appears to be a singularly unfruitful area of study, apart from exceptional theorists such as J. Habermas and K. Offe. Very broadly, a number of schools have developed. On the one hand, there is the 'derivationist school', which is sometimes subdivided between the capital logic and materialist schools. Secondly, there are the followers of the late Poulantzas, often cited as the 'class struggle school'. Finally, there are a number of 'independent State' theorists. Generally, all of these reject the idea of the State as *simply* an instrument of the ruling class. They also resist the idea of a single, unique, universal theory of the State. The actual nature of the State is seen as more dependent on historical factors.

The derivationists concentrate on an 'inner' logic to capital, specifically the process of the falling rate of profit in capitalism. The actual nature and functions of the State are *derived* systematically from abstract political economy. Marx's *Capital* is taken as the key work for reference. Class struggle is expressed through the tension of the falling rate of profit and the attempt to extract surplus value. The State is shaped by this historical process. It is thus derived from the logic and crisis of capitalism. The 'class struggle' school envisages the State as the arena or site of class struggle. This constitutes the relative autonomy of the State, since fractions of classes vie for dominance within the State apparatus. Class struggle is internal to the actual State apparatus. Finally, independent State theory, in Offe and Habermas, has adopted the Weberian idea of the State as a source of power, but rejects the idea of its being solely determined by an underlying logic of capital or fundamental structures. Independent State theorists concentrate on the mediating independent role of the State in the class struggle and process of capital accumulation. The bureaucracy, for example, is seen as virtually an independent mediator between classes. The State is neither a negative result of deep-rooted structures, nor simply a neutral arbiter. Thus, as Offe argues, the State 'does not favour specific interests and is not allied with specific classes. Rather, what the State protects and sanctions is a set of institutions and social relationships necessary for the domination of the capitalist class' and consequently 'while it does not defend the specific interests of a single class, the State nevertheless seeks to implement and guarantee the collective interests of all members *of a class society dominated by capital*' (1984, pp. 119–20).

Offe's argument does not mean that the State can be considered totally independent from capital accumulation. The State is tied into the process of capital accumulation. However, the very development of capitalism has caused the functions and role of the State to be expanded drastically, changing the relationship between base and superstructure. In short the public sector functions of the State have expanded dramatically this century. The State tries to reconcile the needs of capital accumulation with the demands of an electorate whose electoral and financial support are necessary for the mainten- ance of order and legitimacy. The State is thus caught in a crisis of, on the one hand, a pressure to regulate the market and capitalism, and on the other, a demand to free markets from intervention in order to allow the flow of investment and accumulation. The State, therefore, faces contradictory imperatives. Economic restrictions demanded by one large sector of the electorate to moderate capitalism conflict with demands by capitalist groups to minimize State regulation. The one calls for more taxation and public expenditure – high-spending can win votes; the other calls for less taxation and cutting public expenditure. The growth of the public sector of welfare and management of the economy can lead to fiscal crises, namely the ever-widening gap between expenditure and revenue, or the gap between social production and private ownership. The severity of the crisis 'depends upon the production and social relations between corporate capital, local and regional capital, state employees and dependants, and the tax paying working classes at large' (O'Connor, 1974, p. 142, see also O'Connor, 1973). The contradiction is not something that can be easily avoided since intervention is inevitable for the sake of retaining legitimacy; however, accumulation is also necessary for the continuance of capitalism. Jürgen Habermas connects this crisis to a broader framework of economic, motivational, rationality, and legitimation crises. The legitimation crisis is ultimately the situation involving the withdrawal of all loyalty and support when the normative commitment to society has been undermined. Habermas and Offe, who are the most astute and interesting of recent Marxists, have developed these ideas into immensely sophisticated theories of the modern State, often relying on quite eclectic sources outside the terrain of Marxism.

Overall, apart from Offe and Habermas, who have moved so far away from original Marxism and have utilized such diverse intellectual resources in their theories that it might be stretching the point to call them Marxists, the general tenor of theorizing on the State has stayed with the original class theory. There have been a host of complicated and fine distinctions drawn; however, it is still the case that no really overt, clear, normative account of the State has arisen in Marxist thought. The ambivalent concept of class still figures high in the actual appraisal of the State, although no one would now adopt the simple Marxist–Leninist thesis that the State is simply an instrument for the domination of one class by another.

One final question remains to be dealt with: what happens to the State in the class theory? For brevity's sake the writings of Marx and Engels will be used. The simple answer to this question can be found stated quite bluntly in *The Communist Manifesto*. Politics exists in the

State. The State is a condensation of class interests. The superstructure of the State develops on the foundation of class domination. Therefore 'When, in the course of development, class distinctions have disappeared, and all production has been concentrated in the whole nation, the public power will lose its political character' (Marx and Engels, 1967, p. 105). When class disappears then in a sense both politics and the State end. Thus 'The abolition of the State only has meaning for communists as a necessary result of the suppression of classes whose disappearance automatically entails the disappearance of the need for an organised power of one class for the suppresson of another' (Marx quoted in McLellan, 1980, p. 219). This doctrine has been popularly associated with the 'withering away of the State'. In fact it was Engels who uses the phrase, virtually as a biological metaphor. In *Anti-Dühring* Engels comments, in a famous phrase that 'The government of persons is replaced by the administration of things and the direction of the processes of production. The state is not "abolished", *it withers away*' (1976, p. 363). Engels, however, earlier in the text, does explicitly refer to this as 'the abolition of the state' (1976, p. 333). In fact Engels's remarks on the future of the State vary considerably. In 1874 he maintained that the State 'as a result of the social revolution of the future, would vanish'. Political functions would become absorbed into administrative ones. In 1877 the proletariat, by taking over the means of production, would at once abolish the State and it would 'fall asleep' or 'wither away of itself'. Marx had also tentatively spoken of the State being 'smashed' in revolutionary circumstances, although this does not exactly gel with the idea of 'withering'. After Marx's death, Engels was less certain about the immediacy of the withering process. In 1891, for example, he argued that the victorious proletariat could not avoid 'at once paring down the worst aspects of the State, until a new generation grown up in new, free social conditions is capable of putting aside the whole paraphernalia of the State' (for references see Buber, 1949, pp. 101–3). As Martin Buber remarks on this whole process, 'Not only is it no longer the case that the proletariat will abolish the State as State with the nationalisation of the means of production, but also it will, to begin with and right up to the coming of age of the "new generation", merely "pare down" the worst aspect of the State' (1949, p. 102). The problem here is that neither Marx nor Engels had any uniform idea on either what exactly they were abolishing or how any future society would be structured. Lenin's later attempts to attach 'abolition' to the bourgeois State and 'withering' to the proletarian State seems to be simple equivocation, as equivocal as Marx's own distinction between the transitional phases of socialism and communism. Possibly the nearest Marx comes to some kind of formulation about what this future society will look like is his statements on the 1871 Paris Commune in the *Civil War in France*, although this is sometimes contested. Marx, in this work, envisaged the abandonment of a central executive, judiciary and legislature. He also wanted the abolition of the police, army and the like and their functions to be taken on by administrative units elected regularly by decentralized communes. There would also have been little or no pay differentials. The people would form their own militia and co-operative economic framework. In the end this is not a great deal different from Proudhonian federalist anarchism, which was more than likely behind many of the commune ideas in 1871.

There are many problems with the class theory of the State which seem to be insoluble. A lot of these derive from the fact that Marx and Engels did not completely resolve their philosophical concerns with their later emphasis on science and political economy. Many of the comments that Marx specifically makes on the State are intellectually incisive, but they appear randomly and haphazardly, not in any systematic theory. On the Continent, against the Prussian background, Marx showed a definite early interest in the State. On coming to Britain – a political culture which did not invest much time in considering the State – Marx's major systematic works by and large reflect this lack of interest. It is the science of political economy which predominates. Any notion of the State is intepreted through antecedent causes. It is the functions the State performs in the class struggle which are all-important, not the institution itself. Whether from fear of appearing as a Utopian thinker or as a bourgeois theoretician, Marx never constructed a positive normative theory of public power. The State is reduced, in the majority of Marxist writings, to social biography or unspecified objective structures. There is little way of answering a claim that the State functions in the interest of the ruling class or even as a site for class struggle. It is as irrefutable as the 'vulgar Freudian [claim] of a person's actions always being the result of sexual drive, both when he yields to it and when he resists it. Damned if he does and damned if he doesn't' (Jasay, 1985, p. 55).

Marx only touches upon certain issues in his early writings which do seem to be crucial to the State. The State did develop as a response to disorder. It tried to act for harmony, civilization and humanization against a backdrop of civil strife. In this context the State did act, and has acted quite often, as a civilizing influence, shaping, informing and permeating human life with the values of civility. The core to concepts such as civilization, civility, civil, civic and citizen is *cives* (an ordered life in a city). Constitutional States have been engaged in a complex dialectic with the development of both plural group activity and the demand for individual subjective rights. The subtle discussions on individual rights and the tortuous development of civil society and its values is glossed over by Marx. Marx, in scorning individual subjective rights, in ignoring the value of plural group activity (except as manifest in classes), impoverishes the concept of social existence. In fact, if his early comments on participatory democracy or his later remarks on the Paris Commune are anything to go by, Marx regresses in terms of social theory. His values are those of the integrated community, the total life of the Greek *polis*, which has not recognized the significance or importance of subjectivity or individuality. For Marx, subjectivity, individuality and civil society become irksome characteristics of a type of economy which must be superseded. Yet we cannot simply forget subjectivity, it is part of our very existence and the way in which we conceive ourselves. Marx might reply here that it is the bourgeois conception of the individual that he is criticizing. This may be true, to an extent, but if he wished posterity to take him seriously he should have articulated his own 'non-bourgeois' concept of the individual. Marx, however, does not do this and all we are left with is his communal critique of individualism.

The realization of this somewhat regressive, anachronistic quality to Marx's communism and the slightly bizarre and arid aspect to the purely instrumental view of the State, has led many Marxists this century to try to come to terms with the State and individualism. The very attempt by Marxists to do this has led to equally unacceptable solutions. As has recently been pointed out, the cruder instrumental theory makes 'intellectually more exacting Marxists wince. . . . Yet the concept of an autonomous State, a State with a will of its own which keeps surfacing in Marx's early political writings, is even less acceptable; to elevate the State to the rank of a *subject* is revisionism, Hegelian idealism, fetishism' (Jasay, 1985, p. 50). The class theory of the State is, and will remain, caught in this cleft stick. Perhaps its very ambivalence is the source of its popularity.

6

The Pluralist Theory of the State

INTRODUCTION

The term pluralism has a number of connotations in contemporary thought, especially when applied to the State. It is important to gain some clarity of focus before moving on to more substantive pluralist views. There are a number of senses in which we use the term pluralism, some of which overlap with the notion of pluralism employed in the present chapter and some of which do not. These senses will be distinguished as philosophical, ethical, cultural and political.

Philosophical pluralism usually denotes the acceptance of diverse theories of knowledge or frames for understanding the world. Possibly a more precise usage would be epistemological pluralism. This is often closely linked to philosophical scepticism and relativism. In the earlier part of this century, however, philosophical pluralism was associated closely with the pragmatist school. The foremost exponents of pragmatism were William James and John Dewey. In Britain its major protagonist was F. C. S. Schiller. Pluralism in this school was not equivalent to relativism. The pragmatists were concerned with the *application* of ideas. Deliberation was a search for a way to act. Humans do not stand back and spectate. Ideas are our plans of actions. Humans were seen as actors informed by reason. Pragmatists thus argued that knowledge was not fixed but open to perpetual critical change. There was thus no absolute monistic solution to problems; there was no final certainty. All beliefs were open to experiential test and criticism, even ideas which had worked for a time. We could thus be said to live not in a universe but a 'multiverse'. This is the theme behind William James's book *The Pluralistic Universe*. Such a continually open spirit was not sceptical or despairing, it rather implied a continual critical process in the community. A pragmatic community would encapsulate a process of rational enquiry. For pragmatists such as James and Dewey this pluralistic 'action-orientated' view of ideas was contrasted with monistic speculative idealism. A lot of critical energy was directed at idealists such as Hegel and F. H. Bradley. Although this chapter will not be utilising the pragmatist school, none the less many of the key figures to be discussed here, for example J. N. Figgis and H. J. Laski, were aware of, and in some cases claimed to be influenced by, the pragmatists such as James (see Laski, 1925, p. 261). Equally, many of the American political pluralists claimed some ancestry in pragmatism.

Ethical pluralism is akin to philosophical pluralism. In a simplistic sense, ethical pluralism is the recognition of a diversity of ethical goals or ends pursued by individuals or groups. It is often allied to a more sociological or anthropological understanding. The term which is most often used here is cultural pluralism. Cultural pluralism would be the recognition of diverse social practices and customs in different ethnic groups, even within a State. In current jargon, States possessing diverse ethnic groups can be referred to as 'plural societies'. Like ethical pluralism, cultural pluralism, or the notion of a plural society, can be used in a purely descriptive sense, characterizing what is actually the case in certain States. These terms can also be used normatively; namely, that it is desirable or morally preferable that we should live in a plural society and tolerate each others' customs and mores, although this carries its own series of problems with it.

It is important, however, to insist that the pluralism of the present chapter has very little to do with ethical or cultural pluralism. Political pluralists were not advocates of a plural society in the above sense. Many, like Figgis, would have been shocked at such a suggestion. The ideas that will be dealt in the present account were being worked out by theorists in the Victorian and Edwardian eras. The idea of cultural diversity was not such a strong notion at the time, although it was admittedly gaining ground. Behind the pluralism of the present chapter is the idea of basic normative consensus. Certain basic moral premises were assumed to be present. Figgis's own preoccupation with consensus was premised on Christian morality. Individuals were made in the image of God and should be allowed the freedom to make responsible decisions. Figgis, however, was not very optimistic on the future of such assumptions and consensus. With hindsight, it is tempting to see this as a weakness in the pluralist position. There is a sense in which the concept of pluralism, developed at that time, only really worked if there was a background consensus of beliefs between groups. Certain types of behaviour were not permitted, specifically if it caused harm to other groups or individuals. Yet, as Figgis was aware, such a consensus would not necessarily last. In fact, the very existence of group pluralism tended to undermine the effectiveness of such a consensus.

The form of pluralism that will be under discussion is political pluralism. In Figgis's and Laski's terms, it was a different creature to ethical pluralism. On a formal level, political pluralism is a theory which views social life in terms of groups. The primary social entities are groups and they are not created by or even ultimately reliant upon any central authority. Pluralists, as one writer has put it, claim to follow 'the natural lines of authority in the social order' (Hocking, 1968, p. 88). The individual's primary allegiance is not to any abstract government but rather to groups, whether they be trade unions, churches or local clubs. In consequence they deny the absolute necessity of a highly unified legal or political order. Thus, in any social order 'loose-endedness is possible . . . and even desirable' (Sabine, 1923, p. 39). This line of reasoning led many pluralists into a critical stance on traditional ideas of sovereignty and the State. The Hegelian theory of the State, although misunderstood by most pluralists, was identified as an example of what they called the 'monistic State'. This gave rise to a natural affinity with the American philosophical pragmatists, who were equally critical of monism on metaphysical and epistemological grounds. It is important, though, to be clear at the start that not all pluralists rejected the idea of the State. Some reformulated the theory of the State to tie in with their ideas on groups.

One of the major problems in dealing with political pluralism, in both theory and practice, is that the term is used in both a descriptive and normative sense. Secondly, there is no unified or systematic body of pluralistic theory. The investigator is faced with a number of different types of political pluralism, some of which will again have to be ruled out in the present discussion. The descriptive sense of the term applies to the case of the American pluralists. A number of political scientists, beginning with figures such as A. F. Bentley, saw pluralism as a description of the American political system. In this usage, pluralism moves into the area of interest group and pressure group theory. On the other hand, English pluralism, associated with J. N. Figgis, F. W. Maitland and H. J. Laski, was overtly normative. It did not conceive of its function as being that of social scientific description; although there are undoubtedly some more empirical and descriptive elements in their theories. This point moves us into the discussion of types of political pluralism. Apart from American pluralism, associated specifically with political science, and English pluralism (which admittedly was very dependent on the ideas of the German theorist Otto von Gierke), there were a number of other examples. In Britain there were the guild socialists and distributivists; in France, specifically, the syndicalists and anarcho-syndicalists. The European-wide movement of anarchism, specifically the ideas of Proudhon and Kropotkin, also had a strong pluralistic character, although individualist anarchists such as Max Stirner would not fit into this category.[1]

These very diverse strands of theory do not constitute a school but rather a tendency in political thought. The uniting feature of this tendency lies in their critical response to the growth of the State in the nineteenth and twentieth centuries. Increasingly the State, in many European countries, had been taking over more spheres of activity. This often entailed a dominant and critical attitude towards groups within and sometimes beyond territorial boundaries. At various points churches, trade unions and the like came under pressure. Pluralists, amongst others, felt that such activity was an incursion into fundamental freedoms and an abrogation of excessive power by central authorities. Quite often the State was in fact incapable of maintaining such intervention and authority over groups. If there was one primary empirical fact that Figgis and Laski wanted recognized it was the existence of groups. Figgis remarked that 'in regard to the immigration law in South Africa, it was admitted that the Imperial Parliament dare not override the will of the local bodies even though they were doing a manifest injustice to their fellow subjects' (1914, pp. 84–5). Laski was also fond of citing the example of the lack of Parliamentary control of Ulster in 1914 or the resistance to the 1916 Military Service Act by conscientious objectors (1919, p. 45). Both Figgis and Laski drew attention also to Bismark's inability to control the Roman Catholic Church (see Figgis, 1914, pp. 29–30; Laski, 1919, pp. 45–6).

Groups were thus resisting the growth of the State and public power by defending their rights and freedoms. Some, like the communist anarchists and syndicalists, admittedly wished to do away with the State completely. Syndicalism, as one writer put it, 'amounts to a feudal anarchy among contending occupational groups and rejects the state entirely' (Elliott, 1928, p. 100). This has given rise to the judgement that syndicalism was the most thoroughgoing pluralism. A lot depends here on what is meant by pluralism. In fact a number of ideological traditions, including classical liberalism and Marxism, shared some suspicion of the State. The central question for many of these was: could the State really represent a common good in anything except the most minimal sense?[2] Pluralists also shared with some of these other ideological traditions a mistrust of representative democracy. Geographically based representative democracy did not fully represent interests. It gave *carte blanche* to the public authorities to perform actions, supposedly in the national interest or common good. Most often an electorate would not know what they were voting for and the result was a slim majority of those who voted, which in reality was a minority of the population. Many English pluralists wanted democracy to be adapted to functional groups in addition to geographical location.

This opposition to the centrally constituted authority was a theme which many English pluralists traced back to the middle ages, specifically to the fifteenth-century conciliarist movement in the Catholic Church and secondly to the medieval Guild system. The middle ages represented a time of dispersal and diffusion of power. The medievalist Walter Ullman called this the 'ascending thesis' of government. Pressure moved upward rather than downward for specific policies. The conciliarists were often taken as an apt example. Figgis remarked that 'The conciliar movement, more especially as it flowers in the Whiggism of Gerson and the constructive federalism of Nicholas of Cues . . . is a definite assertion within the Church of the needs of a balanced constitution' (1914, p. 146). The conciliarists aimed at the dispersal of power to the church as a whole. The failure of the conciliar movement was regarded by Figgis as a tragedy which had repercussions on subsequent European thought. The victory of papal absolutism over conciliarism led ultimately to the triumph of secular absolute sovereignty and its domination of Europe until the seventeenth century (see Figgis, 1914, p. 150). For Figgis, ultramontanism was a precise equivalent to the secular absolutist notion of the State.

Medieval Guilds were also praised, not only by pluralists such as Figgis, but also by anarchists like Kropotkin and guild socialists like A. J. Penty. The early medieval Guilds were basically 'mutual support groups' which provided aid and insurance, specifically for merchants and craftsmen. The first Guilds developed in the eleventh century in Italy, the Rhineland and the Low Countries and consequently spread throughout Europe, although their origin is still a matter of scholarly debate (see Black, 1984). They varied in size and status, although they usually monopolized a particular craft. They laid down who was to practice a particular trade, and the quality, quantity and price of the goods produced. It was in this context that they formed a hierarchy of masters and apprentices. Guilds provided the basic elements of communal and industrial life in the middle ages. Many nineteenth-and twentieth-century pluralists tended to admire the Guilds partly because they were self-regulating, self-reliant organizations which had been created voluntarily by individuals for a specific function in society. Individuals' needs for work, fellowship and welfare were met within the confines of these groups. They functioned perfectly adequately without the existence of any free market capitalism. They also pre-dated and needed no ratification from any central authority. This probably partially explains why medieval lawyers and scholastics, trained in Roman law, simply refused to look at Guilds. As Anthony Black has pointed out, the pre-eminent fact about Guilds in the context of medieval legal and philosophical thought, is that 'the silence is deafening' (1984, p. 29). If you premise a theory of law on the idea of a sovereign *Imperium* and then go on to deduce all law and societal life out of it, it becomes increasingly difficult to speak sensibly of self-regulating groups which pre-date any centralized authority. In fact the idea of Guilds makes nonsense of such *Imperium*.

The general question, however, remains. What were pluralists suggesting about social existence? Essentially, in the case of the English pluralists, they were reacting to two streams of thought: on the one hand, atomic individualism, which was most closely identified with classical liberalism; and, on the other, monistic Statism, which many pluralists associated with writers such as Bodin, Hobbes, Austin and Hegel. Individualism and monistic Statism in fact were seen as two sides of the same coin. The monistic Statist preferred the notion of separate individuals since they were easier to control. It was groups that resisted. On the other hand, a society constituted by atomized individuals is more easily coerced into a free market order. Ultimately, the imposition of such an order will lead paradoxically to a monistically powerful State.

Humans, for pluralists, were neither isolated atoms, nor were they creatures of centralized States. They were social creatures who worked in groups largely of their own choise. This is the major premise of much pluralist argument. As Otto von Gierke argued, 'What man is, he owes to the association of man with man' (quoted in Lewis, 1935, p. 113). Individuals naturally cohere into groups. These groups, as in the medieval Guilds, were seen to have a life of their own which should be recognized and respected. Their legal and social status should not be a matter of choice by the governing authority. As Figgis argued, the crucial questions for the pluralist are: 'is the life of society ... inherent or derived?'; and as he continues on his particular theme on the Anglican Church (understood as a group): 'Does the church exist by some inward living force, with powers of self-development like a person; or is she a mere aggregate, a fortuitous concourse of ecclesiastical atoms?' (1914, p. 40). The notion of the group also cannot be accounted for simply in terms of the individuals who comprise it. This point is not profoundly significant for all pluralists. However for many, such as Gierke, Figgis and Laski, it was important to stress the independent legal personality of groups. They were real legal persons. They were not simply aggregates of individuals. They had a kind of will and purpose of their own. Most English pluralists also argued that there must be some way of both recognizing groups and adjudicating between them. This point is crucial for their theory of the State.

It was also recognized that individuals naturally would belong to many different groups, often with cross-cutting and conflicting interests and loyalties. It was also part of the maximization of liberty that individuals would have to face multiple choices and commitments. Society is, of necessity, an arena of conflicting loyalties. This process intensifies as societies become more industrialized, affluent and experience increasing divisions of labour. All interests for the pluralists are seemingly worthwhile and deserving of respect, although this argument has several attendant problems which will be examined later. The pluralist society thus claims to respect and reconcile the diverse interests of human beings without thwarting them. Groups would communicate via negotiation, not delegation from some higher authority. Central government would not be a *primus inter pares* or a dominating sovereign authority. Social life is far too complex for such a simple monistic solution. Rather the government would be involved in a process of bargaining and negotiation. This, of course, makes the pluralist case look a lot simpler than it actually is. In fact pluralists varied and were at times extremely ambivalent on the idea of central authority, as one might expect. The pluralists wanted to bring together maximal diffusion of power with some notion of centralized control. Such ideas are not easy to present.

This particular point raises a number of difficulties. It is tempting, after a brief acquaintance with pluralism, to conclude that it could *not* have a theory of the State at all, partly because it is premised on a negative appraisal of the State. As opposed to the Spencerian 'The Man versus The State', pluralists, it can be argued, proposed 'The Group versus The State'. In this view pluralism provides an *alternative* to rule by the State. This is certainly the case for syndicalists and communist anarchists. However, this would be totally wrong as regards the English pluralists. For these latter theorists the group was not a substitute for the State but was integral to it.

One of the key articles which caught the mood of the pluralists just before the First World War was entitled 'The Discredited State' (Barker, 1915a; see also Elliott, 1928, p. 102; Wright, 1979, p. 32). The major theme of the article, which was written largely from a pluralist perspective, was that the traditional monistic sovereign State had been discredited. 'The English State,' Barker argued, 'is . . . accustomed to discredit' (1915a, p. 106). The feudal barons – in constructing the Magna Charta, acting, as Barker says, as good syndicalists – virtually legalized rebellion, making the king's authority a contractual thing. From 1688, Lockeans and exponents of natural rights, specifically rights to property, marked out spheres of activity for the State and civil society. Governing was made a trust and based on consent. Non-conformity, and what Barker calls 'congregationalism', marked out further spheres of private conscience and worship. These movements provided a historical discredit to any centralized notion of the State. Thus, despite the actual growth of the State and the defence of its *Majestas* from Hobbes to Austin, a massive sub-life of groups, Churches, trade unions, had gone on growing, although in English law they were usually seen as trusts. As Barker remarked, 'England is not unlike the University of Oxford – or for that matter any other amoeba. She can throw off by a ready process of fission colleges and delegacies' (1915a, p. 108). These historical movements, coupled with the rich sub-life of groups, had thus brought the State (understood as a monistic sovereign entity) into discredit. Barker concludes that there is nothing to worry about here. A discredited State means, in Barker's terms, that it is working well. No State can be a simple unitary order. It is always a complex multiple entity. It is important to realize here that it is the more absolutist vision of the State which is being discredited not the State *per se*. Barker's State, as it was for most pluralist writers, was a different entity which tried to incorporate and theorize maximal diversity of group life. The difficulties arose in actually giving a theoretical account of such an entity.

In this chapter the English pluralists will be differentiated from other cognate groups. Communist anarchists and syndicalists are not being discussed for the reasons outlined earlier. Pluralism, in the present discussion, is taken to apply to the English pluralists. The key formal elements of the English pluralist vision of the State will then be discussed under the following headings: (1) the centrality of the idea of liberty existing in group life; (2) the critique of monistic sovereignty and the proposals for devolving authority and power; and (3) the concept of the real personality of groups. Finally, these elements will be drawn together to give an overview of the pluralist theory of the State.[3]

VARIATIONS ON A PLURALISTIC THEME

This chapter will deal with those pluralist theorists who could be deemed to have had a normative theory of the State. It is therefore necessary to differentiate them from other schools within pluralism which did not. The main elements of pluralism which tried to theorise a notion of the State are firstly, those in England influenced by the writings of Gierke, namely J. N. Figgis, F. W. Maitland and the young H. J. Laski; secondly, the writings of some of the guild socialists, specifically S. G. Hobson and G. D. H. Cole.

Sociologists had developed more empirical interests in group behaviour in the latter part of the nineteenth and the early twentieth century. Emile Durkheim's *The Division of Labour in Society*, Max Weber's *The Theory of Social and Economic Organisation* and Pareto's *Mind and Society* were all devoted to the empirical social scientific study of the structure and behaviour of groups. In the USA this became the major preoccupation of political scientists, beginning in the early 1900s and reaching its height in the 1950s with writers such as David Truman (see Latham, 1965). One of the early American pluralists, A. F. Bentley, was concerned to direct our attention away from legal and institutional studies towards the behaviour of groups. The political arena was composed of a diverse range of groups all articulating interests, and putting pressure on government. The distincton between types of government was based largely on the way interests were articulated, accomodated and adjusted. All groups were seen as interested in striking some kind of bargain. The government was not there to seek some abstract national interest. The national interest, in a minimal sense, is the final bargain struck between interests in the policy sphere. Policy is the outcome of group pressures. As Latham comments, 'The legislature referees the group struggle, ratifies the victories of the successful coalition.' Public policy is thus 'the equilibrium reached in this struggle at any given moment' (1965, p. 36). Today's loser, it is blithely assumed, will be tomorrow's winner.

Most American pluralists of this ilk assume that the contest between groups will be fair and that there is some kind of lurking normative consensus in the background. Certain types of behaviour are presumably un-American. Practical politics, therefore, for the American pluralist is about bargaining, compromise and trade-offs. There is no normative appraisal of the State, but rather an explanation and partially a justification of what they take to be actually the case in the political processes of the USA. Government is not an impartial umpire. It reflects the dominant coalition on a particular policy – although it will try to maintain some balance. As F. D. Roosevelt remarked, 'The science of politics, indeed, may properly be said to be in large part the science of the adjustment of conflicting group interests' (quoted in Nicholls, 1974, p. 2). This aim is contrary to that of the English pluralists, who would have been deeply critical of the idea that the State becomes a focal point for group pressure, also that policy should emanate from dominant coalitions of groups via the State apparatus. Individuals, in English pluralism, pursue their goals within groups. The State should not be linked to any such partial interests. Each of these groups is recognized as a moral person with a legal status. In American pluralism a group is simply a collection or aggregation of individuals acting in specific roles. Most significantly the American pluralists were not concerned with any normative account of the State as an institution or practice. They were far more interested in examining, empirically, the effects of group pressures on the actual activity of government. Consequently they will not figure in the present discussion.

One of the primary influences on the English political pluralists was Otto von Gierke. Gierke in his massive work *Das Deutsche Genossenschaftsrecht* (a study which he in fact never completed), stressed the social character of humans. Individuals subsist and develop in groups. The associated group is a living whole not a fiction or artifice of the State. Groups are entities with a will and purpose of their own. They also create their own rules and laws. Gierke stressed this latter point. In 1888, German lawyers were drafting a new civil law code. Gierke, like his teacher at Berlin, G. Beseler, wanted the code to reflect old Germanic law, the time-honoured customs of the German *Mark* and *Gemeinde*, feudal records, town charters, guild rules and so on. In effect he wanted a German common law to be recognized. The subject of Gierke's and Beseler's anger was the tradition of Roman law which seemed to be behind the design of the new law code. The patron saint of such Romanism in Germany was the jurist F. C. von Savigny. Law in Romanist terms was the immediate emanation of the sovereign *Imperium*. Lawyers, influenced by Roman law, drew a distinction between private law, which dealt with atomized individuals, and public law, which tended to exalt the State and centralized authority. This argument took no cognisance either of pre-existing customs or established practices. It also ignored the nature of groups. Groups, for example, were viewed either as simple contractual entities between a body of individuals (*societas*) or public law concessions from the State (*universitas*). Gierke, looking at German law and social organization, saw a fundamental conflict between two principles which he called *Herrschaft* and *Genossenschaft*. This conflict dated back to the 800s. *Herrschaft* stressed the role of authority, lordly union and kingship, which developed 'with the help of Roman and Canon law, into State absolutism' (Lewis, 1935, p. 34). It dominated from the sixteenth century onwards. The *Genossenschaft* developed out of early clans. They were free associations or unions (*der Freie Vereinigung*) in which all rights remain with the collective whole. These free associations developed over the medieval period into Guilds and German towns.

It was Gierke's emphasis on the Germanist thesis of law, connected to the *Genossenschaft* idea, that was influential on English pluralist writers such as Figgis and Maitland. Maitland's concern was with how the legal process deals with corporations, companies and the like. Does the law treat these as simple trusts or real persons? Figgis's main interest was in the recognition of the independence of the Church (or Churches) as groups. Laski, influenced by these latter two, became interested in functional decentralization, although later in the 1920s and 1930s he moved away from pluralism to Marxism. Other writers see a difference even in Laski's early days. J. D. Lewis commented that 'In Laski . . . there is more of Rousseau and Proudhon than Gierke' (1935, p. 105).

The guild socialists integrated many of the ideas of Figgis and others. Figgis also thought that guild socialism was a form of pluralism which might be successfully practiced. They recognized the State as 'merely the final bond of a multitude of bodies, Churches, trade Unions, families, all possessing inherent life, a real thing, recognised and regulated by government' (Figgis, 1922. p. 292). The guild socialists' movement was developed in the early Edwardian era, partially as a response to Fabian socialism, which tended, in the Webbs' hands, to be highly Statist in character. It should be noted here, however, that the Webbs never consciously formulated any normative theory of the State. They viewed it largely in a negative instrumental manner. For the guild socialists, the Fabians were simply replacing free market capitalism with excessive bureaucracy (see Wright, 1979, p. 52). The guild socialists, however, were also subject to an number of internal disputes. On the one side, there was a strongly medievalist wing led by A. J. Penty, which will not be referred to in this discussion. Penty argued for small scale handicraft production on a non-machine basis. Industrialism was doomed to 'dissolution and decay' (1917, p. 9). For Penty, some of the early medieval cities contained the true ideals of socialism (1917, p. 4, see also 1906, p. 54). There was, however, little of the medieval nostalgia in G. D. H. Cole and S. G. Hobson, who advocated National Guilds. Critical of Penty's medievalism, they advocated democratic self-governing associations of workers who would be reponsible for an industry in conjunction with the State (see Reckitt and Bechhofer, 1920, p. 1). Despite disagreements with each other, Hobson and Cole attempted some form of *rapprochement* between the State and organized industry (see Wilde, 1924, p. 10). Essentially they were arguing for self-governing industries within some kind of over-arching structure. Thus 'pluralism provided Guild socialism with a political theory which could illuminate the errors of the Fabians and syndicalists alike' (Wright, 1979, p. 40).

Distributivism was closely allied to guild socialism, specifically Penty's more medievalist form. Its chief protagonist was Hilaire Belloc, whose book *The Servile State* 'contributed much to the armoury, and vocabulary . . . of those opponents of State collectivism who had their own alternatives' (Wright, 1979, p. 33). Distributivists accepted the guild arguments on production but insisted on a diffusion of property. To be free a citizen must own private property. This would be protected by co-operative Guilds. Old style capitalism was fading away. The choices facing societies were collectivism 'the placing of the means of production in the hands of political officers of the community'; the servile State, 'in which those who do not own the means of production shall be legally compelled to work for those who do, and shall receive in exchange a security of livelihood'; and finally the distributivist solution, 'in which the mass of citizens should severally own the means of production' (Belloc, 1977, pp. 41–2). Belloc, like the medievalist Penty, did not construct or offer any developed normative account of the State.

English pluralists were deeply concerned about intermediate groups, however these groups were fitted into an overall theory of the State. This draws the guild socialists (in the main) and English pluralists apart from the syndicalists and anarchists, both of whom denied any future role for the State. For Kropotkin, for example, the need was 'to reconstitute society on a libertarian and anti-state basis. Either the State will be destroyed and a new life will begin in thousands of centers . . . or else the State must crush the individual and local life' (1903, p. 44). Thus my main point of reference is English pluralism and Guild socialism.

LIBERTY AND GROUPS

> Above all, we must be willing to put liberty above other ends as a political goal, and to learn that true liberty will be found by allowing full play to the uncounted forms of the associative instinct.
>
> Figgis, *Churches in the Modern State*

There is no doubt of the crucial importance of liberty as a central value in pluralist thought.[4] It is tied to the whole theory of the State as a central value of political association. It is important to recall that a normative theory of the State is necessarily tied in with a range of values and ideals which make sense of social existence. The liberty that the pluralists insisted on was contrasted to the liberty propounded by monistic Statists, specifically those who tried to couple the notion of liberty to the ends of the unitary State. One of the cruder perceptions of idealist thought was that somehow the State defined an individual's freedom. Liberty, in this thesis, was tied to the common good as defined by the State. The pluralists argued that the ends of politics should not be ethically determined in this manner – although it should be added that the pluralists were not advocating, as stressed earlier, ethical pluralism or relativism. They laid stress on diverse goals or ends in the various groups; however, this was premised on the belief in an underlying moral consensus. Thus certain ambiguities remain in this argument which will be taken up later.

Liberty was identified with the dispersal of powers and authority to groups, which many pluralists traced back to the middle ages. The individual who gave the strongest emphasis to the dispersal of power was Acton, who had produced the memorable axiom about all power corrupting and absolute power corrupting absolutely. Acton advised his students at Cambridge that one must 'suspect power more than vice' (quoted in Nicholls, 1975, p. 28). The concentration of power meant the death of liberty. Yet the pluralists did not fall into the opposite argument of individualists such as Herbert Spencer. They did not identify freedom with the individual, specifically the rights of an individual. One of the traditional devices to maintain liberty in constitutionalist and liberal thought was to identify certain fundamental, inalienable rights with individuals. These rights became conventionally enshrined in bills of rights and constitutional documents. For most pluralists such a perspective was unacceptable and too rigid (see Hsiao, 1927, p. 41). Liberty was not primarily the result of the establishment of constitutional rights but rather the dispersal of power amongst natural groups. The individual *per se* did not possess liberty except in the context of groups. In fact it is worth noting that the pluralist notion of society was that of a complex mesh of groups *not* individuals. As one writer has remarked 'it was the contribution of the pluralists to the analysis of freedom to show that the use of the term "society" was an oversimplification which led, on the one hand, to neglect of the complicated forms of behaviour which are included in the term "society". Man's freedom is not to be gained from society, but . . . in society' (Magid. 1941, p. 91). Paradoxically, for Figgis, the origin of the dispersal of power and the consequent protection of liberty lay in religious groupings who were themselves extremely intolerant. Their competitive striving for the right to worship in their own way necessitated the development of group-based freedoms. Thus Figgis remarked with some irony that 'Political liberty is the fruit of ecclesiastical animosities' (1914, p. 101).

Figgis, in fact, added one further argument to the above points. He contended that freedom, in the Christian tradition, was incompatible with individualism. The message of the Gospels is concerned with mutual love and union, not the separate existence of atomized individuals. Christianity was bound up with a mutuality 'which is deeper than can be put into words and changes the whole personality'. For Figgis, 'We must not figure the membership of a church like a heap of pebbles which are unchanged as they lie together; rather is it a union of many diverse elements, all constantly changing and acting upon each other.' Thus, for Figgis, the very idea of pure individualism was completely foreign to the Gospels (Figgis, 1914, p. 261; 1915, pp. 53–4). Of course not all pluralists were interested in this particular Christian line of argument.

All the pluralists were agreed on one crucial point, namely that liberty could only exist in the context of a multiplicity of groups; such group cohesions characterized society. 'The great array of differentiated cohesions', as one writer put it, 'which represent in their totality the free society of modern civilisation, and from which the authority and force embodied in the State have withdrawn themselves, furnish the individual with that great variety of choice which constitutes real freedom' (Unwin, 1927, p. 458; see also Lewis, 1935, p. 27).

It is important to realize that the pluralists were not arguing that individual autonomy is impossible. They insisted that group life more effectively guaranteed the liberty and conscience of the individual. No one group could absorb all the interests of an individual. As M. P. Follett argued, 'no one group can enfold me, because of my multiple nature . . . no number of groups can enfold me' (1920, p. 295). This point ties in closely with Laski's perception of groups. Whereas Cole had argued that humans will be fulfilled in the various association of society, Laski, like Follett, maintained that no one or collection of groups could fulfil individuals (see Magid, 1941, pp. 61–2). Associations grow out of the free action of individuals. Human personality develops within such a multiple range of choice. It was thus that Gierke spoke of 'the building from below of associations which develop an independent life of their own without crushing out the independent personalities of the individuals' (quoted in Lewis, 1935, p. 27). Like individuals, groups need the freedom to develop. They are not entities which exist by virtue of any centralized authority. Freedom cannot be fought for on an individual level. There were two issues at stake here. On the one count, the individual, except in rare cases, is generally incapable of resisting any action by a centralized State (see Figgis, 1914, p. 52). Only groups can stand any chance against centralized power. They have resources which are not available to the average individual. Freedom in the future, as Figgis put it, is about 'the freedom of smaller unions to live within the whole' (1914, p. 52). On another level, even if the individual was successful in maintaining freedom in relation to centralized power, how could such freedom be maximized without group life? Self-realization and self-development cannot be simple individualistic practices. The general human condition is to live and function with others.

The above point was a central plank in pluralist theory. Human character is essentially social. Development and self-realization is something only to be gained in a corporate whole. Whatever individuals do to develop their potentialities they will rely at some point on others. Nothing can be purely individual. As Laski commented, 'The emphasis upon freedom is made because it is believed that only in such fashion can the ethical significance of personality obtain its due recognition' (1919, p. 121; see also Figgis, 1914, p. 263; Cole, 1917, p. 230). The choice will always be which group or groups will the individual develop within.

It is clear that for the pluralists the good State is one which maximizes freedom. This is a sentiment shared by other ideologies, specifically classical liberalism. However, unlike the classical liberal, pluralists argue that such freedom can *only* develop in the context of multiple semi-independent groups. As Figgis stated, 'The battle for freedom in this century is the battle of small societies to maintain their inherent life against the all-devouring Leviathan of the whole' (1913, p. 266). Pluralists thus resist what Maitland called the 'pulverising, macadamising' tendency of the State. In Ernest Barker's terms they wished the State to be discredited not destroyed.

One important ambiguity in this argument is that, in spite of the pluralist recognition of a diversity of groups and interests, the English pluralists were not ethical pluralists, as pointed out earlier. They were not willing to allow certain types of action which caused harm to other groups. For example, criminal groups would not be tolerated. Also, despite the demand for individual freedom of conscience, there was no inviolable sphere or space for the individual, no clear separation between self- and other-regarding actions. As Figgis argued, 'If the individual only comes to himself as part of a society, his conscience is always partially social. Why should not the society which has made him what he is assert an authority in the last resort coercive against him?' (1914, p. 116; see also Laski, 1919, pp. 54–5). Also in situations of war, limitations on individuals are inevitable. Thus, as David Nicholls argues, 'the pluralists acknowledged that there cannot be an absolute right to the same amount of freedom in all contexts. In a state of siege or during a war there can rarely be as much freedom as in peacetime' (1975, p. 18). The ambiguity which arises in this context is a dual pressure on the pluralist case; maximum diversity in group life does not easily link up with the idea of a normative consensus. The normative consensus allowed the pluralists to propose some form of central authority, to lay down parameters to group activity and to rule out harmful behaviour. Yet exactly how this moral consensus arises in a situation of diversity is not adequately or fully explained. Figgis's own conception of Christian moral principle was, as he was aware, inadequate.

Another important omission in the argument on liberty is any clear discussion of the nature of liberty. What is meant by liberty? The pluralists seemed to be far more precise on the question of *how* liberty is to be preserved (by dispersing power into groups), than on the actual *meaning* of the word. The two issues are, of course, not unrelated. The major problem in dealing with this question is, first, the pluralists do not form a school. They had differing interests. They were often polemical and not primarily interested in the analysis of concepts. Second, apart from Laski (and even here there are qualifications to be made), none were committed political philosophers. Consequently, it is difficult to form a consistent overall picture on liberty. Figgis, for one, was very reliant on Acton's and Mandell Creighton's Whiggish ideas. Figgis commented that for Acton 'The theory of liberty is always concerned at bottom with human character, and is based upon the belief that men should do right from proper motives than that their external actions should be correct' (1914, p. 263). In many ways this makes liberty into a more moralistic positive idea. The manner in which this liberty could be preserved was by separating powers. In this sense, as Nicholls comments, pluralism was 'an adaption to the conditions of the early twentieth century of the traditional whig distrust of power' (1975, p. 26). On the other hand, G. D. H. Cole appeared to accept the more negative thesis on liberty, but he also tended to change his view with every book he wrote. Bertrand Russell also adopted the more negative definition, although he was critical of the liberal tradition and did not want to be associated with Herbert Spencer.

Laski is as equally confusing as the above theorists. In 1919 he tried to combine a more negative idea of liberty with T. H. Green's notion of positive liberty. Laski begins by arguing that Green's idea of liberty understood as a 'positive power of doing something worth doing or enjoying' is more valuable 'than the negative conception because it insists on what, in this age, we feel to be fundamental in liberty – the power of adding something to the quality of the common life' (1919, p. 55). Laski then goes on, on the same page, to argue, with quotations from Acton, that 'the greatest truth to which history bears witness [is] that the only real security for social well-being is the free exercise of men's minds'. Individuals must have a realm 'within which the state can have no rights' (1919, p. 55). Laski appears to lay stress here on the idea of liberty as an assurance that the individual will be protected from interference. This implies a more negative usage of the concept of liberty, which is then combined with 'the emphasis upon the expression of man's creative impulses in group activities' (Deane, 1955, p. 45). Laski's basic difficulty here seems to arise 'from the fact that he is using the idealist formula after having rejected the entire substratum upon which that formula rests' (Deane, 1955, p. 45). By the 1930s, in works such as *The State in Theory and Practice*, Laski, continuing his repudiation of idealist metaphysics and liberal ideas, insists that freedom could not exist under the system of private property based capitalism. He admits that his previous pluralism did not 'sufficiently realise the nature of the state as an expression of class relations' (quoted in Deane, 1955, p. 154; see also Laski, 1935, pp. 209–11). By this period he was largely out of the pluralist fold.

The pluralist view of liberty, as Figgis admits, is 'based politically upon Burke and the great theorists of Whiggism' (1914, p. 261). Despite the conceptual ambiguities, liberty was broadly understood as giving room for individuals to make choices and develop their characters within self-governing communities. It was also closely associated, in the pluralist mind, with the dispersal of powers, specifically in doctrines such as federalism (see Mogi, 1931, p. 312). Figgis, following the lead of Gierke, saw the federal principle stretching back to the middle ages. For Gierke, the great exponent of federalism was Althusius (see Gierke, 1939; Lewis, 1935, p. 78). The liberty of pluralists was not that of what Laski called 'modern liberalism'. They rejected individualist ideas on negative liberty, despite the fact that many of their own formulations would have been acceptable to some liberal writers. Thus, despite the pluralist assertion of the central importance of liberty to their view of the State, the actual concept remains ambiguous.

THE PROBLEM OF SOVEREIGNTY

The second crucial component of the pluralist argument is the attack on centralized monistic sovereignty and the proposal for a dispersal of authority and power to groups.[5] The theory to which pluralists were reacting was the by now familiar one associated with Bodin, Hobbes, Austin and so on. Bodin was the first to employ the term systematically in European thought and it is arguable that he identified it closely to the State. Sovereignty implied a 'supreme power over citizens and subjects unrestrained by law'. It was argued by absolutists that it was essential to any commonwealth to possess such an idea. In fact, sovereignty theory was the linchpin to the whole absolutist theory. Statehood logically implied sovereignty, something that was by nature absolute, perpetual, indivisible and inalienable. The logic intrinsic to the sovereign, which was basically the sovereign of absolutism, was that *something* was supreme in any State. This something, initially a person or persons, was the source of all law and authority. If the sovereign was restrained in any way then logically it would not be sovereign. Thus the sovereign could not legally be resisted. Legal resistance was a contradiction in terms, since it would have to be legitimated by the sovereign. Thus the sovereign monarch was often referred to as the living law. As argued in an earlier chapter, Hobbes, Bodin and Austin differed in the basic components of their arguments. Bodin is specifically problematic because he so clearly integrates limitations into his understanding of sovereignty. This is also true of their attitude to groups within the State. However, Hobbes is fairly unequivocal in his view, describing groups as 'worms in the entrails' of the body politic. Groups were viewed as conglomerates of individual atoms. There was nothing distinctive about families, corporations or a commonwealth. They had no independent autonomous character as groups. Secondly, groups were artificial entities which existed only as concessions from the sovereign. They exist by reason of the sovereign will and can be discontinued at will. This follows logically from centralized sovereignty.

Despite variations and elaborations, specifically with the advance of popular sovereignty, the monistic view of sovereignty characterized much of the discussion of sovereignty though the eighteenth and nineteenth centuries. Sovereignty provided an account of the necessary cohesiveness of the State. As one scholar has argued, 'The desire for an adequate theory of sovereignty was a result of the need for some theoretical ground to justify unity. Thus the theories of sovereignty were theories of unity. The elaboration of the basis of sovereignty were indications of the existence of or need for unity. They were justifications of the State' (Magid, 1941, pp. 66–7; see also Figgis, 1914, p. 85). Writers such as Gierke and Figgis consciously identified the source of this principle of sovereignty with Roman law. The doctrines of *Imperium* and *legibus solutus* were taken on board originally by Popes. Innocent IV was not so innocent for Figgis, in fact he was extremely culpable. The doctrine of the 'plenitude of power' (*plenitudo potestatis*) was adapted by Popes such as Innocent to justify their absolutist claims. Figgis quotes Hobbes, with obvious approval, saying that in the Popes we see 'The ghost of the Roman Empire sitting crowned on its grave' (1914, p. 135). For Figgis, 'the Pope could say *L'Eglise c'est moi* with more complete truth than Louis XIV could have said it of the State' (1914, p. 150). The Renaissance set off a new phase of State autocracy, which was accelerated by civil wars in European societies, and led to a vigorous extension of

Romanist doctrine. This doctrine had continued, for the pluralists, unabated through to the twentieth century. No matter whether the State is democratic, ruled by a Pope or absolutist sovereign, if sovereignty is regarded as inalienable and indivisable, it is thereby destructive of small scale union. For Figgis, 'The great *Leviathan* of Hobbes, the *plenitudo potestatis* of the canonists, the *arcana imperii*, the sovereignty of Austin, are all names of the same thing – the unlimited and illimitable power of the lawgiver in the State' (1914, p. 79). Constitutional lawyers, such as A. V. Dicey and others, simply continued this doctrine into the twentieth century.

The question remains though: why did the pluralists reject this doctrine of sovereignty? The answer to this question is fairly complex. Primarily, the pluralists rejected the idea of *legal* sovereignty. The nub of the issue was that the State did not create law. Pluralists were neither arguing that the law is somehow superior to the State nor were they contesting the role of Parliament. What pluralists objected to was the idea that laws and rights were simply the commands of the sovereign and nothing else. As Gierke argued, in a strongly common-law and historical vein, 'it is not the individual as a human being but the individual as a member of the folk who first appears as the bearer of rights, and the folk-law is not *a* law, but *the* law' (quoted in Lewis, 1935, p. 55). Law originated in the community of groups, it was not the emanation or command of any sovereign. The State was thus bound to respect the autonomous personality of groups. The State may recognize and ratify existing law, but not create it *de novo*. As Laski argued,

> it is clear that the sovereign power is engaged on work which cannot at all reasonably be reduced to the form of a command ... no organisation disposes in actual fact of unlimited force; and we shall fail completely to understand the character of society, unless we seek to grasp exactly how the sovereign is compelled to will things desired by bodies in law inferior to itself. (1925, p. 51)

Another sense of the term which Laski and other pluralists rejected was *political* sovereignty, namely the idea that 'there must be in every social order some single centre of ultimate reference' (1925, p. 44). Such an idea Laski saw as extremely dubious and ethically indefensible. Not only was it factually false that there actually does exist a central power in every State, but there is also no need for such a head. Political studies is often unfortuately dominated by the pervasive myth of central control. Society is really a parallelogram of different forces and group interests. It has no logical requirement for a central authority as a source of law. Ernest Barker, in his 'Discredited State' article, makes similar points to Laski. Sovereignty, he contends, provides only a false sense of unification. It is not the unique property of any associations. 'At different times', Barker argues, 'different societies may claim a final allegiance. . . . No associating idea seems to engulf the whole man' (1915a, p. 117). For pluralists, political sovereignty was as much of a fiction as the isolated individual of classical liberalism. Such an idea took no account of the rich complexity of group life (Hsiao, 1927, p. 50). It also ignores the inherent rights of groups to be autonomous and consequently totally misunderstands the concept of authority (see Magid, 1941, p. 31; Deane, 1955, pp. 25–6; Laski, 1919, pp. 56–7).[6]

Another danger of legal and political sovereignty is that, in certain State theorists, it leads to claims of *moral* sovereignty, where the State is regarded as the embodiment of the common good of all its citizens. The sovereign will is the moral will. All the pluralists rejected the notion of moral sovereignty. As Nicholls points out 'It was the political and moral implications of the concept of sovereignty which led Figgis and pluralists to attack it' (1975, p. 51). Moral sovereignty implied that individuals and groups could not exercise their own independent judgement, which thus undermined their liberty. The moral life of the individual is independent of the government. Cole was the only oddity in this argument. Despite his rejection in some books of the notion of moral sovereignty, he did toy, at one point, with Rousseau's notion of the moral sovereignty in the 'General Will' (see Cole, 1917, p. 82). It is not altogether clear whether Cole was aware of the damaging effect such a notion could have on group theory.

Overall, monistic sovereignty was seen as a fictional thing which had dangerous consequences if taken seriously in political, legal or moral fields. It had arisen at a particular point in the historical development of the State, specifically in situations of civil strife. Bodin and Hobbes were writers who reflected during periods of social and political upheavel. Monistic sovereignty had a definite role to play in such situations. But for the pluralist this role was no longer necessary.

The pluralists did not necessarily advocate the total abandonment of sovereignty, but rather a radical change in its nature. It was no longer envisaged as a central monopoly of power and authority. Authority arises in the multiplicity of associations and groups. Society, by definition, was multicellular and decentralized. As one writer has put it,

Laski's pluralism 'consists in the recognition of the claim to sovereignty of other groups besides the State' (Magid, 1941, p. 54). The State still existed, although its nature needs to be examined carefully. There could be no uniform common will to be represented by a sovereign. Human will is always associated with groups. Thus pluralism saw representation as not only a one-to-one individualistic phenomenon, but also the representation of functional groups. This was the basis of their ideas for reforming democratic practices. Rousseau, amongst other thinkers, had warned against factions and partial interests in a State; but for pluralists these partial interests form the actual substance and pattern of authority in society. Thus it is clear that Rousseau's vision of popular sovereignty was at odds with the pluralistic idea of groups. Pluralists suggested the reorientation of democracy to reflect functional group interests. Territorial representation on its own, which assumed that some homogeneity existed in the geographical units and that people could be represented individually, was not enough.

In practical terms guild socialists suggested a duality of assemblies – one for industrial representation and another for political representation (see Reckitt and Bechhofer, 1920, p. 199). As Cole argued 'There is no universal sovereign in the community, because the individuals who compose that community cannot be fully represented by any form of association. For different purposes, they fall into different groups, and only in the action and interaction of these groups does sovereignty exist' (1917, p. 82). Reckitt and Bechhofer, also argue that 'The sovereignties of the Guild and the State should be equal and opposite' (1920, p. 199). Other pluralist writers adopted similar views on the dual and multiple assemblies (see Laski, 1919, pp. 88–9, 1925, pp. 336–9). Power and authority were envisaged as thus being separated into groups. This was not anarchism but, if anything, 'polyarchism' (see Barker, 1915a, p. 120).

It is, however, difficult to grasp exactly what pluralists, such as Laski and Figgis were arguing. At certain points there is a strong sense that they wished virtually to abandon all discussion of the concept of sovereignty. This might have been the wisest move. The implication was that it was too tainted with legal positivism and monistic ideas to be of any use. Yet, there is also another aspect of their argument which concentrates on the decentralization of power and authority to groups. This decentralization is closely connected with the recognition of the legal personality of groups. At times, pluralists seem to be speaking of the decentralization of sovereignty. Laski, for example, argued that 'Sovereignty, in fact, has necessarily to be distributed in order that the purposes of men may be achieved'

(1919, p. 177). Each group is presumably seen to have its own independent legal status. Sovereignty is therefore not abandoned but pluralized. The major problem with this latter argument is that it makes the concept of sovereignty look vacuous. Sovereignty implies supremacy. How can a whole series of divided group interests be equally supreme? Surely such an idea is nonsensical? On the other hand, the argument on plural sovereignty is no more nonsensical than claims for popular sovereignty. Is it any more reasonable to claim that *all* the people are sovereign than a series of groups?

Some critics have also argued that pluralists do not really effectively expunge even the centralized notion of sovereignty from their theories. One critic accused them of smuggling it in through the back door (Hsiao, 1927, pp. 136–7). In fact Hsiao goes on to describe the pluralists, paradoxically, as being more monistic than the monists. Admittedly, Figgis had spoken of an entity called the 'society of societies'; Gierke had openly discussed the necessity of a sovereign State; Cole argued for the supremacy of a supreme court and later a national commune and so on; all of these exist to *resolve* differences between groups. Pluralists also often tend to treat the State in a narrow political sense, just in relation to government, consequently their notion of sovereignty is very narrow. However, Hsiao goes too far in his criticism. The pluralist notion of the State does have some marked differences from the monistic account. This point will be discussed in the penultimate section. In spite of their vigorous attack on the monistic sovereign State, however, it is not always clear that the pluralists actually succeeded in diversifying authority and power. The authority is rather pushed to a higher level of abstraction where it still carries out the task of reconciling conflicts in society. Nevertheless, most pluralists would still question how far this authority could determine the nature or autonomy of groups.

REAL PERSONALITY AND GROUPS

'Arms-drill as it should be done,' someone said, 'is beautiful, especially when the company feels itself as a single-being, and each movement is not synchronized movement of every man together, but the single movement of one large creature.'

Graves, *Goodbye to All That*

The pluralist arguments on liberty and sovereignty were tied integrally to their theory of group personality. The recognition of the actual existence of the real personality of groups entailed that in these groups authority and liberty would be respected. Pluralist theory is strongly contrasted to the claims of methodological individualism. For pluralists, individuals only subsist in groups — groups which are regarded as real persons. This real personality and life of groups is thus integral to the very existence of liberty and individuality. As Figgis stated, 'to deny this real life is to be false to the facts of social existence, and is of the same nature as that denial of human personality which we call slavery' (1914, p. 42; see also Laski, 1919, p. 121).

The origins of the pluralist idea of real personality lie in the writings of Gierke who correctly traced many of the ideas back to Roman law. Roman Law, particularly from the *Corpus Iuris*, had a conception of groups; however, they were looked upon as aggregates of individuals or concessions from the central authority. Gierke saw this doctrine in the Canonists, Glossators and post-Glossators. Groups were regarded as fictional entities. As argued earlier, Popes such as Innocent IV were seen specifically at fault in propounding this idea. In Germany F. C. von Savigny had systematized these Roman law ideas. Savigny premised his ideas on individualism. The individual is the only juridical entity, the only subject of rights and duties. Personality must coincide with this individual. A group person must therefore be a fiction. One implication of this idea is that the group, in law, is incapable of tort or *mens rea*. Its scope is defined by the State, outside this it is *ultra vires*. For pluralists, all the writers expounding on legal and political sovereignty tended towards the Romanist perspective. For the Romanist, the majority of groups were created by a central authority. They were viewed as offshoots from this sovereign authority, at least in juridical terms. Either they have been created or ratified by the sovereign body or they exist because the sovereign allows it. The demand for juridical consistency in the growth of the State often led to the mistrust of large groups within the body politic. This is a view to be found in such thinkers as Hobbes, Rousseau and Bentham.

The opposition to this movement in Germany was led by Gierke and his teacher Beseler. They contrasted themselves as either realists or Germanists against the Romanists. As argued earlier, Gierke championed the claim of the old Germanic idea of fellowship and group life. He maintained that for Romanists social life was viewed through the dominant State or the isolated individual. There was nothing between. In reality, *de facto*, groups existed as intermediate bodies. These corporate bodies had in fact existed 'time-out-of-mind'.

There was some consciousness of them in fourteenth-century legal theory, specifically in medieval towns. Yet, generally, the scholastic and legal theorists ignored them; although it might be argued that Gierke and other pluralists over emphasized this point.[7] Groups were not the offspring of legislation. If they were actually legally incorporated, it must be remembered that the juridical act of incorporation is not *constitutive* but *declaratory*. This keeps distinct the power, reality and pre-existence of groups from the legal statute. Groups and their rules are real factors in the juridical order of society.

The way British law has coped, and largely still does, with groups is through the doctrine of trusts, which neither recognizes the personality of groups nor views them as simple concessions in the fictional sense. For trust theory, a group originates in a contract which creates the rules and articles of association. If property is involved, the members are viewed as trustees. The property itself should only be used in terms of the purposes and rules of association. As Maitland commented on this, 'The device of building a wall of trustees enabled us to construct bodies which were not technically corporations and which yet would be sufficiently protected from the assaults of individualistic theory. The personality of such bodies — so I shall put it — though explicitly denied by lawyers was on the whole pretty well recognised in practice' (1911, pp. 166–7).

The major problem of trusts arises with unincorporated bodies, specifically non-profit making concerns. The central question at issue here is: should a court be able to determine the internal rules of such bodies? In the case of say a Church, should the court be able to rule on doctrine through the idea of trusts. This example may not seem immediately relevant, especially to the issue of property. Yet the major case to stir the English pluralists into a frenzy of polemics was bound up with such an issue. In the so-called Free Church of Scotland Appeals, a property dispute between two factions of a Church was tied inextricably to Church doctrine. A strong majority group in the Free Church of Scotland wanted to promote union with the United Presbyterians. This union was carried through but was resisted by a vociferous minority called the 'Wee Frees'. They declared that the amalgamation went beyond the original trust terms of the Church and was thus *ultra vires*. They asserted that the original Calvinistic doctrine was being abandoned and that the new union had given up the idea of Establishment. Ultimately the case went to the House of Lords and the Wee Frees won. The act of union of the larger body was declared *ultra vires*. The property of the Free Church thus belonged, in terms of the trust, to the Wee Frees minority.

Without entering into the subsequent tortured history of the Free Church case, the pluralists took this as a key example of the lunacy and bankruptcy of the idea of trusts, specifically when it tried to deal with unincorporated bodies. Property would not necessarily be unrelated to the very constitutive doctrines or beliefs of a group. If a special Act of Parliament had not been passed to apportion the property of the Free Church fairly, the majority section would have been totally dispossessed, simply because certain theological beliefs did not fit in with the trust. As Figgis commented, 'on the one hand the judgment denies to a Free Church the power of defining and developing in its own doctrine; and on the other, while disclaiming interference in theological matters, it practically exercises it under the plea of considering the question whether or no the trust had been violated' (1914, p. 22). If instead of trusts the real personality of the church had been recognized then 'the question as to whether or no the new theology . . . was in agreement with that of the old Free Kirk would have become one of fact, not of law, and in that case the overwhelming majority in favour of the union would probably have been sufficient evidence' (1914, p. 22).

The question remains here though: what did the pluralists mean by real personality? We have encountered arguments on the personality of associations in earlier chapters, specifically on absolutism. There is a natural sense of suspicion in the idea that we should regard groups as persons, although even in recent academic writings one can find the idea being used.[8] The suspicion arises from one particular contemporary sense of a person. The shorthand idea of a person is that it refers to a thinking, intelligent being, capable of reason and self-reflection and instantiated in a single body. This is very close to the first and later standard medieval usage from Boethius – *Persona est naturae rationabilis individua substantia* (the individual subsistence of a rational nature). A series of ideas is now attached to this meaning. A person can make choices, is self-conscious, aware of a sense of past, present and future, possesses certain values, interests and purposes which are consciously pursued, can cite intelligible reasons for their actions and consider themselves responsible and free. Some might add to this the ability to formulate thought and language. Such a complex idea is, however, central to much of our moral and religious discourse in the West. The idea that such a concept could be applied to groups seems monstrous.

There are, though, a number of points to take on board when considering the idea of personality. The word derives from the Latin term *persona*, which initially was the mask worn by actors in Rome. It came to refer to both the actor and the part or role played. It was thus easily adaptable for use in legal transaction. The word 'party' is equivalent in some of its uses. It did not refer to the human being or any inner qualities. It was not a way of differentiating humans from animals, rather it referred to the roles being played. This explains, partially, the use of the term by early Christian fathers in relation to the Trinitarian God; three persons did not necessarily mean three separate people. Another fact to bear in mind is that earlier civilizations did not have any real concept of the individual person, which is now a norm in our own cultural discourse. This is not just the point that primitive groups gave priority to the community. As one recent historian has argued,

> The student of the Greek Fathers or of Hellenistic philosophy is likely to be made painfully aware of the difference between their starting point and ours. Our difficulty in understanding them is largely due to the fact that they had no equivalent to our concept 'person', while their vocabulary was rich in words which express community of being. . . . Western individualism is therefore far from expressing the common experience of humanity. Taking a world view, one might regard it as an eccentricity among cultures. (Morris, 1972, p. 2)

In contemporary discussion of the concept of persons, it is also far from clear that it necessarily even relates specifically to humans. If a person is identifable by certain qualities – the ability to form purposes, make choices, communicate and so on – then it can be argued that certain animals must be included under the rubric 'person' and certain humans (the mentally insane, young children), must be ruled out. Peter Singer has coined the phrase 'non-human persons' to cover the case of animals (1979, pp. 93ff). It is therefore the case that a person is not necessarily identical with a single physical human centre. It also may not apply to humans at all. Person indicates certain qualities which are in no way tangible or synonymous with finite physical units of experience.

Against this background it should not be too far-fetched to see the notion of personality being attached to collective entities – groups – partly because they possess many attributes or qualities associated with individuals and also because they play certain roles or parts. Most pluralists recognized that there were different senses of the concept of a person; Ernest Barker saw three. The pyschological implied the power or capacity of self-consciousness; the ethical indicated that the individual was self-conscious and self-determining according to certain principles. Finally, legal personality stressed a power or capacity for legal action and the possession of certain rights and duties (Barker, 1934). A juristic person must be capable of acting as a whole in furtherance of an interest in law and must also have a unifying intelligent purpose, which makes its actions intelligible in law. It is important to remember that even if one wished to limit the use of the term juristic person to individual human beings, this still, under various legal systems, would rule out certain categories of human being who would not count as juristic persons. Under Roman law, women did not count as juristic persons. Under contemporary British law, the human foetus and the Downs syndrome child do not appear to count in the same way as mature adults.

This juristic person might still be regarded as a fiction or artifice of law, even on an individual level. The pluralists argued, however, that the juristic person is *not* a simple artifice. It is a natural entity with a real personality which should be confirmed in law. A group grows naturally from a permanent end being pursued by a number of individuals (see Figgis, 1914, p. 42). Such groups mould individual lives. They were seen to have a principle of growth within them, similar to an organism (see Magid, 1941, p. 12). Corporate groups could also be said to have an independent will in pursuing a particular purpose which united their several members. The purpose is not something conferred by a higher authority. The group is a unified agency with a definite purpose and capability for action. Its reality may not be immediately perceived, but as Gierke remarked, 'The living unity of the association we cannot see nor perceive sensually. But neither can we perceive the whole personality of an individual' (quoted in Lewis, 1935, p. 58). Thus pluralists argued that corporate groups and natural individuals are two species within the one genus of the person. The whole personality is perceived through certain attributes.

One must, however, be careful here. None of the pluralists, including Gierke, argued that the group person was biologically real. The ideas of committed organic theorists such as J. K. Bluntschli were rejected by Gierke. Yet the concept of a person attached to a human individual is also not biologically real. It is as much a result of artifice. As Nicholls comments, all the pluralists 'in their more clear-sighted moments . . . saw that *all* legal personality (including that of the individual) is "articifial"' (1975, p. 70). In addition, they were not trying to argue that a juristic group person is precisely equivalent to a human individual. There were many propositions applicable to human persons that were not applicable to group persons. Groups cannot marry, they need humans to function and speak for them and so on. In spite of not being biologically real, the pluralist were not arguing that groups were fictions. Groups were real persons in a juristic and normative sense. The same point holds for individual humans. Even if some pluralists used the concept 'organic' somewhat freely in relation to groups, the juristic view was their primary emphasis (see Maitland, 1900, p. xxiii).

Ernest Barker tried to get away from all the implications of the organic metaphor by relocating personality as an 'organising idea' in groups. The ancestry to this notion lies in the philosopher Bernard Bosanquet. Bosanquet had argued that the human mind was ruled by certain dominant organizing ideas or purposes. These ideas were seen as the basis to the will. The will structured and was reinforced by action; the actions determined the circumstances of the agent. The stronger ideas gave a clearer, more rational, status to the person uniting, in a systematic way, the faculties and potentialities of the mind (see Vincent and Plant, 1984, p. 109). As an individual mind coalesces around organizing ideas, so a group becomes a person when its members possess a unifying purpose. Individuals in this sense are seen as analogous to the various faculties and potentialities of the mind. Thus Barker argues that 'There is a college mind, just as there is a Trade Union mind, or even a "public mind" of the whole community; and we are all conscious of such a mind as something that exists in and along with separate minds of their members, and over and above any sum of these minds' (1915b, p. 74).

Despite the philosophy of personality, one simple point was being insisted on by the pluralists. Unincorporated groups (groups not given a statutory status) were real entities with a distinctive life of their own, which formed the basis of human liberty and a transformed understanding of sovereignty and authority. In a mundane sense the necessity of treating groups as juristic persons was, and has been, born out in legal practice. As has been recently pointed out,

> Since 1930 the English courts, and also the legislature, have shown a strong determination to render groups, whether incorporated or unicorporated, more accountable collectively for their actions. In doing so the courts have brought into general use expressions which would have astonished earlier generations of lawyers. It is now normal in cases dealing with a corporate

body to speak of its 'psyche', [and] 'its directing mind and will'. (Hallis, 1978, p. ii)

For example, in the judgment of Denning in *H. L. Bolton (Engineering) Co. Ltd v. T. J. Graham and Sons Ltd (1957) 1 QB 159 CA*, Denning remarked, 'A company may in many ways be likened to a human body. It has a brain and a nerve centre which controls what it does. It also has hands which hold the tools and act in accordance with directions from the centre' (quoted in Hallis 1978, p. iv). In this context, the idea of legal personality obviously still has considerable practical and theoretical purchase in legal and political thought.

THE PLURALIST STATE

The pluralist theory arose in the context of a somewhat negative appraisal of the monistic theory of the State. It is therefore difficult to find an overall coherent view. There are often marked changes in perspective which only adds to the complication. The pluralists, as argued earlier, engaged in extensive criticism of certain notions of sovereignty, the State and law; however, they did not all reject the State. They were trying to theorize an idea of the State incorporating maximal diversity of group life and some kind of central authority. It is often thought that the pluralists could not have a theory of the State. Thus, it is often puzzling when it is seen that, for example, Gierke was a fervent believer in monarchy, the Prussian dominance of the Reich and State sovereignty. Gierke stated, for example, that 'we understand by "State" the highest and most inclusive among the collective entities, intangible but intellectually recognisable as "real", which human social existence erects above individual existence. For us this collective entity is the enduring, living, willing and acting unity formed by a whole folk' (quoted in Lewis, 1935, p. 63). The State, for Gierke, was different to other associations or collective persons 'in that it has no similar person above it'. In other words, Gierke thought of it as sovereign. He was also prepared to see the boundaries between groups and the State as very flexible. Yet, in the final analysis, 'the problems and competence of political authority will always project themselves into *every* sphere of human social life' (quoted in Lewis, 1935, p. 86). The English pluralists did not go as far as Gierke, but none the less, they accepted that there was a pluralist conception of the State. Some respond to this by arguing that the State was smuggled in through the backdoor. Therefore, although beginning with an attack on the State, the pluralists end up by bringing it in surreptitiously (Hsiao, 1941, pp. 136–7; Ellis, 1923, p. 590; Wright, 1979, pp. 47–8). There is something to be said for this view, with specific reference to theorists such as Cole, but it is unfair as a complete picture of the whole movement.

There are two major problems in dealing with the pluralist theory of the State. First, apart from the formal agreement on notions such as liberty through group life, plural sovereignty and group personality, pluralists were still imprecise in their terminology on the State. Second, they differed in their actual accounts of what the State is.

The imprecision in terminology applies to the concepts of society, State and government. For some pluralists, the State seemed to be shorthand for the government. As Laski argued, 'A theory of State . . . is essentially a theory of the governmental act' (1925, p. 28). The same point was also made by Cole (1917, p. 71). In this view, the State is understood minimally and is identified with the political institutions and processes of government. It is also distinct from the notion of society – society usually denotes the whole collection of functionally associated groups. Cole, however, in a Rousseauesque vein, distinguished the 'community' from 'society'. Behind the State and society stands community. 'Society', he argues, 'is the mechanism of the communal will; but that will resides only in the community' (1917, p. 72). No other pluralist goes down this path. Cole also spoke of the State resting alongside the organized Guilds, sharing sovereignty. The State is simply the territorially based political organization, politically representing the body of citizens as a whole.

There is, however, a stronger, more adequate sense of the State in pluralism, although it is never resolved as to whether this State is a person. This idea tries to incorporate the diversity of groups in some form of totality. The State is, in Figgis's phrase, to be regarded as the 'society of societies' (1914, p. 49). This second view of the State, understood as a collectivity of living groups united in a single political entity, is difficult to articulate. The State is not simply equivalent to government. It is the public power of the whole collection of groups. It should be noted, though, that Figgis himself is not wholly clear on this point.

The lack of precision in their language confuses the actual accounts of the State. We can begin with Cole and the guild socialists. Cole is, as stressed, the most confusing of the pluralists (see Ellis, 1923, p. 589; Nicholls, 1975, pp. 86–7; Wright, 1979, pp. 34,47). In his earlier work, *Self-Government in Industry* (1917), the State is defined as 'the political machinery of government in a community'

(p. 71). The whole complex of institutions 'for common action in the community' is society (p. 72). He goes on to maintain, like Laski, that the State is one amongst many groups – although by the next page he seems to be arguing that the purified State is plurally sovereign (pp. 81–3). In more substantive detail, he speaks of a national Guild Congress representing all the industrial guilds, existing alongside a political parliament representing citizens as 'consumers'. Both organizations are sovereign. Over and above these is another body to resolve conflict between the Guild Congress and Parliament. This is a federal representative body – a joint congress of Guilds and the State, which would have ultimate coercive power. Cole envisages this body mediating between the State and the Guilds! In his later book, *Social Theory*, the State becomes 'that association which deals with those things "which affect all its members more or less equally and the same way"' (1920, p. 99). It is conceived of as having a regulative and co-ordinating role. It still represents citizens as consumers in terms of prices, incomes and the like, and also regulating personal relations in terms of marriage, divorce and care of children. Ultimate coercion resides more definitely than earlier work in another co-ordinating institution which acts as an appellate body: a supreme court of functional equity (1920, pp. 86–7). In his final definitive statement, *Guild Socialism Restated*, Cole's hostility to the idea of the State comes to fruition, although once again in a haze of terminology. The State, as understood in the previous two works, is substituted by a complex organization of consumers, a conjunction of a co-operative council and a collective utilities council. Civic guilds are envisaged as representing non-economic interests such as health and cultural councils. Industrial guilds are seen to exist alongside other bodies representing the producer and professional groups. Over and above these exists, once again, a renamed ultimate co-ordinating body, which is designated 'the national commune'. It is representative of functional and territorial divisions. Its duties are, first and foremost, resolving the conflicts between groups, the settlement of constitutional issues, the control of the army and navy, and the ultimate settlement on prices, incomes and national economic relations. This body is emphatically not to be regarded as the State. (Cole, 1980, pp. 119–24). Some modern critics in fact agree with Cole on this point (see Vernon, 1980, pp. xxxix and xL). Liberty was to be defended for Cole by decentralization. He was not alone in this idea, it was a common feature among all the pluralists. The fact that Cole limits the State initially to a political entity, government, and eventually tries rules it out altogether should not disguise the fact that all the functions of the State and many of the commonplace features associated with it were still present except with other names, such as national commune.

Cole's views on the State were contested by fellow guild socialists. The most well-known of these was S. G. Hobson, specifically in his book *National Guilds and the State* (1920). He disagreed with Cole's separation between consumers and producers, thus initiating a rigid twofold structure. Guilds can represent individuals in both aspects, since the two cannot, in fact, be separated (1920, pp. 30–1). For Hobson, the State must not be sullied by economic concerns, these can be left up to the Guilds. The State is the 'expression of the life of the citizen community'. Its business is essentially a spiritual mission (pp. 105–7). The State must also, for Hobson, be kept distinct from government. The nation, on the other hand, is the whole body of citizens – the State being the 'vocal organ' of the nation (p. 101). It represents the whole people as the organized expression of citizenship. It protects the consumer and producer. Government is the organization 'that works out in detail the will of the citizens expressed through the state' (p. 105). The government derives its authority and has its function defined by the State. For Hobson, Guilds derive their authority from the State. Although this appears more unitary than Cole's veiled State, as Anthony Wright points out, 'Hobson's assertion of the sovereign supremacy of the state turned out to mean *less* role for the state, because its concern was spiritual rather than economic, than did Cole's denial of such sovereignty' (1979, p. 41).

Laski, like Cole, shifted in his views, although he was manifestedly less confusing. In his early writings, the State is more or less identified with the governing machinery, but the difference is that it is viewed as one association amongst many. It did not differ in substance from a trade union or Church. Its power was persuasion rather than outright force. The real personality of groups negated the central role for the State, although – unlike Figgis – Laski did argue that the State had a personality. As one writer has remarked, Laski 'sometimes argues that the will of the State is no more than a competition with the wills of other groups. . . . At other times he indicates that the will of the state is formed by the struggle that takes place among competing wills' (Deane, 1955, p. 35). Laski was thus suspicious of all forms of centralized Statism and bureaucracy whether it be Fabianism, Marxism or the New Liberalism (see Deane, 1955, pp. 59–72). His early interest was essentially administrative decentralization and a revivified federalism. The ideas of the

French theorist Leon Duguit were very influential on Laski at this point. By the late 1920s, however, Laski shifted his view to the recognition of the distinctiveness of the State apart from all other associations. It is seen as a 'coordinating agency' in the vein of Cole. In his *Introduction to Politics* (1931), Laski argued that the essence of the State was its ability to 'enforce its norms upon all who live within its boundaries'. It was still functioning, as in earlier works, for the benefit of the 'highest and best life' for its members, but it was distinct from other groups. By the 1930s Laski's views had essentially shifted away from pluralism altogether to a Marxist theory. The State became simply the represention of class interests.

Figgis, and to a certain extent Gierke, represent the closest approximation to the idea of a pluralist State. Figgis states his central problem 'as the relation of smaller communities to that "*communitas communitatum*" we call the state' (1914, p. 8). For Figgis, unlike the early Laski and Cole, the State is distinct from all other types of association or group. Figgis is not absolutely clear, but what he seems to be saying is that the State must be understood in a complex sense. Primarily, it is a 'synthesis of living wills' (1914 p. 92). These 'living wills' are basically the multiple number of group persons existing within a territorial boundary. The State, in its completest sense, is this collectivity of partially autonomous groups forming a single entity. It is in this sense, as Nicholls points out, that Figgis intentionally entitled his book Churches *in* the modern State, not as Laski and Cole might have entitled it, Churches *and* the modern State. The State is the summation of group life and is constituted by groups, although it did not create them. It represents the totality. In representing the whole it is distinct from all other groups. It acts through certain organs such as government. It is important to realize here that intrinsic to this collective entity is the recognition of independent group persons. Thus there is no way that this argument could be used to justify the total dominance of the government. The government is also not identified with the State. Rather, as Hobson argued, it carries the authority of the whole State at the highest level of generality. The total system of wills is channelled into a single will which prevents injustices being committed by individuals or groups, secures basic rights, and recognizes and regulates groups. In this sense it possesses some sovereingty and distinctness, since it adjusts the relation of all the groups. If the State withdraws recognition from a group it does not thereby destroy it, although it does undermine its credibility. Fraud or corruption are possible areas of interference in group life – although Figgis himself is not very clear on the precise limitations to interference. The State thus integrates, but does not absorb, groups. Figgis envisages the State as incorporating, in its widest sense, the community of wills of all groups and individuals within a territory. The focus of that will appears in certain governing institutions. However, that which constitutes the will of the State is the plurality of independent groups. As Gierke argued, the State is 'but the last link of the chain of collective units developed as persons' (quoted in Lewis, 1935, p. 63). It is arguable here that Figgis acknowledged that the State could be understood in both a broad and a narrow sense. The broad idea is the totality of groups, the 'synthesis of living wills'; the narrow understanding is the focus of that synthesis in government.

The pluralist State is not sovereign in any conventional sense, partly because it is constituted by bodies whose self-governance and partial independence is fully recognized *within* the very idea of the State. These bodies possess real juristic personality. The focus of the State in government holds the various groups to account for many areas of their activity. Implicitly though, such a body recognizes the diverse centres of authority. Thus the pluralist State has been defined as one 'in which there exists no single source of authority that is all competent and comprehensive' (Hsiao, 1927, p. 8). The function of the governing body is not to exercise unlimited power but rather to superintend and adjust the relations between groups and individuals in the interests of justice, order and liberty. A pluralist State thus embodies continual debate, criticism and compromise between groups. It is 'an association of individuals, already united in various groups each with a common life, in a further and higher group and more embracing common purpose' (Barker, 1915b, p. 177).

CONCLUSION

One of the clearest problems of pluralism is the fact that there is no school, only a general tendency. The majority of the pluralist writers that have been dealt with here were not political philosophers. They were often not precise in their use of terminology. Some obviously followed a line of thought which led them to doubt the existence of the State. There is a strong sense of this latter point in Cole. His line of thought appears closer at times to Proudhon's and Kropotkin's anarchist federalism. The pluralist State, however, is a complex vision which tries to incorporate maximal diversity of group life within an over-arching authority. Pluralists thought that this was the way in which human liberty and self-development could be maximized.

Another problem of the lack of unity and precision in pluralist writings is that they did not answer, or in fact at times even identify, many of the intrinsic problems in their position. It is clear that they did not deal with a crucial issue; namely, that groups can be as oppressive, mean-minded and destructive of liberty as any State. This is a point which is also ignored by many anarchists. If it could be demonstrated that many groups are oppressive, presumably this would provide a sound reason for pluralistic writers themselves to question the nature of groups. Furthermore, if it could be demonstrated that the centralized State can maximize human liberty and self-development better than groups, this also would be a good reason for pluralists to become monistic Statists. Groups are not always a bulwark against tyranny and oppression. They may be the oppressors; they also may be dominated by oligarchic elites. In this sense the central State can liberate individuals from groups. Pluralists did not face these questions. They also neglected to examine the precise nature or degree of intervention that could be exercised by a State over groups. The discussions of Figgis, Laski and Cole subsist on generalities, speaking of regulation and co-ordination. There are no precise arguments offered for parameters to State or group activity. It is clear that they would have wanted regulation of some groups such as the Mafia, but the argument is never spelt out. Lurking behind the pluralist condemnation of some group activity is the concept of consensus. Figgis and other pluralists obviously believed that there were common concepts of liberty, self-realization and the like. Such an argument is manifest in the idea of a government acting as a focus for the collectivity and that some groups will automatically be outlawed. Yet there is a tension within the pluralist argument here. Groups have independent personalities. If they have independent personalities, surely it is possible that they might have different concepts of justice and the like? How can a collective good be constituted out of a plurality of goods? The pluralists seem at times to conjure this collective good out of thin air. In this sense, the interdependance and mutual respect between groups looks increasingly fragile. Surely the idea of co-operation, specifically in cases like Cole's Guild Congress and political Parliament, looks rather unworldly and remote. This has led many critics to the view that decentralized authority is a pretty empty idea. If one interpreted the pluralists as saying that sovereignty was devolved among groups, then it is arguable that divided sovereignty is not sovereignty at all. In fact some have gone on to argue that many pluralists try to slip in indivisible sovereignty in institutions such as Cole's National Commune. Although it is true that it is difficult to make out a case for divided sovereignty and it might have been better for the pluralists to have completely avoided the term, none the less they were indicating something significant about the nature of authority. Human beings are subject, in practice, to a range of differing and often conflicting loyalties. Many of these may be, and often are, far stronger and more immediate than any loyalty to a central State. It is these loyalties which are most significant and meaningful to the average citizen. Yet those who wish to argue that pluralists have brought the State back surreptiously, to oversee group activity, are mistaken. The main thrust of the pluralist position is to argue for a notion of the State. This pluralist State is mediated by a complex vision of group life which cannot be ignored.

7

Do We Need a Theory of the State?

This book began with the question: what is the State? This can be answered on formal and substantive levels. The formal answer to the question is that the State is a public power above both ruler and ruled which provides order and continuity to the polity. It might be tempting to bring in other factors here – for example those examined in the first chapter, such as territory and monopoly of force. Though these are indicators of Statehood, many of them are open to question and contestable. Monopoly of force is obviously significant, but is vague and requires considerable elucidation. The crucial formal and necessary factor in the meaning of the State is that it is a continuous public power. When we ask what we mean by this public power, where it is situated and how one describes it, we come upon a second substantive level of answers. It is the description of the character of public power which leads us directly into theories of the State. The major body of discussion in literature on the State falls in this substantive area. Therefore we must look at the theories which have been offered to explain the character of public power when answering the question: what is the state? Before addressing this question another point should be cleared up. Theories of the State in the nineteenth and twentieth centuries can be divided into two broad categories, the juristic/normative and sociological/historical. This distinction is not necessarily exhaustive and there is a strong case to be made out that the two overlap. The juristic/normative theories try to characterize the nature and ends of the State. These theories are usually wide-ranging. They make assumptions about human nature, fundamental values and human needs, and try to link these with institutional structures. The State embodies fundamental human values and aspirations, and most classical political theorists believed that they were articulating the essence of the State when describing these values. Such a position is now not so easy to entertain. Yet this

·does not undermine the profound significance of the State in our own lives, it only makes assessment of the State that much more urgent. We have examined some of these juristic/normative theories in this book.

Sociological/historical theories are concerned to explain the phenomenon of the State from a different perspective. The State is usually seen as a particular element within the broader category of society, or as an *ad hoc* result of unrelated historical or economic factors. Since the development of the disciplines of sociology and anthropology this outlook has become a popular method of analysis.

There is some truth to the claim that history is usually more complex, messy and pragmatic than philosophical ideas and theories would have us believe. There is something abbreviated and fragmentary about theories of the State which may also take little account of the rich profusion of historical data. Absolutist theory, for example, in the reign of Louis XIV, seemed completely out of touch with the everyday realities of French political life. Yet if one concentrates too avidly on the historical path there is a danger of getting lost in the multiplicity of details. The historical study of the State neglects two other factors. First, when studying history we are not actually impartially examining uncontested empirical events. We always study history through intercolators, reportage and so on. There is *no* way round this. When examining this 'evidence', we must take into consideration: (1) the intepretation, language, words and intentions of the historical actors; and (2) our own conceptual world and how we interpret what is being said. Even the most bland description of State activities will involve conceptual assumptions, however unconscious. Perception functions through concepts. There-fore there is no way that one can simply avoid discussing theories or concepts of the State. The second factor to bear in mind is that the State is not primarily an empirical entity at all. We cannot touch or see a State. It is nothing but a mental category, although it may be an extremely concrete one. In some societies it becomes a customary disposition in the population. In this sense, it becomes a subliminal aspect of institutions. We have now become so accustomed to living with the State that we can forget this point. We do not realise that the State is a mode of being and a complex of values, as well as an institutional structure. The grasp of such a category is not primarily gained from history but from theory and philosophy. In fact the two elements should not really be at loggerheads. History and theory should intermix: their relation is symbiotic.

The same points hold for the sociological treatement of the State.

The matter is of course not as clear-cut as presented here. There are many sociologically orientated theorists who have hovered between the more explanatory and normative views on society and the State. Marx is one theorist that fits into this mould. Durkheim also, although offering a sociological explanation of the State, none the less, in the preface to his *Division of Labour in Society*, propounds a normative view of pluralistic syndicalism.

Non-Marxist sociologists, in general, have tended to avoid the State. The discipline was late in developing and grew in societies where States were already well established and taken for granted. Sociologists thus tended to concentrate on other problems. Disciplines, such as constitutional law and political philosophy, dealt with the State; thus 'When it came to defining domains, the state, being central to other disciplines was "off limits" to sociology' (Poggi, 1978, p. x; see also Badie and Birnbaum, 1983). Apart from Marx and Engels, Max Weber was the major theorist to deal with the State, although many of his ideas are not really fully developed. Poggi indicates the limitations of the sociological approach when he confesses that 'A limitation of my approach is that it does not consider the development in political theory and ideology that accompanied the formation of the modern state. It has no room for Marsilius of Padua, Locke, or Hegel, or for the interaction between their thought and the politics of their time' (1978, p. xii). As in the case of historical study, the lack of attention to ideas is a fundamental weakness.

The more sociological approach to the State is actively pursued by many political sociologists and proponents of comparative politics who can be subdivided broadly into functionalists (including neo-functionalists) and developmental theorists. Both sets of theories are concerned with the economic and social preconditions to the existence of nation States as opposed to other types of social structure; with types of State and what causes them to appear; and, finally, with the determination of what factors give rise to the responsiveness and durability of States (see Tilly, 1975, p. 602). The key functionalist writer was Talcott Parsons. He maintained that the emergence of the State was bound up with the differentiation, automization, institutionalization and universalization of political processes. Following on from Durkheim, Talcott Parsons argued that the State was a unique product of the division of labour in advanced industrial societies. Specialized organizations develop in relation to this division of labour and become centred on the State. The existence of the State thus implies certain preconditions such as industrialization. In consequence, the State can be described as a collection of specialized agencies associated with the division of labour of advanced industrialized societies. Its function is to mediate and reduce conflict and tension between sectors of society. States come into being when they possess enough resources to be able to dominate the peripheries and actually reconcile tensions.

Developmental theory only differs from functionalism in seeing definite stages in the growth of the State, which are identified in the evolution towards the advanced industrial societies. This thesis is central to modernization theory. The Western industrial State is seen as a standard rational model for developing countries to emulate, if they wish to modernize. The growth of all societies is seen as progressive, rational, continuous, uniform and endogenous. Thus, like functionalists, development theorists argue that the State, understood as a set of specialized and centralized agencies, arises at a certain level of industrialization and division of labour. It serves certain mediating functions within this process and is thus linked very precisely to a stage in the economic development of society. The history of the State from the medieval period is one of changing economic practices and modernization in industry which leads inexorably to a particular form of organization that we call the State. Political scientists who use functionalist ideas have tended to concentrate their attention on issues such as the problems of mobilization in societies, political socialization and political culture. As one recent writer has stated, 'Political scientists lost interest in talking about the state as such twenty or thirty years ago. As they did so, they took to the discussion of societies, political systems and nations' (Tilly, 1975, p. 617).

It should be stressed that developmental theory is not Marxist, although Marx undoubtedly held some similar notions. In fact the idea that societies move through stages is of quite ancient heritage. The developmental link with the economy and industrialization is the relatively novel aspect and one of the first to adopt it in political sociology was A. F. K. Organski in *The Stages of Political Growth* (1965). Subsequently it became a popular analytical device for a number of noted American political scientists such as Samuel Verba, Gabriel Almond and S. M. Lipset. Much of the initial literature in the discipline of comparative politics developed along these lines. Lipset, for example, in his *Political Man*, tried to articulate precise measurements for the development of States (Lipset, 1971). In this body of literature, American, capitalist, liberal democracy usually turns out to be the high point of State evolution.

The major drawbacks of such ideas are, first, the unproven notion that differentiation and the division of labour automatically lead to rationalization and the development of the State. In fact States can, and often have, initiated industrialization. Also States do not always mediate conflicts within themselves. They often create conflicts. The idea of developmental stages is also suspect, especially if it is being advanced as a social scientific hypothesis. It is a normative conceptual scheme imposed on the world, not empirically derived from it! Finally, it is assumed by developmental and functionalist theorists that the State is unproblematic. Their theories are examining preconditions and offering explanations of how the State develops. They do not tell us *what* the State is. The State is saturated with values and ideas which are not dealt with; and yet it is these which make sense of it. To understand the State we must get to grips with the normative theories. Normative theory can interact fruitfully with historical and sociological analysis, but these are not substitutes for it.

The disadvantage of sociological and historical theories is that they do not take us much farther with understanding the formal answer to the question: what is the State? They would also not be very helpful in answering the question: do we need a theory of the State? Unless, of course, the questioner was seeking an empirical theory. The answers to these questions lie in theories of public power. In summary, the substantive answers to the question offered in this volume are as follows:

1 In absolutist theory the public power *is* the absolute sovereign person (whether fictional or real) embodying divine right and owning the realm. The sovereign's interests are the State's interests.

2 In constitutional theory the public power *is* the complex institutional structure which, through historical, legal, moral and philosophical claims, embodies self-limitation and diversification of authority and power and a complex hierarchy of rules and norms, which act to institutionalize power and regulate the relations between citizens, laws and political institutions.

3 In ethical theory the public power *is* the *modus operandi* of the citizens, groups and institutions of a constitutional monarchy, directed to the maximal ethical self-development and freedom of the citizen body. It is the unity of the cognitive disposition of the individual with the purposes of institutional structures and rules.

4 In class theory the public power *is* the institutional form of the

condensation of dominant class interests, which is ultimately directed at the accumulation of capital and the defence of private property.

5 In pluralist theory the public power *is*, in general terms, the synthesis of living semi-independent groups (understood as real legal persons). Groups are integrated not absorbed. Narrowly focused public power implies a government acting for the common good of groups.

Within these broad definitions are general indications of the types of polity which might be present. There are, however, a variety of institutional, administrative and governmental arrangements which might be seen within each of these theories. The theories lay down broad parameters within which the public power functions. They do not always lay down precise institutional arrangements. There is no reason, for example, for a constitutional theorist to opt necessarily for a Parliamentary arrangement or a complete separation of powers. The ethical theory is more precise than the others, although other Hegelians did not follow Hegel down his particular path. The English Hegelian, Bernard Bosanquet, thought that the Hegelian theory could be tied into the the British Parliamentary framework.

It is impossible to divorce any of these theories from values. There is a definite link between a theory of the State and a conception of human capacities, powers and potentialities. The constitutional theory, involving a complex of limitations, can neither be separated from these limitations nor the values of individual liberty and rights which are upheld through these limitations. The values, in other words, are constitutive of the theories. Similarly, the pluralist belief in the value of liberty being upheld through the recognition of the real personality of groups, cannot be prised away from the idea of the State as the synthesis of living wills. We are so used to thinking of the State as some kind of attentuated abstract entity, usually centred on government, that it is difficult to conceive of it as a holistic theory. In this sense, we need to broaden our conception of the State. When we say that the State is a public power, which focuses our attention on authority and the relations of authority, we also need to ask *what* that public power is understood to be and why it is situated there. Simple-minded contrasts between collectivist as against minimalist views of the the State – which still proliferate in much academic discussion – are not just unhelpful, but downright misleading.

The idea of the State is, therefore, open-ended. There are descriptive components to it and it can be used as a tool of analysis.

It is not, however, a passive concept. It is more than anything constitutive of political reality. It embodies a sense of social order within which citizens are integrated. Individuals are not integrated simply by force, but rather by establishing the unique rational character of the public power in individual minds. Individuals have a disposition towards the State. This is the source of the legitimacy of the State, although, of course, populations may not feel this allegiance and may in certain situations challenge the legitimacy. We are though, State-creatures whose development, welfare and future cannot be divorced from the State. It is not something that we can shrug off.

One final question remains which forms the title to this chapter: do we need a theory of the State? Again the answer to this question depends on the kind of theory being sought and who 'we' refers to. It is doubtful that we *need* another sociological or historical theory. The question requires a normative response. There has been a neglect of normative theory on the State. Possibly we do not need a new theory, but we should pay more attention to the existing body of theory. We need to ask ourselves about the nature of the State, what is its function or end. It is first and foremost a mental category which informs the attitudes of individuals towards authority. It is also intimately linked to assumptions about human capacities and powers. The State is now the major condition of civilization and most of the values and practices that we associate with it. This does not mean that conflict is eliminated. In many ways the State is as much a danger as a blessing. It has the potentiality for horrendous destruction as well as life. Thus it is crucially important to have some theoretical awareness of the State. It should not simply be taken for granted. We need the theory to grasp the complex processes of social existence and to make sense of them. We should also realize that to innovate in State theory is potentially to change the character of our social existence. Theoretical change can alter our practice. To theorize about the State is to think about and potentially change the ends of social existence. If, for example, we argue that the end of the State is the achievement of the good life for all citizens and that this entails the guarantee of both material and cultural goods, then such an argument could have far-reaching consequences not only on the way in which we conceive both the substantive policies of the State and its institutional structures, but also on individual lives. It is such evaluations which are central to understanding the State.

C. B. Macpherson has asked who the 'we' refers to in the chapter question. He argues that there are three 'we's': (1) those who accept liberal democratic States and defend the status quo; (2) those who believe that present societies do not live up to the normative ideals of liberal democracy and believe that the State should conform to moral values; and (3) those, like Marx, who reject the present State. Macpherson contends that it is the second and third categories who need a theory of the State. He seems to feel most sympathy for the third group, although he confesses that 'Marx's theory was certainly normative as well as analytical, and the role of the state was crucial to his whole theory, yet he did not provide more than fragments of a theory of the state' (1977, p. 229). How the two elements in this quotation hold together is left unexplained; however, Marx does have interesting things to say about the changing character of the State in relation to political economy, but any fragmentary proposals which are made, as argued in chapter 5, are regressive in character. As Macpherson notes, in relation to Marx, 'The theory of the State does have to come back from political economy to political philosophy' (1977, p. 243). Another important omission in Macpherson's article is that he shows little or no awareness of the rich complexity of State theories. There seems to be a liberal democratic capitalist State and an unspecified Marxist one. Such a judgement is simplistic.

The 'we' must refer to *all* who live in States. All who are concerned about social life now and in the future should think critically about the State. It is too important to leave alone or to others. We are now in a fascinating era of the development of States. The existence of the State implies a system of States recognizing each other. Any future theory of the State will have to take cognisance of this international dimension. One important factor to take on board here is the increasing recognition of the vulnerability and interdependence of States as well as the increasing demands in industrialized States for regionalism, localism and devolution of authority. States, in other words, are subject to greater local and international forces than previously.

In considering the future of the State we should not neglect the crucial fact that it is 'concerned with the framework of values within which public life should be conducted and with the effective exercise of public authority in the pursuit of these values' (Dyson, 1980, p. 271). It is impossible to separate the 'State-as-it-ought-to-be' from the 'State-as-it-is'. The State is permeated with values. It is no use bewailing its existence or trying to roll it back. Rather we need to articulate clearly what it is; namely, how we understand the the nature of the public power and also what *is* valuable in social existence and consequently to seek it, within the parameters of civility, in the State.

Notes

1 THE NATURE OF THE STATE

1 Skinner remarks that, 'I hope to indicate something of the process by which the modern concept of the State came to be formed. . . . I shall seek to show, that the main elements of a recognisably modern concept of the State were gradually acquired' (1978, Vol. 1, p. ix). This implies that the State has slowly evolved or developed.

2 Mitteis (1975) speaks of the 900s, Post (1964) of the 1100s, Strayer (1970) 1100 up to the 1600s, Skinner (1978) and Tilly (1975) the 1500s.

3 This particular point will receive considerable expansion in subsequent chapters, specifically chapter 2. The basic thesis is that all law originates in the State itself, therefore the nature of law must be tied into the very nature of the State. This idea is often contrasted to the natural law thesis, where law is seen to originate outside the sphere of the State.

4 In fact the term *societas* seems to derive from a much older principle, *ercto non cito*, which probably dates back to old Roman or even Etruscan law. This was primarily a principle concerned with family property. The idea of the more abstract consensual contract is a later product.

5 It is in fact arguable that the early linkage of *societas* to family property draws it closer to notions of community and fellowship.

6 There is another side to Bodin, which has caused considerable scholarly debate; namely, that he placed constitutional limits on the sovereign. This particular issue will be examined in chapter 2.

2 THE ABSOLUTIST THEORY OF THE STATE

1 A clearer picture of the debates on absolutism will be gained when chapter 3 (where constitutionalism is defined and discussed in detail) has been read.

2 For Pope Gregory VII it was the duty of monarchs to obey the commands of the Pope. No one was exempt from such universal government. As Gregory stated 'For the see of St Peter decides and judges celestial things, how much more does it decide and judge the

earthly and secular' (quoted in Ullman, 1975. pp. 102–3; see also R. W. Carlyle and A. J. Carlyle, 1936, Vol. IV, pp. 190ff).

3 This point should not be given too much emphasis. Monarchs still relied heavily on local enforcement of order and collection of revenue.

4 For a general overview of the senses of sovereignty, see Chapter 1, in the section entitled 'Cognate Concepts of the State'.

5 It is important to grasp that I am moving between different senses of sovereignty. Absolute sovereignty could refer to a monarch or to an assembly (such as Parliament or the Estates-General). In legal terms the assembly could still be viewed as a single person; however, it would be an artificial person (*persona ficta*). Hobbes and Bodin, although admitting that an assembly (Hobbes more so than Bodin), could be sovereign, none the less preferred monarchy – the natural person. Absolute sovereignty was distinct from the idea of mixed or shared sovereignty which combined various elements like monarchy, aristocracy and a representative assembly. This idea became characteristic of certain constitutional writers. Sovereignty was not one person, fictional or natural, but mixed between elements. As an idea it was repudiated by Bodin and other absolutist writers. For Hobbes and Bodin, either you have a sovereign or you do not, you cannot have a mixed or shared sovereignty.

6 This section on property theory is deeply indebted to the work of Herbert Rowen (1961, 1980).

7 It should be noted that I am not implying that any of these theorists were divine rightists. I am simply pointing out the origins of reason of State. The link between divine right and reason of State is a much later product of the era of absolutism.

3 THE CONSTITUTIONAL THEORY OF THE STATE

1 Quentin Skinner has argued that Figgis takes this point too far, particularly on the Jesuits (see Skinner, 1978, Vol. 2. pp. 182–4).

2 Pamphlets such as the anonymous *Vox Populi: Or, the People's Claim to their Parliament's Sitting, to Redress Grievances and to Provide for the Common Safety, by the known Laws and Constitutions and Nation* (see Resnick, 1984, p. 100).

3 Formalized in the Parliament Bill (1911).

4 This section is very much indebted to the work of Vile (1967) and Richter (1977).

5 We only have to recall the opening lines of the American Declaration of Independence (1776) to see these points – 'We hold these truths to be self-evident, that all men are created equal, that they are endowed by their creator with certain unalienable rights, that among these are life, liberty and the pursuit of happiness.'

4 THE ETHICAL THEORY OF THE STATE

1 On the Burkean aspect of Hegel's thought see Pelczynski's introduction to Hegel (1964).

2 On the question of the Hegelian State in terms of international politics see Verene (1980), also Vincent (1983).

3 These figures included Goethe, Herder, Hölderlin, Schiller and Winckelmann.

5 THE CLASS THEORY OF THE STATE

1 This judgement needs to be qualified by the historical fact that Marx's writings at that time were largely in more liberal newspapers and journals. He would presumably have had to tone down his views on class and communism.

2 Engels did provide his own particular idiosyncratic assessment of the period in his *Ludwig Feuerbach and the End of Classical German Philosophy* (1886).

3 Marx does discuss these ideas in his *Civil War in France*, yet he does not reconcile this discussion with his critique of the State.

6 THE PLURALIST THEORY OF THE STATE

1 There are a few terminological points to be made here. I have mentioned the anarchists and syndicalists in this overview, and occasionally in the chapter, for two reasons. First, they adopt a critical stance to the vision of the monistic State, and second, they envisage the future of social existence in terms of groups. These two points are characteristic of the pluralistic tendency in political thought. However, they are very formal characteristics. There is no school of pluralism. Also I am not arguing that anarchists are the same as syndicalists. There are marked theoretical differences. Yet there are also two reasons why I have not utilized anarchism and syndicalism in this chapter. First, they both took an overtly negative view of *any* concept of the State; second, their idiosyncratic characterization of the nature of groups is dependent on the fact that no State should exist. My concern in this chapter is with those pluralists who tried to construct a normative theory of the State in the context of group life. Therefore I have focused primarily on the English pluralists – namely: Figgis, Laski, Maitland and also some of the guild socialists such as Cole and Hobson. It would need a separate chapter to deal with anarchism and syndicalism and their view of the State, although I am not convinced that they really had a developed theory of the State.

2 As argued, syndicalists and communist anarchists rejected even this minimal sense of the State.

3 I am deeply indebted to the work of David Nicholls in this chapter: see Nicholls (1974, 1975).

4 As one scholar has put it, 'It was not just a theory of the State that the work of Figgis, Cole and Laski, elaborated. It was rather a series of attempts to show in what senses we can be free in modern society' (Magid, 1941, p. 8).

5　One of the problems in understanding the pluralists on this point is to know whether they actually wanted the dispersal or distribution of sovereignty to groups or whether they wanted to abandon the actual concept of sovereignty completely as too tainted with the ideas of Hobbes and Austin. In the latter alternative they could still speak of the dispersal of power and authority but without the problems of discussing sovereignty.

6　The use of monistic sovereignty was also regarded as wrong-headed in international politics. There are too many intermediate groups within and between States to interpret international affairs simply in terms of the interaction of sovereign States.

7　Hsiao notes that 'it is certainly safe to say that the Innocentians were not so foolish as to suppose that the State, in recognising the legal personality of corporations, creates the corporations' (1927. p. 35).

8　In a recent scholarly book on international politics, the author comments that 'a treaty of union founds a body that possesses personality, but it is more than merely the technical "legal" personality of the typical international organisation. . . . The "personality" formed by union is an original capacity to act akin to that possessed by the States themselves. It is a "real" personality' (Forsyth, 1981, p. 274).

Bibliography

Allen, J. A. 1957: *A History of Political Thought in the Sixteenth Century.* London: Methuen.

Althusser, L. 1969: *For Marx.* Harmondsworth, Middx.: Penguin Books.

1971: *Lenin and Philosophy and other Essays.* New York: Monthly Review Press.

Althusser, L. and Balibar, C. 1970: *Reading Capital.* London: New Left Books.

Anderson, P. 1977: The Antinomies of Antonio Gramsci. *New Left Review,* no. 100.

Armstrong, A. H. and Markus, R. A. 1964: *Christian Faith and Greek Philosophy.* London: Darton, Longman and Todd.

Austin, J. 1880: *Lectures on Jurisprudence.* London: John Murray.

Avineri, S. 1968: *The Social and Political Thought of Karl Marx.* Cambridge: Cambridge University Press.

1979: *Hegel's Theory of the Modern State.* Cambridge: Cambridge University Press.

Badie, B. and Birnbaum, P. 1983: *The Sociology of the State,* trans. A. Goldhammer. Chicago: Chicago University Press.

Barker, E. 1915a: The Discredited State. *Political Quarterly,* no. 5.

1915b: *Political Thought in England From Herbert Spencer to the Present Day.* London: Williams and Norgate.

1934: Introduction to Gierke's *Natural Law and the Theory of Society, 1500 to 1800,* 2 vols. Cambridge: Cambridge University Press.

1948: *Social Contract: Essays by Locke, Hume and Rousseau.* Oxford: Oxford University Press.

1979: *Greek Political Theory.* London: Methuen.

1967: *Principles of Social and Political Theory.* Oxford: Oxford University Press.

1966: *The Development of Public Services in Western Europe 1660–1930.* New York: Archon Books. First published 1944, Oxford: Oxford University Press.

Barry, N. P. 1981: *An Introduction to Modern Political Theory.* London: Macmillan.

Belloc, H. 1977: *The Servile State*. Indianapolis: Liberty Classics. First published 1913, London: T. N. Foulis.

Bernstein, J. M. 1984: From self-consciousness to community: act and recognition in the master-slave relationship. In Z. A. Pelczynski (ed.), *The State and Civil Society*.

Black, A. 1984: Guilds and Civil Society. London: Methuen.

Blackburn, R. (ed.) 1972: *Ideology in the Social Sciences*. London: Collins.

Blackstone, W. 1765–9: *Commentaries on the Laws of England*, in 4 vols. Oxford: Clarendon Press.

Bluntschli, J. K. 1895: *The Theory of the State*. Oxford: Oxford Univerity Press.

Bodin, J. 1962: *The Six Bookes of a Commonweale*. A fascimile reprint of the translation by R. Knolles in 1606, ed. by K. D. McRae. Cambridge, Mass.: Harvard University Press.

Bosanquet, B. 1895: *Essentials of Logic*. London: Macmillan.

1899: *The Philosophical Theory of the State*. London: Macmillan.

1898: Hegel's Theory of Political Organism. *Mind*, VII.

Boucher, D. 1985: *Texts in Context*. Hague: Martinus Nijhoff.

Buber, M. 1949: *Paths to Utopia*. London: Routledge and Kegan Paul.

Bultmann, R. 1956: *Primitive Christianity*. London: Collins.

Burns, J. H. 1959: Sovereignty and Constitutional Law in Bodin. *Political Studies*, VII.

Butler, C. 1977: *Hegel*. New York: Twayne.

Butterfield, H. 1950: *The Whig Theory of History*. London: G. Bell.

Carlyle, A. J. and Carlyle, R. W. 1903–36 *A History of Medieval Political Theory in the West*, 6 vols. London: William Blackwood and Sons.

Carnoy, M. 1984: *The State and Political Theory*. Princeton, NJ: Princeton University Press.

Carver, T. 1982: *Marx's Social Theory*. Oxford: Oxford University Press.

Cassirer, E. 1946: *The Myth of the State*. New Haven: Yale University Press.

Cheyette, F. L. 1978: The Invention of the State. In Bede Karl Lackner and K. R. Philp (eds), *Essays on Medieval Civilization: The Walter Prescott Webb Memorial Lectures*. Austin: University of Texas.

Chrimes, S. B. 1936: *English Constitutional Ideas in the Fifteenth Century*. Cambridge: Cambridge University Press.

Church, W. F. 1941: *Constitutional Thought in Sixteenth Century France*. Cambridge, Mass.: Harvard University Press.

(ed.) 1969: *The Impact of Absolutism in France: National Experience under Richelieu, Mazarin and Louis XIV*. New York: Wiley.

1972: *Richelieu and Reason of State*. Princeton, NJ: Princeton University Press.

Clark, G. L. and Dear, M. 1984: *State Apparatus: Structures and Language of Legitimacy*. London: George Allen and Unwin.

Cole, G. D. H. 1917: *Self-Government and Industry*. London: G. Bell.

1920: *Social Theory*. London: Methuen.

1980: *Guild Socialism Restated*. New Brunswick: Transaction Books. First published 1920, London: Parsons.

Connolly, W. E. (ed.) 1969: *The Basis of Pluralism*. New York: Atherton.

1983: *The Terms of Political Discourse*. Oxford: Martin Robertson.

(ed.) 1984: *Legitimacy and the State*. Oxford: Basil Blackwell.

Cranston, M. 1962: *What are Human Rights?*. New York: Basic Books.

Deane, H. A. 1955: *The Political Ideas of Harold J. Laski*. New York: Columbia University Press.

Delisle-Burns, C. 1915–16: The Nature of the State in view of its External Relations. Symposium with B. Russell and G. D. H. Cole, *Proceedings of the Aristotelian Society*, XVI.

D'Entrèves, A. P. 1939: *The Medieval Contribution to Political Thought*. Oxford: Oxford University Press.

1967: *The Notion of the State*. Oxford: Oxford University Press.

1970: *Natural Law*. London: Hutchinson.

Denzer, H. (ed.) 1973: *Jean Bodin: Proceedings of the International Conference on Bodin in Munich*. Munich: Verlag C. H. Beck.

Dewey, J. 1927: *The Public and Its Problems*. London: George Allen and Unwin.

Dicey, A. V. 1902: *Introduction to the Study of the Law of the Constitution*. London: Macmillan.

Dickinson, H. T. 1977: *Liberty and Property: Political Ideology in Eighteenth Century Britain*. London: Methuen.

Dodge, G. H. 1980: *Benjamin Constant's Philosophy of Liberalism*. Chapel Hill: University of North Carolina Press.

Dowdall, H. C. 1923: The Word State. *Law Quarterly Review*, XXXIX.

Durkheim, E. 1967: *The Division of Labour in Society*, trans. G. Simpson. New York: Free Press.

Duncan, G. 1983: Political Theory and Human Nature. In I. Forbes and S. Smith (eds), *Politics and Human Nature*. London: Francis Pinter.

Dunn, J. 1979: *Western Political Theory in the Face of the Future*. Cambridge: Cambridge University Press.

Dyson, K. H. F. 1980: *The State Tradition in Western Europe: A Study of an Idea and Institution*. Oxford: Martin Robertson.

Eccleshall, R. 1978: *Order and Reason in Politics: Theories of Absolute and Limited Monarchy in Early Modern England*. Hull: University of Hull.

Ehrenberg, V. 1960: *The Greek State*. Oxford: Basil Blackwell.

Elliott, W. Y. 1928: *The Pragmatic Revolt in Politics: Syndicalism Fascism and the Constitutional State*. New York: Macmillan.

Ellis, E. D. 1920: The Pluralist State, *American Political Science Review*, XIV.

1923: Guild Socialism and Pluralism. *American Political Science Review*, XVII.

Engels, F. 1976: *Anti-Dühring*. Peking: Foreign Languages Press.

Evans-Pritchard, E. E. 1940: *The Nuer*. Oxford: Oxford University Press.

Femia, J. 1981: *Gramsci's Political Thought: Hegemony, Consciousness and the Revolutionary Process*. Oxford: Clarendon Press.

Figgis, J. N. 1913: *The AntiChrist and Other Sermons*. London: Longmans Green.

1914: *Churches in the Modern State*. London: Longmans Green.

1915: *The Fellowship of the Mystery*. London: Longmans Green.

1922: *The Divine Right of Kings*. Cambridge: Cambridge University Press.

1956: *Political Thought from Gerson to Grotius*. Cambridge: Cambridge University Press.

Findlay, J. N. 1972: The Contemporary Relevance of Hegel. In A. MacIntyre (ed.), *Hegel*.

Finley, M. I. 1973: *Democracy: Ancient and Modern*. London: Chatto and Windus.

Fiori, G. 1970: *Antonio Gramsci, Life of a Revolutionary*. London: New Left Books.

Flathman, R. 1972: *Political Obligation*. New York: Atheneum.

Follett, M. P. 1920: *The New State*. London: Longmans Green.

Forsyth, M. 1981: *Union of States: The Theory and Practice of Confederation*. Leicester: Leicester University Press.

Fox, P. W. 1960: Louis XIV and the Theories of Absolutism and Divine Right. *Canadian Journal of Economic and Political Science*, XXVI.

Franklin, J. H. 1973a: Jean Bodin and the End of Medieval Constitutionalism. In H. Denzer (ed.), *Jean Bodin: Proceedings*.

1973: *Jean Bodin and the Rise of Absolutism*. Cambridge: Cambridge University Press.

1978: *John Locke and the Theory of Sovereignty: Mixed Monarchy and the Right of Resistance in the Political Thought of the English Revolution*. Cambridge: Cambridge University Press.

Frege, G. 1950: *The Foundations of Arithmetic*. Oxford: Basil Blackwell.

Friedrich, C. J. 1964: *Transcendent Justice: The Religious Dimensions of Constitutionalism*. Durham, NC: Duke University Press.

1968: *Constitutional Government and Democracy: Theory and Practice in Europe and America*, 4th edn. London: Blaisdell.

Fuller, L. 1966: *The Law in Quest of Itself*. Boston: Beacon Press.

Gallie, W. B. 1955–6: Essentially Contested Concepts. *Proceedings of the Aristotelian Society*, 56.

Gaus, G. F. 1983: *The Modern Liberal Theory of Man*. London: Croom Helm.

Gellner, E. 1983: *Nations and Nationalism*. Oxford: Basil Blackwell.

Gierke, Otto von 1900: *Political Theories of the Middle Ages*, trans. F. W. Maitland. Cambridge: Cambridge University Press.

1934: *Natural Law and the Theory of Society*, trans. Ernest Barker. Cambridge: Cambridge University Press.

1939: *The Development of Political Theory*, trans. B. Freyd. London: George Allen and Unwin.

Giesey, R. E. 1973: Medieval Jurisprudence in Bodin's concept of Sovereignty. In H. Denzer (ed.) *Jean Bodin: Proceedings*.

Giesey, R. E. and Salmon, J. H. M. 1972: introduction to F. Hotman,

Francogallia. Cambridge: Cambridge University Press.

Gilmore, M. P. 1941: *Arguments from Roman Law in Political Thought 1200–1600*. Cambridge, Mass.: Harvard University Press.

Glass, S. T. 1966: *The Responsible Society*. London: Longmans.

Gough, J. W. 1955: *Fundamental Law in English Constitutional History*. Oxford: Clarendon Press.

Gouldner, A. 1980: *The Two Marxisms: Contradictions and Anomilies in the Development of Theory*. London: Macmillan.

Gramsci, A. 1971: *Selections from the Prison Notebooks*, (eds) Q. Hoare and G. Nowell-Smith. London: Lawrence and Wishart.

Graves, R. 1985: *Goodbye to All That*. Harmondsworth, Middx. Penguin Books.

Greenleaf, W. H. 1973: Bodin and the Idea of Order. In H. Denzer (ed.), *Jean Bodin: Proceedings*.

1983: *The British Political Tradition: The Ideological Heritage*, Vol. 2. London: Methuen.

Habermas, J. 1976: *The Legitimation Crisis*. London: Heinemann.

Hall, E. B. 1961: Introduction to *The Political Testament of Cardinal Richelieu*. Madison: University of Wisconsin Press.

Hallis, F. 1978: *Corporate Personality: A Study in Jurisprudence*. Aalen: Scientia Verlag. First published 1930, Oxford: Oxford University Press.

Harris, H. S. 1972: *Hegel's Development Towards the Sunlight 1770–1801*. Oxford: Oxford University Press.

Harris, N. 1968: *Beliefs in Society*. Harmondsworth, Middx. Penguin Books.

Hart, H. L. A. 1961: *The Concept of Law*. Oxford: Clarendon Press.

Hegel, G. W. F. 1892–6: *Lectures on the History of Philosophy*, trans. E. S. Haldane and F. Simson, 3 vols. London: Routledge and Kegan Paul.

1948: *Early Theological Writings*, trans. T. M. Knox and R. Kroner. Chicago: Chicago University Press.

1964: *Hegel's Political Writings*, trans. T. M. Knox. Oxford: Oxford University Press.

1966: *Texts and Commentary*, trans. and ed. W. Kaufmann. New York: Doubleday Anchor.

1967: *The Philosophy of Right*, trans. T. M. Knox. Oxford: Oxford University Press.

1971: *The Philosophy of Mind*, trans. W. Wallace. Oxford: Clarendon Press.

Hexter, J. H. 1973: *The Vision of Politics on the Eve of the Reformation: More, Machiavelli and Seyssel*. London: Allen Lane.

Hinton, R. W. K. 1973: Bodin and the Retreat into Legalism. In H. Denzer (ed.) *Jean Bodin: Proceedings*.

Hirschman, A. O. 1982: *Shifting Involvements: Private Interests and Public Action*. Princeton, NJ: Princeton University Press.

Hobbes, T. 1839–45: *The English Works of Thomas Hobbes*, (ed.) Sir W. Molesworth. London: Bohn.

Hobbes, T. 1968: *Leviathan*. Harmondsworth, Middx.: Penguin Books.

Hobhouse, L. T. 1918: *The Metaphysical Theory of the State*. London: George Allen and Unwin.

Hobson, S. G. 1920: *National Guilds and the State*. London: G. Bell.

Hocking, W. E. 1968: *Man and the State*. New York: Archon Books.

Hotman, F. 1972: *Francogallia*, (eds) R. E. Giesey and J. H. M. Salmon. Cambridge: Cambridge University Press. First published 1573.

Hsiao, K. C. 1927: *Political Pluralism: A Study in Contemporary Political Theory*. London: Kegan Paul.

Ilting, K.-H. 1971: The Structure of Hegel's *Philosophy of Right*. In Z. A. Pelczynski (ed.), *Hegel's Political Philosophy: Problems and Perspectives*.

James I 1918: *The Political Writings of James I*, (ed.) C. H. McIlwain. Cambridge, Mass.: Harvard University Press.

Jasay, Anthony de 1985: *The State*. Oxford: Basil Blackwell.

Jay, R. 1984: Nationalism. In R. Eccleshall, V. Geoghegan, R. Jay and R. Wilford (eds), *Political Ideologies: An Introduction*, London: Hutchinson.

Jessop, B. 1983: *The Capitalist State*. Oxford: Martin Robertson.

Johnson, N. 1980: *In Search of the Constitution: Reflections on State and Society in Britain*. London: Methuen.

Kantorowicz, E. 1957: *The King's Two Bodies*. Princeton, NJ: Princeton University Press.

Kaufmann, W. (ed.) 1970: *Hegel's Political Philosophy*. New York: Atherton.

Kelsen, H. 1945: *The General Theory of Law and State*, trans. A. Wedberg. New York: Russell and Russell.

Keohane, N. O. 1980: *Philosophy and the State in France: The Renaissance to the Enlightenment*. Princeton, NJ: Princeton University Press.

King, P. 1974: *The Ideology of Order: A Comparative Analysis of Jean Bodin and Thomas Hobbes*. London: George Allen and Unwin.

Knox, T. M. 1967: Introduction to Hegel's *Philosophy of Right*. Oxford: Oxford University Press.

Krader, L. 1968: *The Formation of the State*. Englewood Cliff, NJ: Prentice-Hall.

Kroner, R. 1948: Introduction to *Hegel's Early Theological Writings*. Chicago: Chicago University Press.

Kropotkin, P. 1903: *The State: It's Historic Role*. London: Freedom Press.

Laski, H. J. 1919: *Authority in the Modern State*. New Haven, Conn.: Yale University Press.

1925: *The Grammar of Politics*. London: George Allen and Unwin.

1931: *Introduction to Politics*. London: George Allen and Unwin.

1935: *The State in Theory and Practice*. London: George Allen and Unwin.

Latham. E. 1965: *The Group Basis to Politics*. New York: Cornell University Press.

Lewis, J. D. 1935: *The Genossenschaft Theory of Otto von Gierke*. Madison: University of Wisconsin Press.

Lewis, J.U. 1968: Jean Bodin's 'Logic of Sovereignty'. *Political Studies*, XVI.

Lewy, G. 1960: *Constitutionalism and Statecraft during the Golden Age of Spain: A*

Study of the Political Philosophy of Juan de Mariana S.J. Geneva: Libraire E. Druz.

Lipset, S. M. 1971: *Political Man.* London: Heinemann.

1984: Social Conflict, Legitimacy and Democracy. In W. E. Connolly (ed.), *Legitimacy and the State.*

Lousse, E. 1964: Absolutism. In H. Lubasz (ed.) *The Development of the Modern State.*

Lowie, R. H. 1927: *The Origins of the State.* New York: Harcourt Brace.

Lubasz, H. (ed.) 1964: *The Development of the Modern State.* New York: Macmillan.

MacIver, R. M. 1926: *The Modern State.* Oxford: Oxford University Press.

Macpherson, C. B. 1977: Do we need a Theory of the State? *Archives Européenes de Sociologie,* XVIII.

MacIntyre, A. (ed.) 1972: *Hegel: A Collection of Critical Essays.* New York: Doubleday Anchor.

1981: *After Virtue: A Study in Moral Theory.* London: Duckworth.

McGovern, W. H. 1940: *From Luther to Hitler: The History of Fascist Nazi political Philosophy.* Boston, Mass.: Houghton Mifflin.

McIlwain, C. 1910: *The High Court of Parliament and its Supremacy.* New Haven, Conn: Yale University Press.

1939: *Constitutionalism and the Changing World.* Cambridge, Mass.: Harvard University Press.

1966: *Constitutionalism: Ancient and Modern.* New York: Cornell University Press.

McLellan, D. 1979: *Marxism after Marx.* London: Macmillan.

1980: *The Thought of Karl Marx.* London: Macmillan.

McRae, K. D. 1962: Introduction to Jean Bodin's *The Six Bookes of a Commonweale.* Cambridge, Mass.: Harvard University Press.

Magid, H. M. 1941: *English Political Pluralism.* New York: Columbia University Press.

Maitland, F.W. 1900: Introduction to Gierke, *Political Theories of the Middle Ages.* Cambridge: Cambridge University Press.

1908: *The Constitutional History of England.* Cambridge: Cambridge University Press.

1911: Moral Personality and Legal Personality. Appendix C in D. Nicholls, *The Pluralist State.*

Maritain, J. 1958: *The Rights of Man and Natural Law.* London: Bles.

Marshall, G. and Moodie, G. C. 1967: *Some Problems of the Constitution.* London: Hutchinson.

Marx, K. 1909: *Capital: A Critical Analysis of Capitalist Production.* London: William Glaisher.

1971: *The Early Writings,* (ed.) D. McLellan. Oxford: Basil Blackwell.

1974: *Hegel's Philosophy of Right and Marx's Commentary,* (ed.) H. Kainz. Hague: Martinus Nijhoff.

Marx, K. and Engels, F. 1967: *The Communist Manifesto.* Harmondsworth, Middx.: Penguin Books. First published 1888.

1968: *Selected Writings*. London: Lawrence and Wishart.

1970: *The German Ideology*, (ed.) C. J. Arthur. London: Lawrence and Wishart.

Meinecke, F. 1957: *Machiavellianism: The Doctrine of Raison D'Etat and its place in modern history*, trans. Douglas Scott. London: Routledge and Kegan Paul.

Merriam, C. E. 1900: *History of the Theory of Sovereignty since Rousseau*. New York: Columbia University Press.

Miliband, R. 1972: The Capitalist State: A Reply to Nicos Poulantzas. In R. Blackburn (ed.) *Ideology in the Social Sciences*.

1973: *The State in Capitalist Society*. London: Quartet Books.

Mitteis, H. 1975: *The State in the Middle Ages: A Comparative Constitutional History of Feudal Europe*, trans. H. F. Orton. Amsterdam: North–Holland.

Mogi, S. 1931: *The Problem of Federalism*. London: George Allen and Unwin.

Morris, C. 1972: *The Discovery of the Individual*. New York: Harper and Row.

Mousnier, R. 1979: *The Institutions of France Under the Absolute Monarchy*. Chicago: Chicago University Press.

Mulgan, R. G. 1977: *Aristotle's Political Theory*. Oxford: Oxford University Press.

Nicholls, D. 1974: *Three Varieties of Pluralism*. London: Macmillan.

1975: *The Pluralist State*. London: Macmillan.

Nisbet, R. 1970: *The Sociological Tradition*. London: Heinemann.

Oakeshott, M. 1956: Political Education. In P. Laslett (ed.) *Philosophy, Politics and Society*. Oxford: Basil Blackwell.

1975: *On Human Conduct*. Oxford: Clarendon Press.

O'Connor, J. 1973: *The Fiscal Crisis of the State*. New York: St Martins Press.

1974: *Corporations and the State: Essays on the Theory of Capitalism and Imperialism*. New York: Harper and Row.

Oestreich, G. 1982: *Neostoicism and the Early Modern State*, trans. D. McLintock. Cambridge: Cambridge University Press.

Offe, K. 1984: *Contradictions in the Welfare State*. London: Heinemann.

Organski, A. F. K. 1965: *The Stages of Political Growth*. New York: A. Knopf.

Orridge, A. W. 1981: Varieties of Nationalism. In L. Tivey (ed.), *The Nation State*.

Parker, D. 1983: *The Making of French Absolutism*. London: Edward Arnold.

Parry, G. 1978: *John Locke*. London: George Allen and Unwin.

Pateman, C. 1979: *The Problem of Political Obligation*. Chichester: Wiley.

Pelczynski, Z. A. (ed.) 1971: *Hegel's Political Philosophy: Problems and Perspectives*. Cambridge: Cambridge University Press.

(ed.) 1984: *The State and Civil Society: Studies in Hegel's Political Philosophy*. Cambridge: Cambridge University Press.

Pennock, J. R. and Chapman, J. W. (eds) 1979: *Constitutionalism*, Nomos XX. New York: New York University Press.

Penty, A. J. 1906: *The Restoration of the Guild System*. London: Swan Sonnenschein.

1917: *Old Worlds for New*. London: George Allen and Unwin.

Peters, R. S. 1967: *Hobbes*. Harmondsworth, Middx.: Penguin Books.

Pitkin, H. 1972: Obligation and Consent. In P. Laslett, W. G. Runciman and Q. Skinner (eds), *Philosophy. Politics and Society*, Oxford: Basil Blackwell.

Plant, R. 1974: *Community and Ideology: An Essay in Applied Social Philosophy*. London: Routledge and Kegan Paul.

1982: Jürgen Habermas and the Idea of the Legitimation Crisis. *European Journal of Political Research*, 10.

1984: *Hegel*. Oxford: Basil Blackwell. First published 1973, London: George Allen and Unwin.

Plato 1970: *The Laws*, trans. T. J. Saunders. Harmondsworth, Middx.: Penguin Books.

Pocock, J. G. A. 1957: *The Ancient Constitution and the Feudal Law*. Cambridge: Cambridge University Press.

1972: *Politics Language and Time: Essays on Political Thought and History*. London: Methuen.

Poggi, G. 1978: *The Development of the Modern State*. London: Hutchinson.

Popper, K. 1950: *The Open Society and its Enemies*. Princeton, NJ: Princeton University Press.

Post, G. 1964: *Studies in Medieval Legal Thought: Public Law and the State 1100–1322*. Princeton, NJ: Princeton University Press.

Poulantzas, N. 1968: *Political Power and Social Class*. London: New Left Books.

1972: The Problem of the Capitalist State. In R. Blackburn (ed), *Ideology in the Social Sciences*.

1978: *State, Power and Socialism*. London: New Left Books.

Powicke, F. M. 1936: Reflections on the Medieval State. *Transactions of the Royal Historical Society*, XIX.

Proudhon, P.-J. 1970: *Selected Writings*, trans. E. Frazer. London: Macmillan.

Raphael, D. D. 1970: *Problems of Political Philosophy*. London: Macmillan.

Reckitt, M. B. and Bechhofer, C. E. 1920: *The Meaning of National Guilds*. London: Cecil Palmer.

Rees, J. C. 1969: The Theory of Sovereignty Restated. In W. J. Stankiewicz (ed.), *In Defence of Sovereignty*.

Resnick, D. 1984: Locke and the Rejection of the Ancient Constitution. *Political Theory*, 12.

Richter, M. 1977: *The Political Theory of Montesquieu*. Cambridge: Cambridge University Press.

Ross, A. 1961: On the concept 'State' and 'State organ' in Constitutional Law. *Scandinavian Studies in Law*, 5.

Rothbard, M. N. 1978: *For a New Liberty: The Libertarian Manifesto*. London: Collier Macmillan.

Rowen, H. 1961: L'Etat c'est moi: Louis XIV and the State. *French Historical Studies*, 2.

1980: *The King's State: Proprietary Dynasticism in Early Modern France*. New Jersey: Rutgers University Press.

Rubinstein, N. 1971: Notes on the word *stato* in Florence before Machiavelli. In J. G. Rowe and W. H. Stockdale (eds) *Florilegium Historicale: Essays presented to William K. Ferguson*. Toronto: University of Toronto Press.

Sabine, G.H. 1923: Pluralism: A Point of View. *American Political Science Review*, XVII.

Salmon, J. H. M. 1959: *The French Wars of Religion in English Political Thought*. Oxford: Clarendon Press.

1973: Bodin and the Monarchomachs. In H. Denzer (ed.) *Jean Bodin: Proceedings*.

Schacht, R. 1972: Hegel on Freedom. In A. MacIntyre (ed.) *Hegel*.

Schochet, G. J. 1975: *Patriarchalism in Political Thought*. Oxford: Basil Blackwell.

1979: Introduction: Constitutionalism, Liberalism and the Study of Politics. In J. R. Pennock and J. W. Chapman (eds), *Constitutionalism*, New York: New York University Press.

Shennan, J. H. 1974: *The Origins of the Modern European State 1450–1725*. London: Hutchinson.

Siedentrop, L. 1983: Political Theory and Ideology: The Case of the State. In D. Miller and L. Siedentrop (eds) *The Nature of Political Theory*, Oxford: Clarendon Press.

Simmons, A. J. 1979: *Moral Principles and Political Obligations*. Princeton, NJ: Princeton University Press.

Singer, P. 1979: *Practical Ethics*. Cambridge: Cambridge University Press.

Skinner, Q. 1978: *The Foundations of Modern Political Thought*, in 2 vols. Cambridge: Cambridge University Press.

Stankiewicz, W. J. (ed.) 1969: *In Defence of Sovereignty*. Oxford: Oxford University Press.

Strayer, J. R. 1970: *On the Medieval Origins of the Modern State*. Princeton, NJ: Princeton University Press.

Stuart-Hughes, H. 1979: *Consciousness and Society*. Brighton, Sussex: Harvester Press.

Tawney, R. H. 1921: *The Acquisitive Society*. London: G. Bell.

Taylor, C. 1975: *Hegel*. Cambridge: Cambridge University Press.

1979: *Hegel and Modern Society*. Cambridge: Cambridge University Press.

1983: Use and Abuse of Theory. In A. Parel (ed.) *Ideology, Philosophy and Politics*. Ontario: Wilfred Laurier Press.

Tierney, B. 1982: *Religion, Law and the Growth of Constitutional Thought 1150–1650*. Cambridge: Cambridge University Press.

Tilly, C. (ed.) 1975: *The Formation of National States in Western Europe*. Princeton, NJ: Princeton University Press.

Tivey, L. (ed.) 1981: *The Nation State: The Formation of Modern Politics*. Oxford: Martin Robertson.

Tönnies, F. 1955: *Community and Association*. London: Routledge and Kegan Paul.

Tuck, R. 1979: *Natural rights theories: Their Origin and Development*. Cambridge: Cambridge University Press.

Tucker, R. 1961: *Philosophy and Myth in Karl Marx*. Cambridge: Cambridge University Press.

Unwin, G. 1927: *Studies in Economic History*. London: Macmillan.

Ullman, W. 1975: *Medieval Political Thought*. Harmondsworth, Middx.: Penguin Books.

Verene, D. P. (ed.) 1980: *Hegel's Social and Political Thought: The Philosophy of Objective Spirit*. Brighton, Sussex: Harvester Press.

Vernon, R. 1980: Introduction to G. D. H. Cole, *Guild Socialism Restated*. New Brunswick: Transaction Books.

Vile, M. J. C. 1967: *Constitutionalism and the Separation of Powers*. Oxford: Clarendon Press.

Vincent, A. W. 1983: The Hegelian State and international politics. *Review of International Studies*, 9.

(ed.) 1986: *The Philosophy of T. H. Green*. Aldershot, Hants.: Gower.

Vincent, A. W. and Plant, R. 1984: *Philosophy Politics and Citizenship: The Life and Thought of the British Idealists*. Oxford: Basil Blackwell.

Wartofsky, M. W. 1977: *Feuerbach*. Cambridge: Cambridge University Press.

Wheare, K. C. 1958: *Modern Constitutions*. Oxford: Oxford University Press.

Wilde, N. 1924: *The Ethical Theory of the State*. Princeton, NJ: Princeton University Press.

Willoughby, W. W. 1896: *An Examination of the Nature of the State: A Study in Political Philosophy*. London: Macmillan.

Woodhouse, A. S. P. (ed.) 1966: *Puritanism and Liberty*. London: Dent.

Wright, A. W. 1979: *G. D. H. Cole and Socialist Democracy*. Oxford: Clarendon Press.

Wootton, D. (ed.) 1986: *Divine Right and Democracy*. Harmondsworth, Middx: Penguin Books.

Yates, F. A. 1975: *Astraea: The Imperial Theme in the 16th Century*. Harmondsworth, Middx: Penguin Books.

Index

Absolutism, 34–5, 44, 90, 113, 185, 198–9;
    backcloth to constitutionalism, 77;
    and civil war, 77; and cosmic order,
    47, 66; definition of, 47; empirical
    factors and, 48; and enlightened
    despotism, 46; and feudalism, 47; and
    monarchy, 26–7, 227; and
    nationalism, 26–7; and the papacy, 48;
    and Roman law, 47–8; and the State,
    45–76; summary on, 75–6, and
    totalitarianism, 46
Acton, Lord, 107, 193–4, 197
administration, 30–2, 162
Agreemens of the People, 97
Alexander V (Pope), 86
alienation, 156
Allen, J.W., 59
allodialism, 61–4
Almain, J., 86, 88
Althusius, J., 86, 89, 107, 110
Althusser, L., 171–5
anarchism, 10, 31, 41, 44, 132, 184, 185
ancien régime, 120–1
Anderson, P., 170
Anglican Church, 187
Aragonese Privileges (1285–7), 107
Aquinas, T., 68, 104, 105–6, 107
Aristotle, 4, 5, 8, 12–13, 22, 32, 79, 83, 103,
    125, 131
Armstrong, A. H., 104
Asquith, H. H., 116
Aufhebung, 163
Austin, John, 56, 57, 58, 186, 188, 200, 229
Austin, J. L., 42
authority, 20, 32, 37–9
Avineri, S., 158

Badie, B., 220
Bakunin, M., 150, 163
Balibar, C., 172

Barker, E., 13, 17, 79, 109, 188, 196, 201,
    202, 207–8, 209, 215
Barry, N. P., 5
Basel, Council of, 86
Bauer, Bruno, 153
Bauer, Edgar, 153
Bechhofer, C. E., 192, 202
Belloc, H., 192
Bentham, J., 26, 44, 58, 111
Bentley, A. F., 183, 189
Bernstein, E., 164
Bernstein, J. M., 124
Beseler, G., 190–1, 204
Bettelheim, B., 164
Beveridge, W. H., 118
Beza, T., 88, 89, 107
Bildung, 125, 140
Bill of Rights (1689), 97, 98, 106
Birnbaum, P., 220
Black, A., 60, 113, 140, 185, 186
Blackstone, W., 100, 102, 105
Blackwood, A., 67, 68
Bluntschli, J. K., 4, 5, 21
Bodin, J., 7, 8, 34–5, 44, 45, 47, 67–8, 71,
    81, 87, 89, 93, 186, 198–9, 201, 226,
    227
Boethius, 206
Bolingbroke, Lord, 80
Bonaparte, N., 120
Bonham case, 94
Borgia, C., 18
Bosanquet, B., 7, 125, 130, 136, 140, 209,
    223
Bossuet, J.-B., 50, 64, 72–3
Boucher, D., 8
Bracton, H., 11, 79, 85
Bradley, F. H., 182
Bryce, J., 98
Buber, M., 178
Buchanan, G., 110

Budé, G., 19
Bukharin, N., 166
Bultmann, R., 13
bureaucracy, 64–5, 137–8, 157–8; *see also*
  administration
Burke, E., 24–5, 80, 94, 104, 121, 228
Burns, J. H., 59
Butler, C., 124
Butterfield, H., 8, 82

cabinet, 30
Calvin, J., 48, 67, 87
capitalism, 113–14
Carlyle, A. J., 52, 54, 110, 227
Carlyle, R. W., 52, 54, 110, 227
Carnoy, M., 151, 168, 173
Carver, T., 152, 153
Cassirer, E., 18
Charles I, 96, 99
Cheyette, F. L., 14
Chrimes, S. B., 94
Church, W. F., 19, 53, 57, 68, 69–70, 72
Cicero, Marcus Tullius, 48, 67, 87
civil service, 30, 137–8
civil society, 112–14, 132, 134–6, 156–8,
  169–70
civil war, 48, 49, 52, 70; English, 36, 80,
  90–1
class, abolition of, 178; and administration,
  162–3; and civil society, 156–7; and
  factory inspectorate, 162; and
  Hegelian State, 156–9; and history,
  148–9; and the human subject, 180;
  and materialism, 153–60, 166–7;
  meaning of, 149; and political power,
  151; and property, 151, 158;
  traditional theory of, 152–60; types of,
  150
Clement VI (Pope), 86
Coke, E., 11, 79, 84
Colbert, Jean, 49
Cole, G. D. H., 31, 189, 192, 195–7, 201–3,
  211–18, 228, 229
Coleridge, S. T., 25
command theory of law, 53
communes, 10
communism, 10, 31
communitas communitatum, 214; *see* pluralism
community, 10, 24–6, 140–2; of realm, 85
conciliarism, 33, 82, 85–6, 87–8, 185
Connolly, W. E., 38, 39, 42
consent, 109, 135, 188
Constance, Council of, 86
Constant, B., 27, 96, 111
constitution, the ancient, 92–4; the Anglo-
  Saxon, 80, 93; Arthurian, 93;

balanced, 98–103; British, 96, 98; and
  checks and balances, 98–103; as
  entailed inheritance, 92; façade, 81;
  Frankish, 80, 88–9; Gothic, 80, 88–9,
  93; in Greece, 13, 79, 83; in Holland,
  97; mixed, 98–103; in Pennsylvania,
  97; senses of, 79–80; and separation of
  powers, 100–2; and sovereignty, 36,
  37; in Sweden, 97; in the United
  States of America, 96, 97; written,
  96–8
constitutionalism, 45–6; and absolutism,
  45–6; and civil society, 112–14; and
  conciliarism, 82, 85–6; consent and,
  109; and contractualism, 106–9; and
  conventions, 95–6; and democracy, 81,
  111–12; duty and right, 88; and
  ethical theory, 122; and federalism,
  81; and feudalism, 84–5; law and,
  113–14; and liberalism, 116–18; on
  liberty, 114–16; as limitation theory,
  77–9; and the market, 114; and
  natural law, 83, 103–5; origins, 82–91;
  and popular sovereignty, 81, 109–10;
  on public and private realms, 112–13;
  and rights, 105–6; and Roman law,
  45, 47–8, 84, 87; trivialization of,
  81–2; and value of the person, 115;
  values of, 80, 111–12
contract, 22–3, 24, 106–9
conventions, 95–6; *see* constitutionalism
Counter-Reformation, 89, 110
Covenant of the League of Nations, 97
Cranston, M., 106
Croce, B., 165, 166
Cromwell, O., 97
crown, 30, 85, 133, 137; in Parliament, 37,
  101; prerogatives of, 53
Cusa, Nicholas of, 86, 185

Darwin, C., 164
Dahrendorf, R., 26
Deane, H. A., 197, 198, 201, 213
Delisle-Burns, C., 7
Della Volpe, G., 164
democracy, 44, 81, 103, 111–12; and
  auxiliary precautions, 111; functional,
  185, 202–3; geographical, 185, 202–3;
  and liberalism, 112; and pluralism,
  185
D'Entrèves, A. P., 104, 105
derivationist school, 175–6
Dewey, J., 2, 116, 167, 182
dialectic, 126
Dicey, A. V., 37, 96, 200
Dickinson, H. T., 67, 68

Digges, Dudley, 67
Disraeli, B., 25
distributivism, 184, 192
divine right, 48, 50, 65–9, 75, 227;
    arguments of, 67–8; and Tory Party,
    69
Dowdall, H. C., 18
Duguit, L., 22, 214
Duncan, G., 43
Dunn, J., 27
Durkheim, E., 22, 25–6, 140, 189, 220
Dyson, K. H. F., 4, 7, 10, 11, 17, 18, 19, 30,
    42, 123, 167, 225

Eccleshall, R., 47
Ehrenburg, V., 12
Eliot, T. S., 24
Elliott, Y. L., 77, 184, 188
Ellis, E. D., 211
empire, 10, 22; Holy Roman, 15, 66;
    Roman, 32–3
Engels, F., 147–75; *see* Marx and Marxism
Enlightenment, 27
enterprise association, 120
epistemological break, 173; *see* Marx and
    Marxism
essential contestability, 42–3
estado, 17
estates, 17–18, 89, 93; assemblies, 14–15,
    34, 76, 86, 137–8, 140; General, 88–9,
    93
ethical life (*Sittlichkeit*), 139–43; *see* ethical
    theory
ethical theory: *ancien régime* and, 120–2; and
    bad States, 131; and bourgeois
    individualism, 122, 132, 134–6; and
    Burke, 121–2; and civil society, 132,
    134–6; and constitutional order, 133,
    136–9; and corporations, 139–43; and
    dialectic, 126; and the family, 139–43;
    and folk religion, 141–2; and the
    French Revolution, 120–1; and *Geist*,
    120, 122–3; and history, 123;
    metaphysics of, 120, 123–31; and
    system of philosophy, 126–7; and
    reason, 127; and the understanding,
    127
ethnos, 12
European Charter on Human Rights, 97
Evans-Pritchard, E. E., 10
Exclusion Crisis, 93

Fabianism, 192, 213
Factory Inspectorate, 162; *see* class theory
fascism, 143, 172
federalism, 11, 37, 81, 185, 198, 213, 215

Femia, J., 165, 166
feudalism, 14–15, 23, 27, 30, 33–4, 84–6;
    and assemblies, 14–15, 34, 76, 86; and
    property, 61
Feuerbach, L., 124, 152, 153–6
Fichte, J. G., 27, 122, 153
Figgis, J. N., 17, 23, 48, 62, 65, 68, 70, 82,
    90, 93, 107, 182–5, 187, 189, 191,
    193–7, 199, 200, 202–4, 206, 208, 211,
    213–16, 227, 228, 229
Filmer, Sir R., 60, 68, 99
Findlay, J. N., 126
Finley, M. I., 12
Fiore, G., 167
Flathman, R., 39
folk-religion, 141–2
Follett, M. P., 195
Forsyth, M., 229
Fourier, C., 152
Fox, P. W., 65, 72
Francis I, 49, 86
Franklin, J. H., 47, 51–2, 57
Free Church of Scotland Appeals, 205–6
free market economy, 114, 132, 134–6; and
    Guilds, 186, 192
Frege, G., 9
French Revolution, 26–7, 120–1, 132
French Wars of Religion, 34, 52, 67, 88
Friedrich, C. J., 98, 115
Fromm, E., 26
Fronde, 76
Fuller, L., 56

Gallie, W. B., 42–3
Gaus, G. F., 116
Geist (Spirit or Mind), 120, 123–7;
    Feuerbach's critique, 153–4; Marx's
    critique, 154–8
general will, 26, 201
Genossenschaft, 190–1
Gentile, G., 143
Germanism, 191, 204–5; *see* Romanism and
    Roman law
Gerson, Jean, 86, 185
Gierke, Otto von, 23, 25, 34, 110–11, 184,
    186, 189, 190–1, 195, 198, 199, 200,
    204, 205, 208, 210, 215
Giesey, R., 58, 59, 89
Gilmore, M. P., 47, 62
Gobineau, Arthur de, 27
Godelier, M., 164
Goethe, J. W., 122, 228
Golden Bull of Hungary (1222), 107
Gough, J. W., 94, 109
Gouldner, A., 164
government, 29–32, 100–1

Gramsci, A., 164–71, 172, 173, 174
Greeks, 5, 7, 10, 11–13, 83, 122, 131–2, 133, 158; and German thought, 122; on legislative and executive, 13; and natural law, 103–4; and society, 22
Green, T. H., 116, 118, 197
Greenleaf, W. H., 24, 47
Gregory VII (Pope), 48, 226
Grotius, H., 18, 105, 107
Groups: functional, 185; and individualism, 194–5; and interests, 182–5, 189–90; liberty and, 193–8; nature of, 186–7, 190; personality of, 187, 191, 203–10; polyarchy and, 202; pressure, 183–4; and sovereignty, 198–203
Grundnorm, 36
Guilds: democracy and, 192; industrialism and, 192; medieval, 14, 23, 34, 85, 185–6, 192; national, 192; and Roman law, 186; and socialism, 23, 25, 34, 85, 185–6, 192

Habermas, J., 38–9, 165, 175, 176, 177
Hall, H. B., 71
Hallis, F., 210
Harris, H. S., 125
Harris, N., 124
Hart, H. L. A., 20
Hayek, F., 26, 42, 116–17, 120
Heads of the Proposals (1647), 97
Hegel, G. W. F., 2, 7, 8, 25, 27, 113, 119–46, 152, 153–8, 160, 169, 170, 182, 186, 220, 223, 228
hegemony, 167–9
Heidegger, M., 42
Henry II, 49
Herder, G., 27, 122, 228
Herrschaft, 191
Hess, M., 153
Hexter, J. H., 18–19
Hinton, R. W. K., 56, 59
Hirschman, A., 24
Hobbes, T., 7, 8, 34, 40, 44, 47, 50–60, 67, 74, 81, 105, 106, 108, 186, 188, 198–9, 200, 201, 227, 229
Hobhouse, L. T., 116, 118, 144
Hobson, J. A., 116, 118
Hobson, S. G., 189, 192, 213, 214, 228
Hocking, W. E., 183
Hölderlin, F., 122, 228
Horner, L., 162
Hotman, F., 34, 80, 88–9, 93, 110
Hsiao, K. C., 194, 201, 203, 211, 215, 229
human nature, 43–4, 223–4

Ilting, K. H., 133, 141–2

Imperium, 32–3, 37, 54, 186, 199
individualism, 24, 112–18; and the Greeks, 13, 141–2; and pluralism, 186, 194–5, 204
industralization, 27
Innocent III (Pope), 48
Innocent IV (Pope), 66, 199
Instrument of Government (1653), 97
interest groups, 183–4, 189–90; *see* groups and pluralism

James I, 63
James II, 97
James, William, 180
Jasay, A., 179, 180
Jessop, B., 152
Johnson, N., 96, 98
judicial sphere, 100–2
jurisdictio, 85
Justinian, 58, 73, 84, 104

Kant, I., 122, 126, 128, 152, 153
Kantorowicz, E., 31
Kaufman, W., 144
Kelsen, H., 36
Keohane, N. O., 45, 46, 56, 72, 87
Keynes, J. M., 118
King, P., 46, 52, 56
kingship, 65–6
Knox, T. M., 135, 136, 139
koinonia, 12
Korsch, K., 165
Krader, L., 10
Kroner, R., 124, 126
Kropotkin, P., 10, 184, 185, 193, 215

Laski, H. J., 23, 31, 182, 183, 184, 187, 189, 191, 195–8, 200, 201, 204, 211–14, 216, 228, 229
Latham, E., 189–90
law: canon, 8, 14, 15; civil, 8, 63, 113–14; common, 11, 92–4; command theory of, 53; constitutional, 58; and convention, 95–6, 80; fundamental, 63, 87, 92–4; and groups, 205–6; and *leges imperii*, 58–9, 62; living, 35; natural, 83, 103–5, 226; Roman, 11, 15, 22–3, 32–3, 35, 50, 54, 66, 84, 87, 89, 186; rule of, 11, 114; and sovereignty, 32–3, 36, 66; of Trusts, 205–6
legibus solutus, 33, 54, 84, 91, 199
legislative, 13, 29, 53–4, 100–2, 137–8
legitimacy, 20, 37–9
legitimation crisis, 38, 176–7
Lenin, V. I., 161, 167

Leo I (Pope), 48
Levellers, 93, 94, 97
Lewis, J. D., 191, 195, 198, 200, 210, 215
Lewis, J. U., 54
Lewy, G., 90
lex regia, 33, 35, 84–5
liberalism, 6, 45, 81, 116–18, 196, 198
libertarianism, 10, 193
liberty, 114–18, 189, 193–8, 216
Lilburne, J., 93
Lipset, S. M., 38, 221
Locke, J., 8, 26, 40, 80, 81, 90, 101, 102, 105–6, 107–9, 117–18, 220
Louis XIV, 17, 29, 46, 47, 48, 64–5, 67, 68, 72, 74, 75–6, 96, 199, 219
Lousse, E., 46, 47
Lubasz, H., 6
Lukács, G., 165, 171
lumpenproletariat, 150
Luther, M., 48, 70, 87

McGovern, W. H., 144
McIlwain, C., 59, 69, 80, 84–5, 93–4, 98
MacIver, R. M., 22
McLellan, D., 162, 170, 178
Macpherson, C. B., 224–5
McRae, K. D., 53, 59
Machiavelli, N., 18–19, 48, 69–70, 143
Machiavellianism, 70
Madison, J., 111
Magid, H. M., 194, 195, 199, 201, 202, 208
Magna Charta (1215), 85, 93, 107, 188
Mair, J., 86, 88
Maitland, F. W., 23, 93, 99, 183, 189, 191, 196, 205, 209
Mariana, Juan de, 89–90, 107
Maritain, J., 105–6
Markus, R. A., 104
Marshall, G., 95
Marsilius of Padua, 68, 220
Marx, K., 1, 22, 25, 42, 134, 147–80, 225, 228
Marxism, 1, 45, 147–80; and capital logic school, 175–6; and class struggle school, 174; and derivationists, 175–7; economic tendency of, 147–8; and epistemological break, 173; and fiscal crisis, 177; and Hegelianism, 166; and independent State theorists, 176–7; and legitimation crisis, 176–7; and materialist school, 175–6; as praxis philosophy, 146, 177; voluntaristic and scientific, 164–5, 172
Maslow, A., 26
materialism, 152–60, 166
Mazarin, Cardinal, 49, 64

Meinecke, F., 18, 70–1, 143
mercantilism, 49
Merriam, C., 56
Merum Imperium, 84
Miliband, R., 174–5
Mill, James, 111
Mill, J. S., 112
Mitteis, H., 14, 226
modernization, 27
Mogi, S., 198
Molesworth, Viscount, 89
monarchomachs, 88
monistic State, 183, 186, 188, 193, 195
Montesquieu, Baron de, 100–3, 142
Moodie, G. C., 95
Mornay, Philippe de Plessis, 88, 89, 107
Morris, C., 207
Morris, W., 25
Mousnier, R., 46
Mulgan, R. G., 13
Mussolini, B., 143

nation: and sovereignty, 36; and State, 5, 26–9, 36
national commune, 212, 213, 217
nationalism: classifications of, 27–8; French, 26; Irish, 27; nature of, 26–9, 36
natural law, 103–5, 226; *see* law
Nicholls, D., 190, 194, 196, 201, 208, 214, 229
Nietzsche, F., 154
Nisbet, R., 24
normative theory, 41–2
Nozick, R., 40–1, 118

Oakeshott, M., 5, 23, 120
obligation, 37–9
O'Connor, J., 177
Oestreich, G., 107, 108–9
Offe, K., 38, 175–7
office theory, 51, 61–5, 91
Organski, A. F. K., 221

Paine, T., 93, 98
Pareto, W., 189
Parker, D., 47, 72, 75–6
Parker, H., 91
Parliament, 33, 91, 93, 96, 98
Parry, G., 117–18
Pateman, C., 39, 109
Pelczynski, Z. A., 133, 142, 228
Penty, A. J., 185, 192
personality: of groups, 187, 191, 203–10; in Hegel's thought, 137; in Hobbes, 74; and impersonality of State, 75; origin

of, 73; and *persona ficta*, 35, 73–4, 208; real and artificial, 203–10; and Roman law, 73; senses of, 73–4, 206–10; of State, 8–9, 21, 73–4, 206–10
Peters, R. S., 56
phalanx, 12
phratry, 12
phyle, 12
Pitkin, H., 39
Plant, R., 26, 39, 118, 125, 126, 141, 209
Plato, 12, 83, 99, 103, 106
Plekhanov, G. V., 166, 175
plenitudo potestas, 32–3, 37, 49, 199
pluralism: American, 184, 189–90; and anarchism, 184, 215, 216, 228; and Anglicanism, 187; and Christianity, 194; and consensus, 182–3; and critique of democracy, 185; cultural, 182; descriptive sense of, 183; and diffusion of power, 187, 188; and distributivism, 184, 192; English, 184, 190; and English law, 209–10; ethical, 182, 193, 196; and Free Church of Scotland, 205–6; and government, 187; and group personality, 189, 190, 203–10; and growth of State, 184; and guild socialism, 184, 185, 191–2, 211–13; and individualism, 186; and interest groups, 183; and liberalism, 196, 198; on liberty, 189, 193–8, 216; normative sense of, 183; philosophical, 181; political, 182–3; and political science, 183–4; and polyarchy, 202; and pragmatism, 181–2; and rights, 194; and self-realization, 195–6; senses of, 181–3; and sovereignty, 189, 198–203, 215; and syndicalism, 184, 185, 189, 192, 193, 228
Pocock, J. G. A., 67, 94
Poggi, G., 220
polis, 5, 7, 10, 11–13, 83, 122, 131–2, 133, 158
political economy, 134, 152
politics: and ethics, 13; and pluralism, 183–4, 189–90; science of, 12, 45, 183, 189; and theory, 40–3
politiques, 34, 66, 70
polyarchism, 202
Popper, K., 144
populus, 35–6, 109–10
Post, G., 15–16, 18, 226
Poulantzas, N., 164, 171–5
pragmatism, 181–2
pressure groups, 183–4, 189–90
property, 61–5, 158, 192
Protestantism, 87

Proudhon, P.-J., 152, 163, 179, 184, 191, 215
Prynne, W., 88
public power, 19, 21, 30, 52, 218, 222–3; and private, 112–14
public services, 30
public welfare, 17
Pufendorf, S., 105, 107

racial theory, 27
raison d'état, 69–73
Raphael, D. D., 5
Rawls, J., 40, 108, 116
Reckitt, M. B., 192, 202
Rees, J. C., 31
Reformation, 48, 67, 87, 132
Regierung, 30
Renaissance, 18, 66
resistance theory, 87–8
Resnick, D., 227
Respublica Christiana, 15
Richelieu, Cardinal, 19, 49, 64, 69–70, 72–3, 74
Richter, M., 99, 100, 102, 227
rights: bill of rights, 80, 98; Bill of Rights (1689), 97, 106; and consent, 109; and contractualism, 108; duties and, 106; and liberalism, 117–18; natural and human, 105–6
'right reason', 94
Roman law: and constitutionalism, 84; and Germanist thesis, 191, 204–5; and Guilds, 186; and natural law, 104; and personality theory, 73–4
Romanism, 191, 204–5
Roosevelt, F. D., 190
Ross, A., 9
Rothbard, M., 23
Rousseau, J.-J., 8, 107, 110, 201, 202
Rowen, H., 61, 62, 64, 65, 227
Ruge, A., 153
Russell, B., 197
Ryle, G., 8

Sabine, G. H., 183
Saint-Simon, Henri de, 152
Salmon, J. H. M., 52, 89
Sartre, J.-P., 171
Savigny, F. C. von, 191, 204
Scarman, Lord, 98
Schelling, F. W. J., 122, 124
Schiller, F., 122, 141, 228·
Schiller, F. C. S., 181
Schochet, G. J., 68, 109
self-realization, 195–6
separation of powers, 30, 37, 100–2

Seyssel, Claude de, 81, 83, 86–7, 93
Sidney, Algernon, 89
Simmons, A. J., 109
Singer, P., 207
Skinner, Q., 8, 19, 34, 47, 49, 52, 53, 54, 57, 63, 69, 84, 87, 88, 117, 226, 227
Smith, A., 113, 122, 134
societas, 22–3, 191, 226
society, 22–4, 118, 201–2
sociology, 219–22
Soto, Domingo de, 89–90, 107
sovereignty: and absolute theory, 45–60; and Bodin, 34–5; *de facto* and *de jure*, 35; and democracy, 111; and Dicey, 37; and divine right, 50, 65–9; and general will, 110; and Hobbes, 34; and the law, 36, 37; legal, 200; and legislative power, 53–4, 67; limitations on, 34, 58–60; and living law, 35; the logic of, 34–5, 51, 55; the marks of, 53; and the monarchomachs, 34; and natural law, 105; parliamentary, 91, 98; in a person, 31, 35, 73–5, 227; and pluralism, 189, 198–203, 215; political and moral, 37, 200–1; popular, 26, 35–6, 44, 81, 87–8, 90, 109–11; and property theory, 50, 61–5; and reason of State, 69–73; and Roman law, 32–3, 35, 50; shared, 37
species being, 154
Spencer, H., 188, 194, 197
Stäel, Madame de, 111
Stoics, 23, 103
Strauss, L., 104
Strayer, J. R., 226
Stuart-Hughes, H., 164
Staat, 17
State: absolutist theory of, 45–76; and academic study, 2; and administration, 29–34; antecedents of, 11–16; class theory of, 147–80; in classical political theory, 2; and community, 24–6; constitutional theory of, 77–118; developmental theory and, 220–1; discredited, 188, 201; essential contestability of, 42–3; ethical theory of, 119–46; etymology of, 16–19; formal features of, 19–21, 42, 220; formal theory of, 218; functionalist theory of, 220–1; and government, 29–34; and Greeks, 11–13; and human nature, 43–4; juristic–normative theory of, 218, 222–5; medieval theory and, 13–16, 69–70; and monism, 183, 186, 188, 193, 195; and nation, 26–9; pluralist

theory of, 181–217; and politics, 4–6; and public power, 19, 21, 30, 52, 218, 222–3; reason of, 69–73; sceptics, 2; and society, 22–4, 112–14, 118; and sociological theory, 219–22; tradition, 2, 10–11; values of, 6–9, 223–5; the word, 13–14, 69–70
stateless society, 2, 5, 10–11
stato, 18
status, 16–18
Suárez, F., 68, 89–90
syndicalism, 23, 184–5, 189, 192, 193

Tawney, R. H., 25
taxation, 30, 49, 63–4, 68
Taylor, C., 40, 121, 140–1
teleocratic association, 120
territory, 11, 19
textualism (and contextualism), 7–8
theocratic rule, 65
theory, 40–3
Tierney, B., 8, 62, 84, 86
Tilly, C., 14, 220, 221, 226
Tocqueville, Alexis de, 134
Tönnies, F., 25
transformative criticism, 154–5
Triennial Act (1694), 97
Truman, D., 189
Trusts (Law of), 205
Tuck, R., 105
Tucker, R., 152, 155, 158
two bodies theory, 31
two swords theory, 66
tyrannicide, 90

Ullman, W., 14, 47, 65, 85, 185, 227
Ulpian, 16
ultramontanism, 185
United Nations Charter, 97, 106
universitas, 22–3, 191
Unwin, G., 195
Urban VI (Pope), 86
Utopia, 10

Verene, D. P., 228
Vernon, R., 212
Vile, M. J. C., 100, 101, 227
Vincent, A. W., 118, 209, 228
Vitoria, Francisco de, 89–90, 107

Wartofsky, M., 153, 154
Webb, Beatrice, 192
Webb, Sidney, 192
Weber, M., 25, 38, 138, 176, 189, 220
Wheare, K. C., 95
Whig Theory of History, 82

Whigs, 107, 185, 197, 198
Wilde, N., 192
Wildman, J., 93, 94
William III (and Mary), 101
Willoughby, W. W., 30
Winckelmann, J. J., 122, 228
Woodhouse, A. S. P., 93, 94
Wootton, D., 36

world history, 123
Wright, A. W., 188, 192, 211, 213

Yates, F. A., 66

Zeno, 83
Zwingli, H., 48, 67